# Rising Sun Victorious

# ALTERNATE HISTORY
# FROM GREENHILL BOOKS

# Rising Sun Victorious
## The Alternate History of How the Japanese Won the Pacific War

Edited by Peter G. Tsouras

Greenhill Books, London
Stackpole Books, Pennsylvania

*Rising Sun Victorious*
first published 2001 by Greenhill Books,
Lionel Leventhal Limited, Park House, 1 Russell Gardens, London NW11 9NN
and
Stackpole Books, 5067 Ritter Road, Mechanicsburg, PA 17055, USA

*British Library Cataloguing in Publication Data*
Rising sun victorious: the alternate history of how the Japanese won the Pacific War
1. World War, 1939–1945 – Campaigns – Pacific Ocean
I. Tsouras, Peter
940.5'426

ISBN 1–85367–446–X

*Library of Congress Cataloging-in-Publication Data*
Rising sun victorious : the alternative history of how the Japanese won the Pacific War/
edited by Peter G. Tsouras
p.   cm.
Includes bibliographical references.
ISBN 1-85367-446-X
1. World War, 1939–1945—Campaigns—Pacific Ocean.   2. World War, 1939–1945—
Japan.   3. Imaginary wars and battles.   I. Tsouras, Peter.
D767.R575   2001
940.54'26—dc21                                         00-066094

Typeset by DP Photosetting, Aylesbury, Bucks
Printed and bound in Great Britain by
Creative Print and Design (Wales), Ebbw Vale

# CONTENTS

# ILLUSTRATIONS

**Pages 97–112**

# MAPS

*All maps by John Richards, except maps 9 and 10 by John H. Gill, and map 15 (CINCPAC).*

# THE CONTRIBUTORS

CHRISTOPHER J. ANDERSON is a lifelong student of World War II and the Associate Editor of *MHQ: The Quarterly Journal of Military History* and *World War II* magazine. He is the author of several volumes in Greenhill Books' series *G.I.: A Photographic History of the American Soldier*, and is working on a history of the 327/401st Glider Regiment.

JAMES R. ARNOLD is a professional writer who specializes in military history. He has published over twenty books roughly divided into three major topic areas: the Napoleonic era; the American Civil War; and the modern period. His two most recent books are a Napoleonic campaign study, *Marengo and Hohenlinden: Napoleon's Rise to Power* and *Jeff Davis's Own: Cavalry, Comanches, and the Battle for the Texas Frontier*. He has also contributed numerous essays to military journals, including the British *Journal of the Society for Army Historical Research* and the American journals *Army History*, *Army Magazine*, and *Navy History*. His chapter in this book reflects his interest in the influence of intelligence and espionage upon military events.

JOHN D. BURTT is the editor of *Paper Wars Magazine*, an independent review journal devoted to wargames. In his day job persona he is an advisory nuclear engineer consulting for the U.S. Nuclear Regulatory Commission. However, his real love is military history. A former marine sergeant and a veteran of Vietnam, he holds a Master's degree in military history and is pursuing a PhD in the same field. He has written for *Command Magazine*, *Strategy & Tactics*, and *The Wargamer*, and was the original editor of *CounterAttack* magazine.

WADE G. DUDLEY returned to academia after almost two decades with Proctor & Gamble, to earn a Master's degree in maritime history and nautical archaeology from East Carolina University in 1997 and a doctorate in history from the University of Alabama in 1999. He contributed 'Drake at Cadiz' to Sarpedon's *Great Raids in History*, while a monograph, *A Comparative Evaluation of Blockades in the Late Age of Sail*, and a book, *Without Some Risk: A Reassessment of the British Blockade of the United States, 1812–1815*, are due to be published shortly. He is employed as a visiting assistant professor of history at East Carolina University in Greenville, North

9

Carolina, and is currently working on a history of naval blockades and a novel about privateers during the War of 1812.

D.M. GIANGRECO is an editor for the U.S. Army's professional journal, *Military Review*. He has lectured widely on U.S. national security matters, and written six books on military and political subjects, including *Dear Harry ... Truman's Mailroom, 1945–1953: The Truman Administration Through Correspondence with 'Everyday Americans'*, and *War in Korea*. He has also written articles for many U.S. and international publications, including 'Casualty Projections for the U.S. Invasion of Japan: 1945–1946' and 'The Truth About Kamikazes', and on such topics as the Falkland Islands' sovereignty question, decentralization of the Soviet Air Force command and control structure, Persian Gulf pipeline construction, and the human interface with rapidly changing technologies.

JOHN H. GILL is the author of *With Eagles to Glory: Napoleon and his German Allies in the 1809 Campaign*, and the editor of *A Soldier for Napoleon*, providing commentary on the letters and diaries of a Bavarian infantry lieutenant during the Napoleonic Wars. In addition to numerous articles and papers on Napoleonic military affairs and a chapter in *The Peninsular War*, he has contributed chapters to two other alternate history collections, *The Hitler Options* and *The Napoleon Options*. He has a BA in history and German and an MA in international relations. A lieutenant colonel in the U.S. Army, he is assigned to the Defense Intelligence Agency as Assistant Defense Intelligence Officer for South Asia.

DAVID C. ISBY is a Washington-based attorney and national security consultant and adjunct professor at American Military University. He has a BA in history and a JD in international law. A former editor of *Strategy & Tactics* magazine, he has also served as a congressional staff member. He has designed nineteen conflict simulations and been awarded two Charles Roberts awards for excellence in this field. He has written or edited twenty books, including several dealing with World War II: *G.I. Victory*, *The Luftwaffe Fighter Force: The View from the Cockpit*, and *Fighting the Invasion: The German Army at D-Day*.

LIEUTENANT COLONEL FORREST R. LINDSEY USMC (Ret) served nearly thirty years in the United States Marine Corps, including time in combat in Vietnam. His assignments included nuclear weapons testing with the Defense Nuclear Agency, and service as a United Nations Truce Supervisor in Egypt and as an arms control treaty Inspection Team Leader in the former Soviet Union. His artillery duties included battalion operations officer, regimental logistics officer, and commanding officer of the 5th

Battalion, 11th Marines. Upon retirement from active duty in 1996, he continued working with the Marine Corps as Senior Engineer for the Marine Corps Warfighting Laboratory, responsible for weapons experimentation and precision targeting. He has written several articles on professional military issues in the *Marine Corps Gazette*. He has a BSc in mechanical engineering technology and is pursuing a Master's degree in business administration.

FRANK R. SHIRER is a historian with the U.S. Army Center of Military History at Fort McNair, Washington, D.C., specializing in oral history, World War II and the Soviet military. An army veteran with twenty years' enlisted and commissioned service in the U.S. Army, he has served in Field Artillery as a fire direction specialist and forward observer, and received a direct commission in Military Intelligence, where he served as an armored cavalry squadron S-2 and 3rd Armored Division Artillery S-2. He has also served on the DCSINT Staff at the Pentagon, as a Soviet analyst at the Defense Intelligence Agency, and as an order of battle analyst at the U.S. Army Intelligence and Threat Analysis Center. Since retiring in 1994 he has worked for the U.S. Army Gulf War Declassification Project and the U.S. Army Declassification Activity, and has been with the CMH since 1995. He has assisted in the research for several works of military history.

PETER G. TSOURAS is a senior intelligence analyst at the U.S. Army National Ground Intelligence Center's Washington office. He has served in the Army as an armor officer in the 1st Bn/64th Armor Regiment in Germany and subsequently in intelligence and Adjutant Generals Corp Assignments. He retired from the Army Reserve as a lieutenant colonel after serving as a Civil Affairs officer. His assignments have taken him to Somalia, Russia, Ukraine, and Japan. He is the author or editor of twenty books on international military themes, military history, and alternate history, including *Disaster at D-Day*, *Gettysburg: An Alternate History*, *The Great Patriotic War*, *The Anvil of War*, *Fighting in Hell*, and *The Greenhill Dictionary of Military Quotations*.

# INTRODUCTION

The Pacific War was a war of extremes: extremes of distance and climate, of opportunity, chance, boldness, and of technology, from the Samurai sword to the atom bomb. It was, as the Ancient Greeks would have said, the 'Dancing Floor of War'. And in no other theater were there so many possibilities from which the players could choose. Again and again earth-shaking opportunities paraded past Japanese and American commanders and even common soldiers and sailors. History turned on how wisely and how boldly they seized them – or not. The interplay between chance and opportunity is the heartbeat of war. Clausewitz touched on it when he said, 'War is the realm of chance. No other human activity gives it greater scope: no other has such incessant and varied dealings with this intruder. Chance makes everything more uncertain and interferes with the whole course of events.'[1] And Napoleon defined the relationship: 'War is composed of nothing but accidents, and ... a general should never lose sight of everything to enable him to profit from these accidents; that is the mark of genius.'[2] This book examines the ways not taken, the stillborn possibilities that could have grown to mighty events. Each chapter examines a plausible opportunity for decisive advantages to be won by the arms of Imperial Japan.

Each of the ten chapters takes a well-known episode in the history of the Pacific War and spins it off in a new direction. Each is a self-contained examination of one particular battle or campaign in the context of its own alternate reality; the new paths created in one chapter do not run into the next. Since each chapter sets in motion new events, each generates new ground from the historian's perspective. If the Japanese win the Battle of Midway, for example, different historical works will appear in time. These different works appear in the endnotes along with those reflecting actual events. Where the one takes over from the other is the shimmering gateway into alternate history. The use of such 'alternate reality' notes, of course, poses a risk to the unwary reader who may make strenuous efforts to acquire a new and fascinating source. To avoid an epidemic of frustrating and futile searches, the 'alternate' notes are indicated by an asterisk.

My own contribution, 'Hokushin: The Second Russo-Japanese War', does not even address the alternatives of the course of the Pacific War. It examines the very decision to attack the United States. Until the middle of 1941, such a course was not inevitable. Equal weight was given within the

13

Japanese leadership to the proposal to attack the Soviet Union. It could have been Stalin who addressed his nation about a certain date 'which would live in infamy'. More than eighty percent of Japanese divisions were earmarked for such a struggle. The consequences would have been incalculable had the Japanese attack been the straw that broke the camel's back and dragged down the Soviet Union to defeat at Hitler's hands. Wade G. Dudley's chapter, 'Be Careful What You Wish For: The Plan Orange Disaster', explores the consequences of the United States Navy's implementing the plans for war with Japan, in which the Pacific Fleet was to sail into Japanese-controlled waters for the showdown battle. Had the Japanese not attacked Pearl Harbor, just such a scenario might have come to pass. The consequences for the Pacific Fleet, deficient in both training and readiness compared to its Japanese counterpart at the time, are vividly evoked.

Most of the chapters deal with the fluid and desperate months of the early part of the war, when Japanese resources were at their greatest and Japanese martial skills a significant advantage against their opponents. Frank R. Shirer, in 'Pearl Harbor: Irredeemable Defeat', tackles this heady period by refighting Nagumo's battle. What might have happened had Nagumo been sure that it would not be too risky to send in the third wave? James Arnold, in 'Coral and Purple', looks at the loss of one of the United States' few advantages in those fearful months: signals intelligence. John D. Burtt addresses the issue of the character of command in the Guadalcanal campaign, in 'Guadalcanal: The Broken Shoestring'. Had the aggressive and tenacious warrior, Admiral Halsey, not been placed in command, the campaign's desperate naval engagements and severe losses might well have overwhelmed his predecessor despite the valor and success of Vandegrift's Marines ashore.

In fact, it was Admiral Isoroku Yamamoto, commander of the Imperial Japanese Navy's Combined Fleet, who correctly forecast the balance of power between Japan and the Allies, especially the United States: 'If you insist on my going ahead I can promise to give them hell for a year or a year and a half, but can guarantee nothing as to what will happen after that.'[3] Indeed, he was more optimistic than events were to justify. The first great disaster to befall the Japanese occurred at Midway less than seven months after the attack on Pearl Harbor. After that, the initiative slipped away from the Japanese. The weight of American industrial production was so great that Japan was doomed. But the United States' opportunity to marshal its material and human resources was not inevitable. The crucial victory at Midway essentially depended on the decision of a navy lieutenant commander to follow, with his dive-bombers, the last direction given for the Japanese fleet. His aircraft were already low on fuel, and he could easily have decided instead to fly to Midway Island and refuel. History pivoted on one man's intrepidity. What if he had chosen safety first? Forrest R. Lindsey, in

'Nagumo's Luck', shows how the American carriers would probably have gone to the bottom as a result. How would America have begun its way back had the next step been to defend the West Coast? It would have been a different war in which American cities, not Japanese, would have borne the brunt.

John H. Gill and David C. Isby tackle the Japanese invasions that might have been: of Australia and India. Australia's fate hung in the balance at the Battle of the Coral Sea. The battle was essentially a tactical defeat for the U.S. Navy, but it stung the Japanese enough to draw them away from their attack on Port Moresby. Had Coral Sea gone worse, the Japanese invasion fleet would have continued on to seize Moresby. Then Australia would have been cut off and vulnerable. Douglas MacArthur had just escaped to Australia from Corregidor and had been placed in command of Australian and American forces, all green and under-equipped. Against a veteran and victorious army, led by the Tiger of Malaya himself, how would he have fared? John H. Gill, in 'Samurai Down Under', brings to mind the terror of the old cry, 'Hannibal at the gate!'

Few people today realize how unstable the British hold on India was in the panicked months after the fall of Singapore, especially when Admiral Nagumo trailed his coat through the Bay of Bengal. A concerted Japanese push might well have brought down the 200-year-old British Raj and sent the imperial crown of India to Tokyo. Carried away by victory fever, the Japanese could well have been pulled into the subcontinent. Gandhi would have had the opportunity to find out how the Japanese reacted to protest, non-violent or otherwise. British imperialism might then have suddenly looked a little better. David C. Isby, in 'The Japanese Raj', points out how limited Japan's resources were even in the face of incredible opportunity. A land war across the subcontinent might well have been one of the most brutal in the entire Second World War; the scope for human suffering would have only been rivaled in China and Russia.

By June of 1942, Japan's hope of winning the war through offensive strategy was gone. Still, even in the catastrophic years of 1944 and 1945, opportunities appeared. It was only by the slightest of chances that Admiral Halsey's failure to protect the invasion fleet in Leyte Gulf properly did not result in catastrophic slaughter. Christopher J. Anderson, in 'There Are Such Things As Miracles', shows how the luck might have fallen instead to Admiral Kurita. How long would it have taken the United States to recover had Kurita been able to ravage the huge herd of American transports and merchant ships in Leyte Gulf? My own father, Theodore P. Tsouras, was then third officer on the S.S. *Alcoa Pioneer*, a merchant ship in Leyte Gulf filled with fuel and supplies for the forces fighting ashore. He still recalled decades later how hundreds of ships lay at anchor, and none had 'steam up' when the news of the sudden arrival of the Japanese battle fleet spread fear and panic through their crews.

Even at the last moment of the war, the invasion of Japan, with all the weight of a fully mobilized America behind it, was threatened by the severe underestimation of the increased lethality of the Kamikaze in close quarters off the coast of Japan. Looking back at the roll of victories as one island garrison after another was annihilated, the student of the Pacific War might understandably consider the planned invasion of Kyushu in late 1945 to be simply a larger version of these earlier successes. D.M. Giangreco, in 'Victory Rides the Divine Wind', describes the incredible planning for the invasion of Japan which depended upon the closest of timing margins and did not give sufficient credit to Japan's massed suicide weapon, the Kamikaze. The severe loses suffered by the U.S. Navy off Okinawa were not an accurate foretaste of the losses to be suffered off the Japanese home islands themselves by any means. An invasion of Japan would have seen the advantages of the Divine Wind multiplied many times over.

All the chapters in this book point to one inescapable conclusion: the roads not taken could have led to the world resounding with the cry of 'Banzai! Banzai! Banzai!'

Peter G. Tsouras
2001

## Notes

1. Carl von Clausewitz, *On War*, 1.3 (Princeton University Press, Princeton, 1976), p.101.
2. Napoleon, *The Military Maxims of Napoleon*, trans. Burnod (1827), in T.R. Phillips, ed., *Roots of Strategy*, Book 1 (Stackpole Books, Harrisburg, 1985), p.436.
3. Hiroyuki Agawa, *The Reluctant Admiral: Yamamoto and the Imperial Navy* (Kodansha International Ltd, Tokyo, 1979), p.232.

# 1

# HOKUSHIN
# The Second Russo-Japanese War

Peter G. Tsouras

### The Kremlin, November 1939

Stalin gloated. Bundle after bundle of Samurai swords was dumped ostentatiously at his feet by Red Army officers as their commander, Georgii Zhukov, looked on with pride. These were the trophies Zhukov had taken in the Mongolian desert at Nomonhan (Khalkin Gol) in October when he crushed the advance of the Japanese Kwangtung Army into the Soviet protectorate with a masterful orchestration of all arms in overwhelming force. The Japanese 6th Army had suffered at least 21,016 casualties, including 8,629 dead, in what has been called 'a graveyard of reputations'. Soviet casualties had numbered 15,925 with 7,974 dead.[1]

Certainly Stalin had reason to be pleased. His suspicion of Japanese intentions in the arc of Soviet territories from Lake Baikal to Vladivostok had been proved correct. Then he was always pleased when his suspicions were proven correct. The Soviet Far East was a treasure house of minerals and forests and a handy place to lose millions of political prisoners. And Stalin knew how much the Japanese coveted it. Had they not already shamed the Russian Empire in the Russo-Japanese War (1904–5) by snatching Manchuria? Their current adventure to conquer China had not prevented them from building up their Kwangtung Army in Manchuria to a dangerous level. And their intentions had been proved when they sent their Army into neighboring Mongolia, a Soviet republic in everything but name. Well, Zhukov had administered a sound thrashing and thrown the militarists out on their ear; but Stalin had no doubt they would be back. He was not one to be content with a victory. The build-up in the Transbaikal and Far East Military Districts (MD) continued at an accelerated pace.

Tanks and planes flowed east by the thousand to fill out the divisions trained to a high pitch by Army Commander 2nd Grade G.M. Shtern, a brilliant officer whose talents had been unleashed by the Revolution. Shtern had commanded the 39th Corps in the undeclared border war with Japan that had been fought out at Lake Khasan, south of Vladivostok, in 1938. For that performance he had won the Order of Lenin. He had played a tactful but vital supporting role for Zhukov in Mongolia in 1939. Transferred in 1940 to the Finnish Front, he distinguished himself in command of the 8th Army, earned promotion, and was then given command of the Far Eastern MD.[2] He was one of the stars of the prewar Red Army, one of the few left by the purges, something Stalin had not forgotten.

### Lessons learned – or not

Nomonhan had stunned the Japanese Army. Not since its founding during the Meiji Restoration had it been so thoroughly humbled and shamed. Everything was done to hide the catastrophe from the world, and even from Japan. Survivors were isolated and quietly discharged. So many white boxes of ashes had to be shipped back to the homeland that it was done in three shipments so as not to stun the nation.

Stalin was right. The Japanese did covet the Soviet Far East. Even more, they feared the growth of Soviet power to their north, which the shock of Nomonhan did much to feed. They worried about a Soviet attack on their rich Manchurian province while they were deeply involved in China. Not least, the very existence of the monarch-murdering Bolshevik regime was an affront to his Imperial Majesty. By 1934, when Manchuria was finally under Japanese control, offensive war plans were prepared against the Soviet Union. 'This plan laid down the principle that operations against the USSR should be offensive in nature, with the battlefield chosen in Soviet territory from the first, and with the major offensive launched from the eastern front of Manchuria. The final operational objective was set as the vicinity of Lake Baikal.'[3] It was in this direction that the 6th Army had marched in July 1939, only to stumble back in ruin. It was obvious that there were lessons to be learned.

The defense minister, General Hata, responded to the concern of a member of the Diet, 'Please rest assured that we shall not have wasted the blood that was shed on the sands of Nomonhan.'[4] Hata convened a special commission to decide what lessons needed to be learned, and to recommend solutions. There was no lack of first-hand, blunt information from officers who had served in the campaign. But this was not the Japanese Army's first warning of the might of materiel. In 1938 they had engaged the 19th Division against the Soviet 39th Rifle Corps, commanded by Shtern, at Lake Khasan, near the Soviet border with Korea. The seesaw fighting was eventually decided by Soviet numbers and weight of material, and the Japanese were driven back. One participant said, 'All we experienced directly was one edge of Soviet combat power.' A general staff expert concluded, 'We learned that Soviet strength was up to expectations, whereas Japanese arms and equipment had to be improved and reinforced.' On top of the experience of Lake Khasan, the Japanese Army was finally able to digest four bitter lessons of combat with the Red Army:

(1)   The Soviets were clearly superior in armor and artillery and the ability
      to deliver accurate firepower on a scale that dwarfed Japanese capa-
      bilities;
(2)   Soviet logistics were highly impressive, especially their ability to
      transport large mechanized forces 600 kilometers from a railroad
      head;
(3)   The Soviets were flexible in the application of tactics to different cir-
      cumstances;
(4)   The Soviets were tough fighters, determined to win.[5]

But then things went awry. Faced with attempting to match the Soviet
overwhelming superiority in materiel and production, the Japanese found
themselves with an insurmountable problem. There was no way Japan's
industrial base could match the advanced design, quality, and output of the
Soviet arms industry. The Red Army had used almost 6,000 trucks to
support its forces in the Nomonhan campaign, while there were only 9,000
motor vehicles of all types in Manchuria. Japan was a nation of railroads and
small medieval roads.[6]

But there was a greater and deeper problem. The Japanese Army had
been spared the horrors of World War I; it had only the smallest taste of the
crushing wars of materiel in the Mongolian desert. The salient experience
was still the largely nineteenth-century Russo-Japanese War. Since then, a
perverse mutation of the Samurai code of Bushido had permeated the
Army's thinking. It was an unabashed triumph of the spiritual over the
material. The *Yamato damashii* or spirit of Japan, the distilled essence of the
Japanese nation, was infinitely superior to a reliance on the material aspects
of war. Of course, improvements in firepower and logistics would have to be
made, but the real superiority of the Japanese soldier still resided in his
spirit. The Japanese disadvantage in materiel would be more than compensated by strengthening the will of the soldier. There was more than a
passing resemblance to the French obsession with their own form of spirit,
called elan. That died on the Western Front, its tombstone inscribed with
Marshal Petain's two words, 'Fire kills'.

Petain had come close to ruin as a colonel before the war by his advocacy
of firepower, but rivers of French blood vindicated him. Japanese Petains
after Nomonhan were either ignored or driven out of the service. Harping
on the importance of the material aspects of war was defeatist. At the
beginning of 1941, when the army should have been in high gear implementing lessons learned, Tojo issued a new *senjinkun* (moral code) for the
Japanese soldier, which stated: 'A sublime sense of self-sacrifice must guide
you throughout life and death. Think not of death, as you push through,
with every ounce of your effort, in fulfilling your duties. Make it your joy to
do everything with all your spiritual and physical strength. Fear not to die
for the cause of everlasting justice.'[7]

The artillery school remained satisfied that horse-drawn pack artillery was best suited for the infantry divisions rather than the recommended 150 mm motorized artillery. Only one improvement crept through – the development of a one-ton, 300 mm bunker-busting howitzer shell, designed to smash the numerous concrete *tochka* pillbox emplacements the Soviets had strung along their border. Tank production would be only 573 in 1940, compared to 3,000 for the Soviets. Production was doubled in 1941 to a still meager 1,024, all of models inferior to newer Soviet ones. Aircraft production presented a better picture, with production rising to 4,768 in 1940 and 5,088 in 1941, with the emphasis on fighters. Far worse was the continued reliance on hundreds of thousands of horses for transport; wartime planning called for fewer than 15,000 vehicles to be brought from Japan to support operations against the Red Army.[8] With the beginning of the war in China in 1937, Japanese war industries had been tasked with a great increase in the production of munitions. By 1941 this plan had succeeded so well that the Japanese Army could be kept well supplied in simultaneous wars with China and the Soviet Union.[9]

## Operational Plan No.8 (*Hachi-Go* Plan)

Nomonhan did have a major impact, however, on Japanese war plans. Interestingly, 1943 was chosen as the date by which Japanese preparations would be advanced enough to engage the Red Army in the Far East. That was the same year Hitler had chosen for general war, when the Wehrmacht's strengthening would be complete. Until 1940 Japan's strategy, Operational Plan No.8 (*Hachi-Go* Plan), had been based on a powerful main thrust across the Greater Hsingan Mountain Range into the Lake Baikal region. The advantage lay in the severing of the entire Soviet Far East from Chita to the Pacific. By early 1939, the general staff informed the Kwangtung Army that such plans required the provision of 200,000 motor vehicles and the great expansion of railroads in the region. Nomonhan had been a rehearsal. The Japanese rightly concluded that they did not have the logistics or materiel to support an offensive of that distance. Japanese attention consequently shifted to the northern and eastern theaters.[10]

Compared to striking out into the great void leading to Lake Baikal, vital objectives lay just across the Manchurian borders demarcated by the Amur and Ussuri Rivers. A fact of geographical life in the Soviet Far East was its absolute dependence upon the Trans-Siberian Railway, which – essentially from Blagveshchensk, to Khabarovsk, the Soviet regional administrative and production center, to just north of Vladivostok, the major Soviet port in the Pacific – ran perilously close to the Manchurian border. In particular, the Maritime Province or Primorskiy Kray was vulnerable. It was wedged between the Manchurian border and the Sea of Japan, with the railroad running within easy artillery range of the Japanese for much of the way north of Lake Hanka. The Japanese fortress at Hutou directly overlooked the railway at Iman. So blatant was the threat that the Red Army had begun construction of a defensive belt further to the east, leaving the railway uncovered. Already major elements of the Kwangtung Army were stationed directly across the border south of the lake. It was a bare sixty kilometers to the critical junction of Voroshilov (modern Ussurisk), the fall of which would sever the railway and cut off Vladivostok.

The 1940–1 modifications of *Hachi-Go* confirmed the main Japanese operational thrust in this eastern theater. The western and northern theaters would go over to the defensive. Second phase operations in either of these theaters would depend upon opportunities presented by the success of the first phase along the Ussuri.

*Hachi-Go* called for the eventual commitment of the bulk of the Japanese Army, thirty-two divisions in the first phase and ten or eleven in the second. To the twelve divisions in the Kwangtung Army, ten more would be added from the homeland and ten from the operations in China. The second phase would see another seven divisions from the homeland and a further three or four from China. In the first phase twenty divisions would be massed along the Ussuri under the First Area Army (army group) in three armies. The 3rd and 7th Armies with eight divisions would strike towards Voroshilov; the 5th Army with five divisions would strike at Iman and sever the railway. Remaining divisions would conduct supporting operations or be in reserve. Along the northern front, the 4th Army with four divisions would engage in delaying actions north of the Lesser Hsingan Mountains. Along the western front, the 6th Army, also with four divisions, would engage in holding operations west of the Greater Hsingan Mountains. Second phase operations on the eastern front would have the 3rd and 7th Armies advance upon Vladivostok while the 5th Army struck north to seize Khabarovsk. These objectives were strategically and geographically much less far-reaching than the drive to Lake Baikal, but they had the great, even vital, advantage of minimizing the necessary logistics effort. The emphasis on the capture of Vladivostok had been at the insistence of the Imperial Japanese Navy, which wanted the home base of the Soviet Pacific Ocean Fleet eliminated. For that goal, the Navy would actively participate by massing up to 350 aircraft, from land-based bombers to the planes of the 1st Carrier Division, to cooperate with the 500 aircraft of the Army's 2nd Air Group in surprise attacks to eliminate the Red Air Force in the Maritime Province.[11]

The Red Army's order of battle in this theater was daunting. By 1940 the Japanese had concluded that the Red Army forces stationed from Vladivostok to Mongolia included thirty rifle divisions, two cavalry divisions, nine tank brigades, and one mechanized brigade, a total of 2,800 planes, 2,700 tanks, and 700,000 men.[12] They were roughly correct overall, but the standard of mechanization escaped them. The Red Army actually boasted nineteen rifle divisions, six tank divisions, four mechanized divisions, two motorized rifle divisions, one cavalry division, and ten rifle brigades.[13] Despite the aggregate materiel superiority, the Japanese had the important advantage of interior lines. The Red Army was spread out in a vast arc from Mongolia to the Pacific, depending solely on the vulnerable Trans-Baikal Railway. An important part of the mechanized force was at the western end of the arc in Mongolia and the Transbaikal MD. The Japanese would be concentrating the bulk of their army against the farthest end of the Soviet arc in the Maritime Province, which they estimated would be defended by thirteen divisions. Given that Red Army divisions were about half the strength of Japanese divisions, the advantage became impressive. The Navy's advantage would be even more crushing, with the might of the Combined Fleet available to dispose of an estimated five destroyers, 200 torpedo boats, and seventy submarines. The latter posed a real threat to reinforcement operations across the Sea of Japan.

## A present from the NKVD

In 1938 the first of two incredible intelligence windfalls fell into Japan's lap. The Far East chief of the NKVD, the Soviet secret police, walked across the border on 13 June and defected. General Genrikh Samoelovich Lyushkov had a lot to say. An efficient and vicious climber, he had ridden the opportunities offered by Stalin to reach the top. But underneath he had become disillusioned, poor man, that Stalin was not building the right kind of socialism. Perhaps after putting to death 5,000 people he feared becoming number 5,001. He was ready to help the Japanese. Coming at the height of the purges, he painted a picture of devastation in the command levels of the Red Army. A Soviet officer wrote of the lingering effects of the NKVD's handiwork two years later, in 1940:

> I saw for myself the aftermath of the destruction of officer cadres in the Far East. Almost right after my arrival in Khabarovsk I went with Shtern to review his forces. Two years had passed since the mass arrests had come to an end, but the command pyramid had not yet been restored. Many positions remained unfilled because there were no men qualified to occupy them. Battalions were commanded by officers who had completed military schools less than a year before ... How could anyone have thought that such a gap could be filled?

In the 40th Rifle Division of the 39th Corps, which had played such a role in the Lake Khasan victory, only one officer remained – a lieutenant.[14] Lyushkov went on to paint such a picture of deprivation, despair, and pent-up hatred of the regime that he convinced important circles in the Japanese Army that the Soviet Union was a rotten house ready to collapse if attacked on its own doorstep. Lyushkov's insider views were very impressive, especially when his forecasts were accurate. His reputation grew with the confirmation of his information and his ability to forecast events, not the least of which was the German attack on the Soviet Union. By then he was already acting as the Soviet opponent in Japanese Army wargames,[15] and was being groomed as the governor of his Imperial Majesty's new Maritime Province.

## Go North or Go South?

By July 1940, the strategic tension facing the Japanese national and military leadership had begun to intensify. Japan's war with China had earned it the increasing enmity of the United States, which was leading to one economic restriction after another. Should the Unites States and Britain engage in an economic embargo, especially of oil, Japan would be mortally wounded without a war. Much of the military leadership subscribed to this 'gradual decline' view and advocated a *Nanshin* or 'Go South' strategy to seize the resources of Southeast Asia and the Dutch East Indies. Others advocated a *Hokushin* or 'Go North' strategy, seeing the Soviet Union as the greater threat that must be dealt with first. Adding weight to their argument was the support of the new foreign minister, Yosuke Matsuoka, and the new war minister, General Hideki Tojo, under the second cabinet formed by Prince Konoye. Strengthening their hand was the unease of the Emperor himself at leaving a powerful Red Army to their rear.

Complicating deliberations was Japan's membership in the Tripartite Pact with Germany and Italy, which obligated the other members to come to each other's aid if attacked. As the Germans had initiated the war raging in Western Europe, the Japanese did not feel obliged to enter it against the British, French, and Dutch. But collapse of the last two powers and the desperate straits of the British beckoned the Japanese to exploit their weakness to seize the resource-rich south. The reappearance of Shtern as Commander, 1st Far East Army, was also a source of apprehension for the Japanese, who remembered him from Lake Khasan.[16] The 'Go South' option seemed to have gained the upper hand.

Historians would later identify Matsuoka's visit to Berlin in late March as the pivot upon which Japanese policy turned. Matsuoka had been prepared for some discussion of a joint war against the Soviet Union by the Japanese ambassador, General Hiroshi Oshima.[17] Still, he was thunderstruck by Hitler's blunt and insistent proposal for a joint attack. A flurry of messages flew between Berlin and Tokyo as the formal proposal was transmitted. On his return to Japan through the Soviet Union, Matsuoka was instructed to conclude a neutrality pact with the Soviet Union, which Stalin was eager to sign on 13 April. As with the western allies, Japan was under no treaty obligation to attack the Soviet Union, but Operation Barbarossa – the German plan to invade Russia – had completely changed the equation of power among the nations. If opportunity beckoned against the western colonies to the south, a greater and immediate opportunity now beguiled them from across the Sea of Japan, on their very doorstep. One Japanese general put his finger on the issue when he said that Japan should not 'miss the bus'. When asked about the timing of the operation, the Germans said late May, when the mud had dried in Russia. And yes, there was one more piece of good news. Shtern had been arrested and shot on Stalin's orders.

In Tokyo the lights burned late at the Imperial General Headquarters. Already the senior ministers and flag officers had determined to catch the bus. Matsuoka carried the day by explaining the logic of the anti-Soviet war. An attack to the south would leave a major enemy in their rear while simultaneously gaining three new enemies. A Japanese attack on the Soviet Far East would guarantee the collapse of the Bolshevik experiment. The resulting German domination of Europe would concentrate the western allies in their own backyards. Even the United States would have to choose between Europe and Asia, and there was little doubt where her decision would lay. The Navy was grudgingly won over with the prospect of eliminating the U.S. Navy by a stroke of policy. The commander of the Combined Fleet, Admiral Isoroku Yamamoto, had actually been relieved at the change in the situation. The prospect of a prolonged war of attrition against the United States filled him with dread at the prospect of facing its industrial might and warlike people. He supported the 'Go North' plan and called in a certain staff officer, 'Madman' Genda by name, to plan something special for the first blow from the sea.

### 'There's a rout. Do you understand? *A rout!*'

There was little time to prepare. It was agreed between Germany and Japan that the Japanese blow would follow the German attack by several months to maximize the disruption of Soviet operations, especially the movement of reserves. The Japanese would pick the time that presented the greatest opportunity. They also needed a longer mobilization lead-time than a simultaneous attack would allow. Tojo ordered a general mobilization on 30 April, which sent reinforcements flowing to Manchuria under the *Hachi-Go* Plan under the cover explanation of 'Special Maneuvers'. By 1941 Japan had increased its Army to fifty-one divisions; Tojo's order would concentrate the great bulk of it, 1.3 million men in forty-two divisions (eighty-two percent), for Japan's death struggle with the Soviet Union. Imperial General Headquarters heard with relief of the German postponement of their attack caused by the unexpected campaign into the Balkans triggered by Mussolini's ill-considered attack on neutral Greece.

For the Japanese, the extra month was vital if their armies were to have any time to assimilate their reservists and new units. It also made sense to profit from the withdrawal of Japanese divisions from China and Northern Indochina. They paraded it as a goodwill gesture towards the United States in settling the China problem. Faced with the evaporation of much of the anti-Japanese sentiment at home by newsreels showing Japanese soldiers by the thousands boarding transports for home, Roosevelt could only read the MAGIC intercepts of Japanese diplomatic traffic and shake his head. He could not get Stalin's attention with a sledgehammer. The United States would have to look out for its own interests in the Atlantic now that the Japanese were going to go north. Stalin had had plenty of warning from his own military intelligence, as well as from the Americans, who were reading Oshima's diplomatic traffic, but the bearers of unwanted bad news had only earned firing squads for their dedication to duty.

On 22 June three and half million German and allied soldiers invaded the Soviet Union in Operation Barbarossa. At the same time, the Kwangtung Army was swelling with new divisions and hundreds of thousands of support troops. Over fifty railway station commands were created to bolster the railway system which was pulling the might of Japan to the vast camps hidden in the forests west of the Ussuri River.

General Tomoyuki Yamashita was summoned home on the heels of Matsuoka from his military mission to Germany.[18] As early as 1940 he had been made head of Unit 82, the planning team for the invasion of Malaya. He had kept that post even while on the mission in Europe. Yamashita had a reputation for innovative thinking and decisiveness, and the impressions he had gained around the world showed that he was willing to break with current army thinking. He was particularly impressed with the German coordination of all arms, the employment of armor and airplanes in one seamless effort. To remove a rival for defense minister, Tojo secured him the command of the First Army Area with its growing mass of divisions aimed at the Maritime Province. His chief of staff was General Kitsuji Ayabe, who had accompanied him to Germany and had served in numerous staff positions in Manchuria and specifically in the eastern area of operations.[19]

It was in late April, as the mobilization began to fill the streets with men in khaki, that the second intelligence windfall fell into Japanese hands. Actually, he walked out of the German embassy and into the arms of the Japanese police. He was Richard Sorge, the dean of the German press corps and trusted confidant of the ambassador. Unfortunately, he was also a most adept Soviet agent and the head of the espionage network in Japan. His reports were based on an intimate knowledge of everything that flowed through the German embassy as well as his privileged contacts with the Japanese government and armed forces. Sorge had served in the trenches in the German Army in World War I and came out of them a committed communist. One of his agents had been compromised, and the resulting trail led directly to Sorge. The Japanese police made a clean sweep of his entire organization and even found the records of his radio operator's messages to and from Moscow. From this they were able to conclude that Sorge had diligently been warning Stalin of Japan's aggressive intentions,

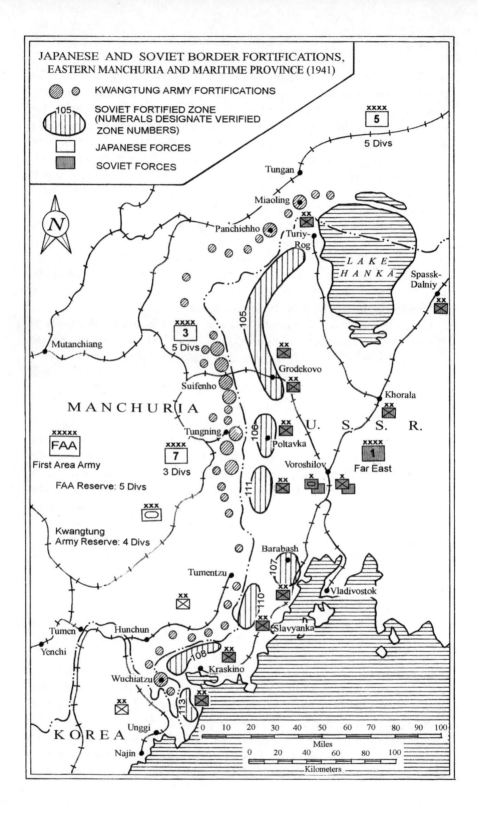

JAPANESE AND SOVIET BORDER FORTIFICATIONS,
EASTERN MANCHURIA AND MARITIME PROVINCE (1941)

KWANGTUNG ARMY FORTIFICATIONS

105 SOVIET FORTIFIED ZONE
(NUMERALS DESIGNATE VERIFIED
ZONE NUMBERS)

JAPANESE FORCES

SOVIET FORCES

XXXX
5
5 Divs

Tungan

Miaoling

Panchiehho

Turiy-
Rog

LAKE
HANKA

Spassk-
Dalniy

Mutanchiang

XXXX
3
5 Divs

105

Suifenho

Grodekovo

Khorala

MANCHURIA

U.   S.   S.   R.

XXXXX
FAA

First Area Army

Tungning

XXXX
7
3 Divs

106

Poltavka

Voroshilov

XXXX
1
Far East

FAA Reserve: 5 Divs

111

XXX

Kwangtung
Army Reserve: 4 Divs

Barabash

Tumentzu

107

110

Vladivostok

Tumen      Hunchun

Yenchi

XX

108

Slavyanka

Kraskino

Wuchiatzu

113

XX

KOREA   Unggi

Najin

0   10   20   30   40   50   60   70   80   90   100
Miles

0    20    40    60    80    100
Kilometers

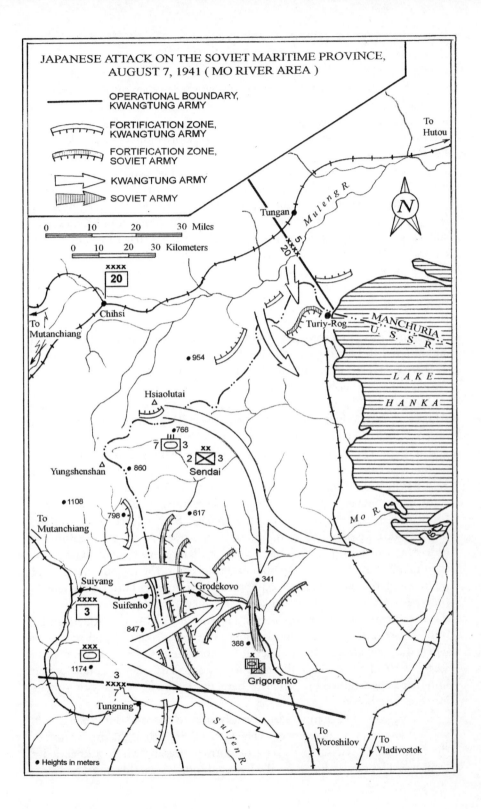

JAPANESE ATTACK ON THE SOVIET MARITIME PROVINCE,
AUGUST 7, 1941 ( MO RIVER AREA )

OPERATIONAL BOUNDARY,
KWANGTUNG ARMY

FORTIFICATION ZONE,
KWANGTUNG ARMY

FORTIFICATION ZONE,
SOVIET ARMY

KWANGTUNG ARMY

SOVIET ARMY

0        10        20        30   Miles

0      10      20      30   Kilometers

N

xxxx
20

To
Hutou

Tungan

Muleng R.

5
xxxx
20

Chihsi

To
Mutanchiang

Turiy-Rog

MANCHURIA
U. S. S. R.

• 954

LAKE
HANKA

Hsiaolutai
△

• 768
7 □ 3

xx
2 ⊠ 3
Sendai

Yungshenshan △   • 860

• 1108

798 •

• 617

Mo R.

To
Mutanchiang

Suiyang

Grodekovo

• 341

xxxx
3

Suifenho

847 •

388 •

xxx
1174 •

3
xxxx
7

x
Grigorenko

Tungning

Suifen R.

To
Voroshilov

To
Vladivostok

• Heights in meters

the first details of the mobilization, and the most intimate confidences shared by the foolish ambassador. For a while Sorge even dutifully reported on Lyushkov's activities. He could have saved himself the effort; Stalin was as incredulous of war warnings from Sorge as he was from his other agents reporting on the Germans. So it came as something of a shock when Lyushkov walked into Sorge's cell in the basement of the Japanese secret police headquarters and offered him a deal. It had helped that the Japanese police had worked on him already – and on his woman.

The short interruption in messages from Sorge to his masters in Moscow had not been noticed. But when they resumed, the contents of his messages suddenly began finding favor at the top. He reported that the mobilization efforts were a ruse to lull the Americans into concentrating on Europe while the Japanese prepared to go south. Reconnaissance conducted by the Red Air Force in the Far East that revealed the enemy build-up was as quickly dismissed as that in the west. Still, if Stalin was pleased, no one objected. As the Germans gobbled up whole Soviet armies on the frontiers and thrust deeper into Russian territory, Stalin reviewed the cables from Sorge in Tokyo and ordered the divisions in the Far East to deploy to the western front.

Shtern's replacement in the Far East was General Iosif Radionovich Apanasenko, an able, energetic, and innovative officer, and a natural problem solver.[20] The war now placed a great burden on all those qualities. Almost immediately upon the outbreak of war the Soviet General Staff had ordered the Far East to send west its entire mobilization reserves of weapons and ammunition. When his staff objected to Apanasenko, he roared back at them, 'what are you talking about? There's a rout. Do you understand? *A rout*! Begin loading up immediately.' He was the only man in the eastern third of the Soviet Union who had a clear understanding of what was happening in the west. Although the General Staff relented on its order, deciding to take only half of the mobilization reserves, soon thereafter the order was sent to dispatch eight of the best divisions to fight the Germans, then four more, then two. Apanasenko dispatched them immediately and poured replacement personnel, equipment, and supplies onto their trains as they passed through Kuibeshevka-Vostochnaya, headquarters of the 2nd Far East Army, near Blagoveschensk. He dutifully complied with the order from Moscow to see that the divisions were fully manned and equipped when they departed. Weeks later four more were ordered west. Within weeks most of the tanks and planes were gone. The irony was not lost on him that as he stripped his cupboard bare, the Japanese were stocking theirs just over the border.[21]

A more educated man would have given in to despair. But Apanasenko was a fountain of positive energy. The General Staff thought the bottom of the barrel had been scraped, but this former peasant who commanded a front was adept at finding a meal where staff officers would starve. So he set to work, and his energy crackled down through every military and civil official in the Far East. If the Japanese thought they could use the extra time provided by Hitler's Balkan detour, Apanasenko was even more happy to get it. Given complete powers by Stalin, he ordered a draconian conscription of all males up to fifty-five years old. He scoured the NKVD's Gulag camps near the border and pressed thousands of prisoners (they called themselves 'zeks') into uniform. He also freed hundreds of officers who had been condemned in the purges. Industry was cranked up to provide new weapons and munitions while training weapons were converted for combat use. He began raising new divisions to replace those sent west.

It was plain to see that the most threatened front would be the border from south of Khabarovsk to Voroshilov. It was in this area that he concentrated his reconstructed formations. At least they would have the fortifications that had been under construction since 1932. The impenetrable swamps made most of the long stretch of frontier between Khabarovsk and Lake Hanka safe on the Japanese side. The danger point was at Iman, opposite the Japanese fort at Hutou. The guns of the fort could easily take the railroad under fire, effectively severing it. For some time the Soviets had been building fortifications in the high ground further east. Apanasenko stationed a rifle division here along with one of his few tank brigades, one with the old T-26 light infantry tanks, mounting 45 mm guns.

On the front from Lake Hanka south, there were three main defensive localities that barred their way in depth. In the north, on the edge of Lake Hanka at Turiy Rog, there was one rifle division. About fifty miles to the south was the linchpin of the front, Fortified Zone 105, at Grodekovo, defended by two rifle divisions. Fifty-five kilometers to the south was Fortified Zone 106, centered on Poltavka and defended by one division. Heading south four more fortified zones, each with its division, defended the narrowing bottom sliver of the Maritime Province. Just south of Lake Hanka, two more rifle divisions and a few tank brigades formed a reserve at Khorala and Spassk Dalniy. The area north of the Mo River consisted of 'rivers and crest lines, without any natural strategic defense line'. The sides of the crests were steep, but travel along the crests was easy. About thirty percent of this area was wooded and easily passable. Along the border between Turiy Rog and Grodekovo ran a dense forest, covered only by observation. South of the Mo was a 'great area of rolling hills with gentle slopes'. There was little forest, and most was tilled land.[22]

Voroshilov was the key to the entire region. It was the locus of the railroad; from it reserves could be shifted to the fortified zones on the frontier. If it fell, the entire region's defense would collapse and seal the fate of Vladivostok, which would be cut off save for mountain roads. So Apanasenko concentrated his mobile reserves here: two tank and several motorized infantry brigades. One of the brigades was armed with the old

T-26 light infantry tanks. The other had the new wonder tank, the T-34, which the General Staff had incredibly overlooked when everything but the junk was ordered west. He gave the command of one of the infantry units to one of his best staff officers, the feisty Ukrainian, Colonel Petro Grigorenko. The T-34s were given to one of the camp veterans, Colonel Sergei Golitsyn. Apanasenko was pleased to see the wonders men like these had done when he inspected their brigades in late August. Grigorenko he knew and respected. Golitsyn was a tank expert and had been one of the Tukhachevskiy crowd and was very lucky to be alive. When they were walking alone through the muddy ruts left by the big steel monsters, Golitsyn stopped the general and looked him in the eye. 'Comrade General, I want to thank you for giving me this chance.' Apanasenko returned his look honestly. 'I want to thank you for giving me the chance to prove that I am not a traitor to the Motherland,' continued Golitsyn. The general clapped him on the shoulder. He knew now they would have a chance.

Even his optimism needed reinforcement at this time. The news from the west reeked of one disaster after another. Right now the Germans were closing in on a huge Soviet concentration pinned to the ground in the defense of Kiev. He wondered if his Siberians, all the men he had sent off to that distant front eleven time zones away, would be in the thick of it.

Apanasenko was still laboring like Hercules when Yamashita struck.

## Banzai! Banzai! Banzai!

The planes came first, taking off at dawn on 7 August from their airfields in Manchuria, Korea, and aboard the four aircraft carriers of the Navy's 1st Carrier Division in the Sea of Japan. Almost a thousand Japanese planes struck the airfields of the Red Air Force from Khabarovsk to Vladivostok. Apanasenko had tried to ensure that his planes would not be slaughtered on the ground as they had been in the west, but his own reconnaissance assets had been thinned and thinned again and there were too many holes. The short distance from the border was just too much of an advantage for the Japanese. They worked over the Soviet airfields, although many of the Red Falcons rose to contest the skies. By the end of the day, Apanasenko's air force was badly wounded. Second and third waves of naval aircraft pounded the Soviet fleet's ships and facilities in Vladivostok and Nahodka. Yamamoto would leave no chance of the Pacific Ocean Fleet recovering.[23]

That same morning Yamashita's three armies on the eastern front sprang forward.

North of Grodekovo, Lieutenant General Masao Maruyama was filled with confidence even in the darkness of the forest. He was cheered by the incessant sound of axes in the hands of the thousands of Chinese coolies at the van of his 2nd Sendai Division. It was a good division, the men well-trained, with many veterans of combat in China and long-service in Manchuria. They had just settled into their comfortable garrison in the division's hometown, the city of Sendai on Honshu, almost 300 kilometers north of Tokyo, when the order had been given to return to Manchuria. Behind them, on the path cleared by the Sendai, came the 7th Tank Regiment and the 3rd Independent Antitank Battalion. He was honored that General Yamashita had given such a critical mission to his division. He would not fail. The spirit of the division was high.

But for the muffling sound of the trees, Maruyama would have heard the drumbeat of artillery on the fortified zone before Grodekovo as two divisions of the 3rd Army attacked the defenses. The 300 mm *tochka* busters were working quite well, but the infantry were paying a terrible price as they fought through one trench line after another. Yamashita knew it would be costly, but he wanted to fix the Soviets' attention on their main defenses. He had absorbed the Blitzkrieg lessons of his German hosts; those lessons followed his own inclinations easily. They were a natural fit. Further south the 7th Army, under General Masaharu Homma, also drew the attention of the Red Army to their defenses around Poltavka. As a special reserve Yamashita held four tank regiments, which he had brigaded into two division-sized formations and put through a month's intensive training with special motorized infantry regiments and designated fighter support. It was the largest mechanized force the Japanese Army had ever assembled, and it would be learning on the battlefield. Once Yamashita broke free of the fortified zones, he would unleash it.

As the reports began to filter back, he was also pleased to see how quickly the fortified zones were being fought through. Many of the pillboxes that interspersed the defenses had been poorly made in the rush to fortify the area after the Manchurian Incident of 1932; many were of wood and earth, and easily destroyed.[24] But the quality of the defenders, the work of the men in those positions, was what had surprised him. In most places the Soviet defense had been tenacious and costly. The artillery was surprisingly well served and was using ammunition on a scale that was alien to the Japanese. NKVD units, especially, were diehards. Lyushkov's predictions were proving badly off. He was prowling around the headquarters somewhere. Yamashita had been briefed by him and taken an instant dislike to him; however useful he was supposed to be to His Majesty, the general felt a palpable distaste for a traitor.

To the north of Lake Hanka, the 5th Army ran into trouble. The Japanese guns at Hutou had successfully taken the railroad under fire, but the army's crossing of the Ussuri River had not gone well. A few bridgeheads had been taken, but they had been isolated. Enemy aircraft from Khabarovsk, which had not been within range of the first strike, were contesting the sky quite well. 'Well,' he commented to Ayabe, ' a plan must have many branches so if one is broken, another can be followed.'[25] The sacrifices in the Iman crossings would still serve a purpose if they pulled the Red Army's reserves to that spot. He had the initiative, a priceless advantage from which he would forge more trouble for the Soviets. He was a patient man who strikes like a cobra when ready.

Apanasenko was on the phone to Moscow. 'Yes, Iosif Vissarionovich, the enemy has been held all along the frontier. The fortified zones have held, for the moment, but the Japanese are grinding through them. They have cut the Trans-Siberian Railroad at several places. Their gunboats have entered the Ussuri from the Sungari River and destroyed several railroad bridges near Khabarovsk.... Yes, they have all been sunk, but raiding parties are attacking bridges and tunnels all the way from Khabarovsk to Blago-veschensk. They have succeeded in only a few places, but most of the damage is minor and can be easily replaced. No, Iosif Vissarionovich, no. I realize that no reinforcements can be spared from the west.... I have concentrated my reserves at Voroshilov to counter any breakthrough.'

He was going to need those reserves soon. The division at Turiy Rog was in trouble. An estimated two of the big Japanese divisions were over-whelming the boys up there. Boys, peasants, *zeks*. Apanasenko was proud of them. He let himself think, 'Russians.' Yes, that's why they are fighting. Not for Stalin. Had that been all, most would have shot their officers and rushed out to meet the Japanese, like so many had happily surrendered to the Germans. But it was Russia they fought for, and there was nothing wrong with Russia that Japan would set right. It was a war of the *narod*, the Russian people. It was easier to realize this than with the Germans, who looked like them. The Russian visceral hatred for the Oriental would be Apanasenko's great weapon. The Mongols had driven this fear to the bone. Nothing in Russo-Japanese relations had proven the feeling misplaced. He then ordered the rifle division from Spassk-Dalniy to help the boys at Turiy Rog.

Yamashita continued to be surprised by the enemy's defense of the fortified zones. What had a German general mentioned to him about the Russians? Yes – 'It is not enough to kill a Russian, you must knock him down, too.' Well, the *Yamato* spirit was doing a lot of knocking down as well. The casualty lists were alarming, but he was proud of his warriors, his Samurai. They were as tough as their grandfathers in the Russo-Japanese War. He laughed quietly. 'Or should I say the First Russo-Japanese War?' His junior officers were on the sword's edge of the fighting, holding their units together and encouraging them to superhuman feats of will and daring, and dying in great numbers – a blizzard of cherry blossoms. The Japanese soldier was being exceptionally well led at the battalion level and was showing a real flare for infiltration through difficult terrain and around enemy strong points.

While the 3rd and 7th Armies continued to pound away at the fortified zones, they also constantly pushed strong forces through the open woodlands and hills between them. These efforts drew more and more of the enemy's reserves to cover a longer and longer front. A supporting attack by a division from Korea tied down more of the enemy far away from the main effort. Still, prisoners were now being taken from the garrisons of fortified zones that had not been engaged to the south. Although Yamashita was an army group commander, that never stopped him from visiting the front. He could feel the rhythm of operations along the 200-kilometer eastern front, could feel the crisis building as the enemy used up his reserves. To the north, the 5th Army had finally expanded its bridgeheads over the Ussuri and pushed inland to seize Iman. A nasty enemy attack with tanks had driven the 9th Division back to the river and handled the 23rd Tank Regiment roughly, but the enemy attack had petered out, impaled on the will of the Japanese soldier, who coolly manned his antitank guns or raced in among the tanks with his Molotov cocktails. A German officer attached to his headquarters remarked that the fighting in the fortified zones reminded him of the trenches in France in World War I. He was visibly fretting over the casualties and missing the window of opportunity that was about to open.

The window simply blew out on the fifteenth day of fighting.

The Sendai's coolies had done their work well. When the last screen of trees fell, Maruyama rushed his division south, leaving a broad road for Yamashita's reserve divisions to pour through. They bypassed the edge of the *tochka* belt to their south and brushed aside a few Soviet cavalry patrols. Maruyama pushed on quickly to the Mo River and the railroad crossing that supplied the enemy at Turiy Rog. The tanks of the 7th Tank Regiment splashed through as his men waded across downstream. It was a shallow river, no great obstacle. Hurry! Hurry! He was everywhere pushing his command along in its long khaki columns, as the Soviets melted away in front of them. Now they were in rolling farmland, the only features the collective farm villages. Here and there Soviet units attempted to defend them, but Maruyama just bypassed them, now heading for the rear of Fortified Zone 105.[26]

He strode up Hill 341, a bump in the earth, but still an elevation. He could see the railroad to Voroshilov five kilometers to the south. The 7th Tank Regiment raced ahead, with his 16th Infantry Regiment close behind.

Five kilometers south of the railroad, on Hill 388, Colonels Grigorenko and Golitsyn were looking north at the column of Japanese tanks and infantry. It would be a race to see who got to the railroad first. Already Grigorenko's infantry were mounted on the backs and sides of Golitsyn's tanks. They rumbled north and crossed the tributary of the Mo and then the railroad, before the Japanese. Even before the tanks came within shooting distance of each other, a battalion of motorized artillery deployed and got in the first shot, its salvo straddling the 16th Infantry. The T-34s opened up at a longer ran than the Japanese Type 98 tanks could hope to reach, their 76 mm guns quickly beginning to find targets as Japanese tanks began to blossom then burn. The Soviet attack would have swept over Hill 341 and Maruyama himself had not a swarm of Japanese planes showed up to strafe and harry the Soviets. A few of the surviving Red Falcons showed up in turn to provide support, enabling the Soviet tanks and infantry to push as far as the base of the hill before the combined weight of Japanese artillery and antitank fire and air attacks finally stopped them. Under the cover of the few remaining Red Air Force fighters, they withdrew back to the railroad.

Over the next week Grigorenko and Golitsyn fended off the determined thrusts of a growing Japanese force trying to cut off Fortified Zone 105. Grigorenko's men were doing well. He had been lucky in this command; most of his men had been in an officer-cadet school, which was shut down. The quality was high, but few were left after a week. Incessant Japanese attacks were inching closer to the railroad. Already the front had swung backwards from Turiy Rog after the Japanese bypassed it. Two divisions were lost there. Then the word came. The enemy had broken through at Poltavka, twenty kilometers to the south, with a horde of tanks. Their orders were to hold open the rear door to let the survivors of the two divisions escape. It was during this desperate attempt that Golitsyn died with his last five tanks. Grigorenko's few men were swallowed up by the rush of fugitives from the fortified zone.[27]

As Yamashita knew it would, the Soviet front had broken wide open. He had stressed it to breaking point and then slipped through every hole he could. It was a simple matter of Judo. The Sendai had done well. Now it was the turn of the tank corps and a matter of forty kilometers to Voroshilov. Outside of the town the Soviet commander threw in his last reserve, the T-26 tank brigade and some infantry. They fought the Japanese tank corps to a standstill, but a draw was the same as a defeat for the Soviets. Japanese infantry divisions flowed around the tank fighting, closed around Voroshilov, and headed south again. The town surrendered. Yamashita rode southwards on the wave of victory to thunderous shouts of 'Banzai!' as he passed the endless columns converging on Vladivostok. It was September 23 – forty-six days since the beginning of the offensive.

On the 26th, he stood looking down at the port city on its peninsula jutting into Ussurisk Bay. A pall of smoke hung over it. He again laughed to himself. Over the years, he had studied in wargames how to seize the fortified Bataan Peninsula in the Philippines, but never Vladivostok. Well, he would leave the siege to General Homma. Homma had always spoken highly of General Nogi's siege of Port Arthur in the Russo-Japanese War. Again he laughed to himself, 'Oh, yes, it should now be called the First

Russo-Japanese War.' His thoughts returned to Homma 'Let's see what he learned about sieges,' he said to his chief of staff.

Yamashita could see Yamamoto's battleships parading back and forth firing their big guns into the city's defenses. The admiral had crushed the minor threat of the Soviet fleet. Most of the submarines had been sunk where they were moored by naval aircraft or smashed up by gunfire. Their crews had been pressed into the Naval Infantry and fed into the defenses of the port. A few had gone to sea to sting the Imperial Navy here and there, sometimes painfully. Yet Yamashita had to admit that Yamamoto had skillfully shown off the Navy's ability. Despite that, the war had been an army victory. Let the Navy try to emulate the Army this winter when it would go south. Now he had to worry about Phase 2 – Khabarovsk, and that same winter – and the message announcing his victory to His Imperial Majesty.

## The Treaty of Manila

The letter to the Emperor was the easy part. Apanasenko fought a tough battle for Khabarovsk, but the game was really up, and even he knew it. The city fell in December, as winter closed down operations for the Japanese. It was never an excuse for inactivity to the Russians, who relocated the center of resistance to Blagoveschensk. He would be remembered for his humane efforts to care for the hundreds of thousands of Russian civilians who fled west with his forces. He also threw open the gates of the camps as he retreated, forcing the camp guards and *zeks* into combat units. Most likely Stalin would have shot Apanasenko had the dictator lived past December, when he disappeared in the chaos of his flight from the fall of Moscow.[28] The Siberian divisions had perished in the great encirclements at Kiev in September and Bryansk and Vyazma outside of Moscow in October. Zhukov was to write bitterly in his memoirs that had those Siberians been kept in reserve, Moscow might have been saved.[29]

Apanasenko survived the disaster in the Far East to hold off Yamashita the next spring, until the Treaty of Manila ended the war.[30] The siege of Vladivostok went on for three months, tying down Homma's 7th Army and earning him an Imperial reproof. Grigorenko, released from Japanese captivity in 1943, became a successful civil engineer in the Russian Eurasian Federation (REF) and wrote the definitive history of the Second Russo-Japanese War. Lyushkov proved a surprisingly good governor of his Majesty's new Maritime Province. In fact, he was too good. The Japanese were never ones to quibble over his ruthlessness, but they did have to take rather drastic notice of his treasonous plans to reunite the province with the REF. Yamashita returned to a hero's welcome and a personal audience with the Emperor. The Tiger of Siberia would be denied nothing.

The Treaty of Manila, signed on March 2, 1942, had been sponsored reluctantly by President Franklin Roosevelt, who had more to worry about with Russia out of the war and a victorious Germany looking wolfishly across the Atlantic. That treaty kept the Philippines for the United States but at the humiliating cost of looking east while Japan moved south in the winter and spring.

## The reality

This story follows actual events until Foreign Minister Matsuoka's visit to Germany in March 1941. In reality Hitler hinted rather broadly about war with the Soviet Union. The Japanese ambassador had been reporting the coming war accurately, but the Japanese did not seem to take it seriously. In this story, Hitler frankly asks for a joint German-Japanese attack on the Soviet Union. There was already considerable tension in the Japanese Government and military about whether to attack the Soviet Union or the Western colonial powers in Asia to acquire their natural resources. Hitler's formal proposal could have concentrated the Japanese on the possibilities and given weight to those who urged Japan to *Hokoshin* or 'Go North'. The mobilization plan and initial campaign plan are those the Japanese had actually devised for such an eventuality in 1941; and Yamashita was actually assigned, during the summer 1941 mobilization of the Kwangtung Army, to army group command of those forces that would have attacked the Maritime Province. The heroic reorganization of the defenses of the Far East was actually accomplished by Apanasenko. He would be killed by a stray bullet fighting the Germans after his transfer to the west in 1943.

## Bibliography

Boyd, Carl, *Hitler's Japanese Confidant: General Oshima Hiroshi and MAGIC Intelligence, 1941–1945* (University Press of Kansas, Lawrence, 1993).

Coox, Alvin D., *The Anatomy of a Small War: The Soviet-Japanese Struggle for Changkufeng/Khasan, 1938* (Greenwood Press, Westport, 1977).

Coox, Alvin D., 'The Lesser of Two Hells: NKVD General G.S. Lyushkov's Defection to Japan, 1938–1945' (*The Journal of Slavic Studies*, September and December 1998).

Coox, Alvin D., *Nomonhan: Japan Against Russia, 1939* (Stanford University Press, Stanford, 1990).

Fuller, Richard, *Shokan, Hirohito's Samurai: Leaders of the Japanese Armed Forces, 1926–1945* (Arms and Armour Press, London, 1992).

Glantz, David, *Stumbling Colossus: The Red Army on the Eve of World War II* (University Press of Kansas, Lawrence, 1998).

Grigorenko, Petro, *Memoirs* (W.W. Norton and Company, New York, 1982).

Hayashi, Saburo, *Kogun: The Japanese Army in the Pacific War* (Greenwood Press, Westport, 1978).

Hoyt, Edwin P., *Japan's War: The Great Pacific Conflict* (Da Capo Press, New York, 1986).

*Japanese Preparations for Operations in Manchuria (Prior to 1943)*, Japanese Monograph no.77 (United States, Department of the Army, Hq. Army Forces Far East, Military History Section, Japanese Research Division [JRD], 1954).

*Japanese Special Study on Manchuria, vol.I: Japanese Operational Planning Against the USSR*

(United States, Department of the Army, Hq. Army Forces Far East, Military History Section, Japanese Research Division [JRD], 1955).

*Japanese Studies on Manchuria, vol.III, part 3, Strategic Study of Manchuria: Military Topography and Geography, Regional Terrain Analysis* (United States, Department of the Army, Hq. Army Forces Far East, Military History Section, Japanese Research Division [JRD], 1956).

Krivosheev, G.F. (ed.), *Soviet Casualties and Combat Losses in the Twentieth Century* (Greenhill Books, London, 1993).

*Political Strategy Prior to Outbreak of War, part III*, Japanese Monograph no.147 (United States, Department of the Army, Hq. Army Forces Far East, Military History Section, Japanese Research Division [JRD], 1953).

Whymant, Robert, *Stalin's Spy: Richard Sorge and the Tokyo Espionage Ring* (St Martin's Press, New York, 1996).

## Notes

1. Alvin D. Coox, *Nomonhan: Japan Against Russia, 1939* (1990), pp.916, 952, 1123. Total casualties were calculated by adding the total battle casualties in the secret Kwangtung Army Report at Appendix J with the number of ill at Table 39.1. G.F. Krivosheev, ed., *Soviet Casualties and Combat Losses in the Twentieth Century* (1993), p.53.

2. Coox, *op.cit.* p.991.

3. *Japanese Special Study on Manchuria, vol.I: Japanese Operational Planning Against the USSR* (1955), p.20.

4. Coox, *op.cit.* p.1001.

5. Saburo Hayashi, *Kogun, The Japanese Army in the Pacific War* (1978), pp.14–16.

6. Alvin D. Coox, *The Anatomy of a Small War: The Soviet-Japanese Struggle for Changkufeng/Khasan, 1938* (1977), p.359.

7. Edwin P. Hoyt, *Japan's War: The Great Pacific Conflict* (1986), p.198.

8. Coox, *op.cit.* pp.1023–5.

9. Hayashi, *op.cit.* p. 25–6.

10. *Japanese Operational Planning Against the USSR*, pp.105–11.

11. *Ibid* pp.79–85.

12. *Ibid* p.44.

13. David Glantz, *Stumbling Colossus: The Red Army in the Pacific on the Eve of World War II* (1998), pp.263–4.

14. Petro Grigorenko, *Memoirs* (1982), p.111.

15. Alvin D. Coox, 'The Lesser of Two Hells: NKVD General G.S. Lyushkov's Defection to Japan, 1938–1945, Part I', *The Journal of Slavic Studies* (September 1998).

16. At this time, forces in the Transbaikal MD and Mongolia were ordered to report directly to Moscow and passed out of the control of the commander in the Far East.

17. Carl Boyd, *Hitler's Japanese Confidant: General Oshima Hiroshi and MAGIC Intelligence, 1941–1945* (1993), p.19.

18. Born in 1885, Yamashita graduated from the Central Military Academy in 1906. After troop and staff assignments as a junior officer, he was selected for grooming as a rising star. After attending the War College in 1916 and attachment to the General Staff in 1917, he was sent on a number of prestigious foreign assignments: military student in Switzerland in 1919, in Germany in 1921, and military attaché to Austria and Hungary 1927. He commanded the 3rd Infantry

Regiment in 1930, and headed the mobilization section of the General Staff in 1931. In that year he played an important role in mediating between rebel officers and the War Ministry and was exiled to command a brigade in Korea in 1937 for apparent sympathy with the rebels. In the war with China he commanded a mixed brigade and served as Chief of Staff to the North Area Army, and then commanded the Kwangtung Army's 4th Division in 1938. In 1939 he was head of 'Unit 82', the planning element for the 'Strike South' invasion of the East Indies, Malaya, etc: cited in Richard Fuller, *Shokan, Hirohito's Samurai: Leaders of the Japanese Armed Forces, 1926–1945* (1992), p.236.

19. *Ibid* p.86.

*20. Born in 1898, Apanasenko joined the Red Army in 1918 and rose to command a cavalry division during the Russian Civil War. After the war he served consecutively as division and corps commander and in 1935 military district deputy commander, then in 1938 commander, of the Central Asian Military District. See N.V. Ogarkov, *Military Encyclopedic Dictionary* vol.1 (Voyenizdat, Ulan Ude, 1983), p.132.

21 Grigorenko, *op.cit.* pp.129–33.

22. *Military Topography and Geography, Regional Terrain Analysis*, pp.66–7.

*23. Minoru Genda, *First Strike at Vladivostok* (Seit Shorin Press, Tokyo, 1946).

24. *Military Topography and Geography, Regional Terrain Analysis*, pp.81–3.

*25. Kitsuji Ayabe, 'The Imperial Sun Rises in the North' (*The Infantry Journal*, Washington, D.C., 1949), p.261.

*26. 'The Battle for the Fortified Zones', *Operations on the Ussuri Front* (Imperial General Headquarters, Tokyo, 1947), p.105.

*27. Petro Grigorenko, *The Struggle for the Far East* (Voyenizdat, Ulan Ude, 1956), pp.223–6.

*28. Anna Akhmatova, 'Dead Birches', *The Broken Millstone: Poems of the Soviet Debacle*, trans. Boris Pasternak (Maybury Hill Ltd, London, 1955), pp.98–102. Akhmatova, considered the greatest lyric poet of the Soviet and post-Soviet periods, wrote the poem cycle of the death throes of Soviet power. The most chilling segment was 'Dead Birches,' based on the most credible story of the death of the tyrant as he fled to Khuibyshev, now Samara, just ahead of the Germans. Although fear of him had mostly evaporated with his power, enough remained for him to be simply abandoned at a railroad siding in an empty car. The siding served Camp 839 of the Gulag. Its guards had disappeared in the engulfing chaos, and the *zeks* wandered about with nowhere to go. They found him in the car. It was Akhmatova's darkest work.

*29. Georgii Zhukov, *Bitter Memories* (Collins, New York, 1952), p.399.

*30. The Treaty of Manila was a ruthless (some would say shameless) display of realpolitik by FDR. In order to save the Philippines and conserve American resources to oppose the German hegemony of Europe, he gave the Japanese carte blanche to overrun the Dutch East Indies and consolidate control of French Indochina. In one of the greatest balancing acts of diplomatic history, he persuaded Churchill to allow Japan to freely import tin and rubber from Malaya. Simultaneously, he hinted at putting a crimp in Japan's oil supply. Faced with the prolonged fighting in Siberia, the prospect of getting so much without a fight bought a Japanese signature at Manila. The wisdom of the treaty was borne out as Britain, reinforced by her untouched empire and left alone by a Japan busy digesting its new acquisitions, hung on against a renewed German onslaught in the summer of 1942 and crushed a German invasion.

# 2
# BE CAREFUL WHAT YOU WISH FOR
## The Plan Orange Disaster

Wade G. Dudley

Secrets abound in times of war, as does what Winston Churchill termed the 'bodyguard of lies' surrounding any important military 'truth'. Some sixty years ago, the failure of American, British, and Russian military intelligence to penetrate Japan's secret stratagems placed the United States Navy on the wrong side of the greatest naval debacle in history. How and why the United States suddenly implemented a version of War Plan Orange that had been abandoned as unfeasible in the 1920s is, perhaps, even more important than the story of the proud warships gutted by its implementation.

### From War Plan Orange to Rainbow 4

In the 1890s, American military staffs began to consider the Pacific as a potential major arena for international conflict. Initially, they envisioned Europeans as the anticipated enemy – one of the earliest plans called for the destruction of a weak French Asiatic squadron in support of America's Open Door Policy in China. The joint American Army and Navy Planning Boards, for the sake of secrecy and perhaps from the awareness that giving names to possible enemies tends to raise levels of international tension, soon devised a color-based system for identifying nations during planning. They designated the United States as 'Blue', the British as 'Red', the Germans as 'Black', and so forth. The acquisition of the Philippines in 1898 increased the emphasis on defensive operations in surrounding waters and necessitated giving consideration to the acquisition and protection of 'stepping-stone' logistical bases from the west coast of the United States to Manila Bay, and onward to the resources and markets of the Orient.

In the first decade of the twentieth century, a new potential enemy emerged in the Pacific. With the Meiji Restoration, Japan had embraced Western-style industrialism and the imperialism which inevitably accompanied it. A modern Imperial Japanese Navy, modeled on the British Royal

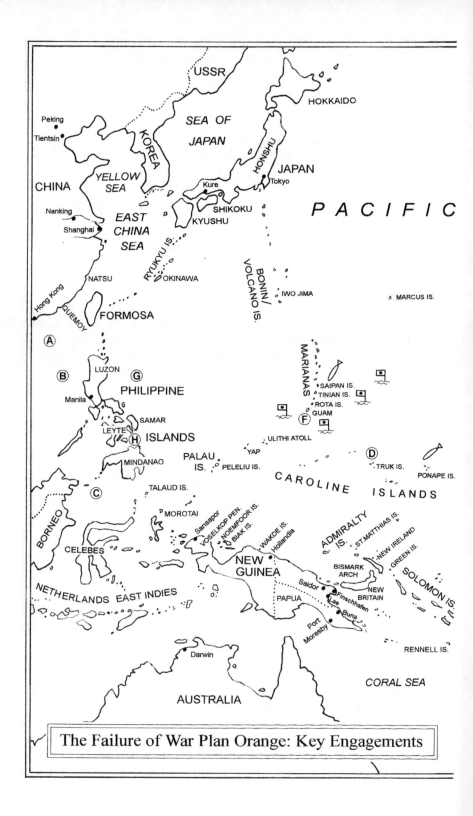

The Failure of War Plan Orange: Key Engagements

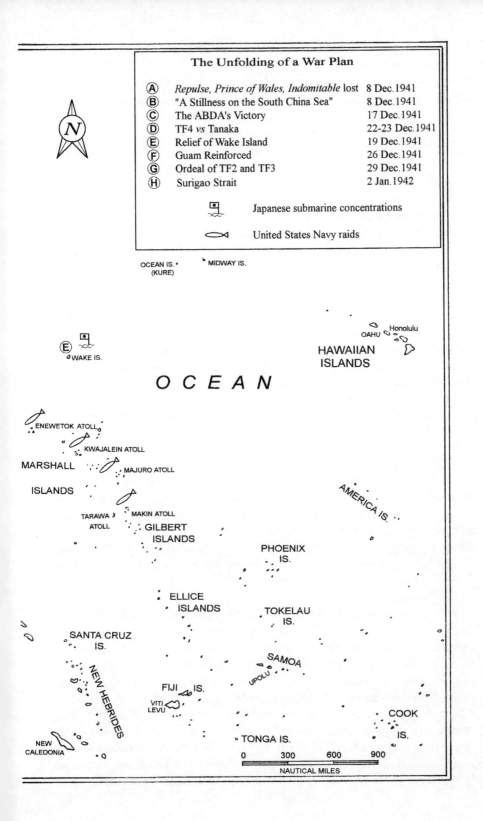

### The Unfolding of a War Plan

(A) *Repulse, Prince of Wales, Indomitable* lost 8 Dec. 1941
(B) "A Stillness on the South China Sea" 8 Dec. 1941
(C) The ABDA's Victory 17 Dec. 1941
(D) TF4 *vs* Tanaka 22-23 Dec. 1941
(E) Relief of Wake Island 19 Dec. 1941
(F) Guam Reinforced 26 Dec. 1941
(G) Ordeal of TF2 and TF3 29 Dec. 1941
(H) Surigao Strait 2 Jan. 1942

Japanese submarine concentrations

United States Navy raids

OCEAN IS. • MIDWAY IS.
(KURE)

(E) WAKE IS.

O C E A N

OAHU Honolulu

HAWAIIAN
ISLANDS

ENEWETOK ATOLL

KWAJALEIN ATOLL

MARSHALL MAJURO ATOLL

ISLANDS AMERICA IS.

TARAWA MAKIN ATOLL
ATOLL GILBERT
ISLANDS

PHOENIX
IS.

ELLICE
ISLANDS TOKELAU
IS.

SANTA CRUZ
IS.

SAMOA

FIJI IS. UPOLU

VITI
LEVU COOK
IS.

NEW
CALEDONIA TONGA IS.

NEW HEBRIDES

0   300   600   900
NAUTICAL MILES

Navy (not to mention trained by that navy, and often using ships built in British shipyards), played the key role in defeating Russia in 1904–5. The naval successes at Port Arthur and Tsushima established the IJN as a force to be reckoned with. In the eyes of American military planners, this impressive display earned Japan its own designation, 'Orange', and actions deemed necessary to counter future Japanese aggression in the Pacific could be found thereafter in War Plan Orange.

The rapid technological shifts resulting from World War I, coupled with post-war diplomatic initiatives and the economic difficulties of a world-wide depression, dictated numerous changes in War Plan Orange between 1919 and 1939. In various guises and with the occasional twist and turn, planning moved from a determined direct defense of the Philippines by the American fleet in the early 1920s, to the anticipated loss of those islands to a superbly trained, well-equipped, and (thanks to its Chinese adventures) veteran Japanese military in the 1930s. By early 1939, Plan Orange called for the recapture of the Philippines after a two to three year methodical advance across the central Pacific, at which time Japan's home fleet would be confronted and destroyed, allowing a close blockade of the home islands (hopefully decisive without the need for an invasion). In mid-1939, with war in Europe threatening to erupt at any moment, War Plan Orange was incorporated into Rainbow 1, a unilateral defense of the western hemisphere against Germany, Japan, and their fascist minions.

By mid-1940 a new plan, Rainbow 4, offered a multi-lateral defense of the western hemisphere, assuming alliances with Great Britain and France. This plan forbade any Blue offensive action in the Pacific – a clear acknowledgment of Germany as the most dangerous of potential opponents. In essence, the United States would abandon the Philippines, Guam, and even Wake Island to a hopeless delaying action against superior Japanese forces. Rainbow 4 allowed Japan a free hand in Asia and the Pacific while the military assets of the United States and its eventual allies knocked Germany out of the war as quickly as possible.

## Japan: options and planning through 1939

The industrialization of Japan's economy may have saved the nation from direct European domination in the late 1800s, but it resulted in a quandary for Japanese leaders. The home islands simply lacked the raw materials to support massive industrialization. Thus the history of modernized Japan became one of aggressively seeking control of Asian resources. Through 1920, military success followed military success, yet European and American diplomats more often than not managed to strip away the fruits of Japanese victory. After 1920 the Japanese government became increasingly dominated by its officer caste, the same men who had found victory to be bittersweet, at best. They knew a reckoning with their foreign tormentors could not be avoided, and the greatest threat appeared to be the United States, a nation with seemingly endless industrial might.

Japanese naval thinking fixated on victory through a single great battle.[1] Before the technological changes during and following World War I, planners envisioned the American fleet being brought to battle near the home islands. As had the Russians at Tsushima, the United States Navy would be debilitated by its extended voyage, considerably improving the odds against a numerically superior American fleet. After the technological changes, the expected interception point moved south and east, its location varying with changing plans from the coasts of the Philippines to the Marshall Islands. With the distance traveled less of a debilitative factor (speed, range, and durability had improved dramatically), the IJN planned an attritional war against the advancing USN. Submarines, land and naval airplanes, and night attacks by light surface units equipped with the superb Type 92 'Long Lance' torpedo, would deplete the American forces by as much as thirty percent before the main battle fleets clashed and decided the issue.

The timing and location of the final battle, as well as the success of the IJN's attritional strategy, depended upon which nation seized the initiative. If Japan struck first (first strike, the surprise attack, being prominent in Japanese military tradition), it could quickly seize the American Pacific bases – the Philippines, Guam, Wake Island, and perhaps even Midway Island and the Aleutians – forcing the USN into a protracted advance of one to two years' duration. This would allow time for the attritional strategy to work; but a danger (almost a certainty) existed that the United States' production capacity would so far exceed that of Japan that the USN would actually be stronger, despite a thirty percent attrition of its starting forces, once it breached Japan's defensive perimeter in the Pacific. If the Americans struck first, especially with the IJN scattered across the Pacific and along the coasts of Asia, disaster would result. Thus, by 1940, as the Imperial Army continued to advance in China, Europe dissolved in flames, and the American people prepared to elect a president to lead them away from or into war, the IJN lacked a truly effective counter to an aggressive War Plan Orange.

## Democracy at work

The Democratic Party nominated Franklin Delano Roosevelt for a third consecutive term as president in 1940. The Republican Party opposed the highly popular Roosevelt with Wendell L. Willkie, a major player in the corporate world but not a man expected to win the heart of the common man, still suffering from the Great Depression. It may never be known exactly who leaked details of Rainbow 4 to the American press, but on October 18 newspaper headlines across the United States screamed 'FDR

PLANS TO ABANDON OUR BOYS IN THE PHILIPPINES TO THE JAPS!'[2] General Douglas MacArthur, caught unprepared by reporters that morning, inadvertently added fuel to the political fire: 'Gentlemen, no American president has ever willingly abandoned an inch of American soil to an enemy, much less thrown away the lives of American soldiers and sailors. Our good President would be the first person to agree with me on that. In fact, I have so much faith in President Roosevelt that I would willingly leave for Manila today.'[3]

The Republican Party knew a possible winning gambit when they saw (or leaked) it, especially with less than a month remaining until the election. Hammered by Willkie on the only issue available and with the polls only a week away, Roosevelt finally offered a statement to the American public via his Sunday radio chat. 'I will no more abandon America's sons than I would my own children. The United States Navy is one of the most powerful forces in the world; should – and I pray it never does – war come to the Pacific, the enemy will be met and destroyed in the Philippines.'[4] Somewhat reassured, voters elected their president to a third term, though not by the expected landslide.

The day after the election, three things of note occurred. In Washington, American naval planners dusted off old copies of an aggressive Plan Orange to use in preparing a new multi-lateral war plan, Rainbow 5. In San Francisco, a vacationing General Douglas MacArthur received orders to take command immediately in the Philippines. And at his office in Tokyo, Admiral Isokura Yamamoto, the man commanding the Japanese Navy, smiled as he read the news from the United States.

## Yamamoto and Plan Z

Isokura Yamamoto towers above the great admirals of history, despite his five foot three inch height. As a young officer, he paced a deck at Tsushima, sacrificing two fingers to Imperial glory. Later, he attended Harvard and served as a naval attaché in Washington, gaining a first-hand understanding of the overwhelming resources and industrial capability of the United States. Throughout his life he excelled at games of skill and strategy – bridge, poker, and shogi (similar to European chess).[5] And it was with great skill that he tackled the problem of defeating the American giant.

In August 1939, Yamamoto found himself at the pinnacle of his profession, commander and chief of the Combined Fleet. Two months later he observed a demonstration of naval air power from the bridge of the carrier *Akagi*. Turning to his chief of staff, the admiral remarked, 'Impressive! If I can use our fast carriers to sink the American fleet in the mud of Pearl Harbor, I shall run wild in the Pacific for a year, maybe two.' From behind the two men, the absent-minded (though brilliant) Captain Kameto Kuroshima murmured, 'Be careful what you wish for, Admiral.' Pressed for an explanation of his less than artful words, Kuroshima replied, 'The mud of Pearl is shallow. If the Americans are the industrial geniuses that you have preached about so often, then they will simply raise the ships and repair them. Far better if the mud is deep, and the victory permanent.'[6] Yamamoto agreed, but lacking the ability to force the USN into a deep water engagement, he assigned Kuroshima the task of planning a preemptive strike on Pearl Harbor. The resulting plan, though offering a strong possibility of tactical success, left both men troubled because it would not force America to negotiate a peace treaty.

Roosevelt's commitment to defend the Philippines changed everything. The strike at Pearl scrapped, Yamamoto officially unveiled 'Plan Z' to the army and navy in September 1941.[7] The plan meshed well with the idea of a Southern Offensive then being championed by the army, one designed to secure quickly the Philippines and Malaysia as a stepping stone to resource-laden India and the East Indies.[8] Plan Z anticipated an immediate advance of the USN from Pearl following the line Midway–Wake Island–Guam–the Philippines, in order to secure American territory, avoid Japanese land-based air and light surface units in the Marshalls, and force the battleline of the IJN into a decisive engagement east or northeast of the Philippines. Without attrition of the USN, the Japanese Combined Fleet, divided as it supported the army, would face anticipated ratios of (USN:IJN) 13:9 in battleships, 20:12 in cruisers, and 60:40 in destroyers by M+20 (the earliest date on which the American fleet should near the Philippine coast). Only in fast carriers, 4:6, and naval air power, 400:500 planes, would ratios favor the IJN. Yamamoto, however, expected the Americans to split their light surface forces in order to support the British and Dutch, to escort troop convoys closely following their main fleet, and to cover the fleet's large logistical train.

Central to Plan Z was a daring scheme to lull the Americans into misusing their carriers. Five old merchantmen would be converted to appear as flattops – including dummy planes on the decks. These vessels, accompanied by the light carrier *Ryujo*, would operate west of the Philippines. If they could fix American attention, Yamamoto's Fast Striking Force of six carriers, supported by two battlecruisers and assorted lighter vessels, would have an opportunity to weaken the USN with repeated strikes once it reached Guam. The carriers would then drive the American fleet through the southern approaches to Manila – either San Bernadino Strait or Surigao Strait – where Yamamoto would be waiting with a gauntlet of destroyers, cruisers, and battlewagons quickly concentrated from forces supporting the Southern Offensive. Surviving elements of the American battlefleet would undoubtedly reach Manila, but there they could be pounded by land-based airplanes, operating from newly captured fields on Luzon or those recently occupied in (formerly French) Indochina. To avoid a change of heart by the

Americans, Guam and Wake Island would not be seized until after the defeat of the USN's main fleet.

Though the Imperial Japanese Army did not smile upon Plan Z, arguing that the fast carriers would be better used covering the invasion of Malaysia and clearing the South China Sea of Allied naval forces, they could not disagree with Yamamoto's logic: 'Only the complete destruction of the American Pacific fleet and the loss of the Philippines will shock the citizens of the United States into a negotiated peace. It will take twenty years and the resources of Asia to allow our nation to achieve industrial parity with our enemy. Samurai of Japan! We *must* have that quick peace!'[9] In the end, all present concurred that land-based aircraft and those surface units scheduled to rendezvous at Surigao Strait would suffice to cover the invasions.

In the following months, as negotiations with an American government angry at continued Japanese expansion in China and obviously preparing for a showdown in the Pacific, moved toward collapse, Tokyo set December 7, 1941, as the date for its assault against Allied territories in the Pacific. Sunrise of that day found Yamamoto off the Philippine coast, aboard the hastily completed super-battleship *Yamato*, wondering how quickly the USN would sortie from Pearl Harbor.

### Kimmel at the helm

Roosevelt's choice of the two key officers responsible for finalizing and implementing the War Plan Orange segment of Rainbow 5 has been debated by historians almost as much as it has been lamented by Americans as a whole. It is not difficult to argue that the self-proclaimed military genius MacArthur's mouth earned him the hot seat; but the much maligned Admiral Husband Kimmel is a different story. War Plan Orange actively sought a big-gun confrontation, and Kimmel was a big-gun admiral, having served on a dozen battlewagons in his career. Though he lacked experience with naval aviation, carriers constituted a virtually untried arm of the United States Navy at that time. Without doubt, Kimmel was the consensus choice to implement War Plan Orange. Even General George Marshall whole-heartedly supported the aggressive Kimmel for the role.

In early November 1941, Kimmel held a conference for his top officers at Pearl. There he presented the plan which would be implemented, as it happened, the following month. In the Philippines, MacArthur, recently reinforced by fifty P-40 fighters and twenty-four B-17 bombers, would fight a delaying action, preserving Manila Bay as a primary fleet anchorage. A British fleet of two battleships, a carrier, and screening elements would similarly defend Singapore, the Gibraltar of the Pacific, as a secondary base for the American fleet. Southward, the ABDA flotilla (a small American-British-Dutch-Australian force built around two heavy cruisers) would be reinforced by the carrier *Yorktown*.[10] It would secure a secondary supply route to the Philippines from Australia, distracting Japanese naval forces in the process.

Task Force 1 – eleven battleships, three cruisers, and eighteen destroyers – under the tactical command of Kimmel, aboard the battleship *Pennsylvania*, would sail on M+2 to Wake Island via Midway, arriving on M+12. In case Wake had fallen, a battalion of Marines in APDs (old destroyers modified as high speed transports) accompanied TF1. A convoy transporting a coastal defense battalion, fifty crated aircraft, and supplies for Wake trailed TF1 by approximately five days. TF1 would sail from Wake for Guam by M+15. Guam, probably lost to the Japanese in the first days of the conflict, would be briefly bombarded and recaptured by the Marines. On or about M+21, the fleet would leave Guam for Manila, arriving off the Philippines no later than M+25 and taking a northern route around Luzon, hopefully forcing the IJN to give battle or face the interdiction of its forces engaged in the invasion of the Philippines. Elements of the victorious TF1 would arrive in Manila by M+28, at the latest.

Task Forces 2 and 3, centered, respectively, on the carriers *Lexington* and *Saratoga*, would sortie from Pearl immediately upon the opening of hostilities. The carrier groups, each protected by a screen of cruisers and destroyers, would scout ahead of the fleet (TF2 to the north, TF3 to the south). Through M+15, the task forces would operate approximately 300 miles forward of TF1. After the relief or recapture of Guam, the carriers would be reined in, to fifty miles, allowing them to fly CAP (Combat Air Patrol) over TF1 as Japanese naval and land-based aircraft became more of a threat.

Task Force 4, composed of the carrier *Enterprise* and the fast battleships *North Carolina* and *Washington* – the last-named warship rushed to commissioning as the Japanese threat loomed – would provide a diversionary force. From either Pearl or its normal cruising station southeast of the Marshalls, TF4 would raid through the Japanese mandates; its high-speed run concluding with a daring assault on Truk, the major IJN base in the area. TF4 would then rendezvous with TF1 near the Philippines around M+22.

On M+30, a large convoy with men and materiel for Guam, Wake, and the Philippines, would leave the West Coast. Task Force 5, composed of cruisers and destroyers, would escort this force to the Philippines – if the Japanese had not yet sued for peace. 'The Japanese will face us because they must face us – or abandon their invasion forces in the Pacific. And their battleline cannot stand against us!' Kimmel stated at the conclusion of the briefing. He was interrupted by the man who would command TF4, William F. 'Bull' Halsey, 'Be careful what you wish for, Admiral!' Ordered by Kimmel to explain his outburst, the unrepentant Halsey warned, 'Somewhere across that water a little yellow bastard is telling other little yellow bastards the same thing; only he's saying that our battleships cannot stand against their carriers. And until those carriers are burning, I say be damned careful what you wish for!'[11] As it turned out, both men were correct to some degree.

At 0800, December 7, an aide awakened Kimmel at his office on Oahu with the news that Japan had just invaded the Philippines. He immediately ordered War Plan Orange to be implemented and prepared to board *Arizona*, rather than *Pennsylvania*. Kimmel had placed the usual flagship of the Pacific Fleet in dry-dock only three days earlier for annual servicing of its shafts, and rather than sail late the admiral ordered it to join the M+30 convoy as reinforcement for his by then theoretically victorious fleet.[12]

An hour later Kimmel's blood pressure soared when he learned that Douglas MacArthur had somehow managed to be taken by surprise. Most of his planes had been destroyed on the ground and the Imperial Army had landed at points across the Philippines with minimal resistance. Turning to Ensign Elmo R. 'Bud' Zumwalt, his newly appointed aide, Kimmel snarled, 'If MacArthur loses my base before I get there, he better have died gloriously – or I will kill him myself!'[13]

As the American fleet began its exodus from Pearl, a last telegram crossed the Pacific to Tokyo.[14] It read, 'Hope to leave for Tokyo tomorrow. Plan to Climb Mount Niitaka next week.' Unknown to the American telegraphist, the sender, Takeo Yoshikawa, had been carefully observing the American base for six months. His telegram, received at the American Desk of Japanese Naval Intelligence and forwarded immediately to *Yamato*, gave rise to cheers among Yamamoto's staff. Their admiral, an avid climber, had picked the phrase 'Climb Mount Niitaka' as the signal that the American battlefleet had entered the fray.

### A stillness on the sea

MacArthur had, indeed, been caught unprepared, despite the obviously critical place of the Philippines in War Plan Orange. Clark Field, outside Manila, bloomed with fires from the prettily arrayed rows of American planes pummeled by Japanese bombers. By 2000 of December 7, only thirty-one fighters, twenty-seven bombers (including five B-17s), and three seaplanes remained operational. Though MacArthur failed to contest the landings in the Philippines, that did not mean resistance melted away. On the contrary, Americans as well as the green Filipino Constabulary fought magnificently on the ground. As early as December 9, General Nasaharu Homma, commanding the Imperial Army's invasion of Luzon, sent a message to Tokyo demanding increased naval air support and additional troops. Yamamoto refused to release his carriers (now lurking west of Guam), partly out of fear that too rapid a success on the ground would cause the American fleet to return to Pearl, thus evading his trap. As a result, considerable friction developed between the army and navy hierarchies. Fortunately for Japan, Yamamoto's threat to resign, following on the heels of naval successes in the South China Sea on December 8, squelched that particular internal conflict.

On December 7, a British force composed of the battleships *Repulse* and *Prince of Wales*, with the carrier *Indomitable* providing air cover, sortied from Singapore to disrupt Japanese amphibious landings along the Malaysian coast. On the following day, *Indomitable*'s CAP found itself swamped by waves of Japanese fighters and bombers. The British lost all three capital ships, but not before scout planes from their carrier reported the source of their numerous attackers – six Japanese flattops, steaming just within maximum range of Clark airfield. For once, MacArthur acted with alacrity, dispatching every available plane to attack the enemy task force. The uncoordinated waves of American planes began their attack as darkness fell across the South China Sea. Short on fuel and blanketed in darkness, few of the bombers and fighters managed to return to Clark, but those that did allowed MacArthur to send his historic message at 2330 that evening, 'Tonight there is a stillness on the South China Sea where once the fleet of Japan roamed at will. I have avenged the brave crews of the *Repulse*, the *Prince of Whales* [sic], and the *Indomitable*. Five carriers of the Japanese navy have been confirmed as destroyed by my heroic American aviators, and another is damaged and presumed sinking.'[15]

Thus Yamamoto won a double victory that day – three British capital ships stricken from the Royal Naval List and MacArthur's reassurance to the world that the carrier might of Japan had been destroyed. Kimmel, steaming rapidly to Wake Island, is reported to have held a dinner party the following evening, neither the first nor the last warrior deceived into celebration while a trap waited patiently mere days ahead. Rear Admirals Wilson Brown (TF2) and Frank Fletcher (TF3), scouting far forward of TF1, breathed sighs of relief. Until that moment, each man had wrestled with nightmares of their single carriers isolated and destroyed by the numerically superior IJN naval air power. Fletcher, always concerned about the fuel levels of his ships, even slowed his advance the following day to replenish. Only aboard *Enterprise*, flagship of TF4, did a senior American officer seem to have doubts concerning the veracity of MacArthur's message. A young flyer overheard Halsey, then suffering from a constantly worsening skin rash, snort, 'That son of a bitch was born an egotistical liar. Even those yellow bastards aren't stupid enough to put six big carriers where his flyers could get at 'em. Doug couldn't sink an outhouse, not even if he dropped a brick one in the middle of Subic Bay. I hope to God that Wil and Frank see through this crap. "Stillness on the sea" – shit!'[16]

## Truk-ing

That no plan survives contact with the enemy is a military truism, and certainly as applicable to Plan Z as to the ill-fated Plan Orange. Yamamoto faced two unexpected problems: the ABDA command, reinforced by *Yorktown*, and TF4 rampaging through the Marshall Islands. Both moves caught the Japanese admiral flat-footed (Yamamoto strongly believed that the USN would sensibly mass its carriers for battle) and demanded immediate attention.

Operating from secure bases in the Netherlands East Indies, the ABDA task force pushed tentatively northward on December 8, threatening to disrupt the valuable convoys supporting the invasions of the Philippines and Malaya. Two days later, Yamamoto dispatched a task force centered around the slightly damaged *Ryujo* and the light carrier *Hosho* to counter the threat. On December 17, after a week of sparring, fighters and bombers from *Yorktown* caught the Japanese carriers in the process of launching a strike against the ABDA task force. In the face of stiff resistance from a reinforced enemy CAP (fighters were already aloft for the planned strike against *Yorktown*), American dive-bombers hit *Hosho* five times, while two torpedoes and three bombs turned *Ryujo* into a flaming hulk. But this victory had a stiff price— *Yorktown* expended 73 planes in the attack, including all of its torpedo-bombers and over half of its fighters. Admiral Karl Doorman, aboard the cruiser *De Ruyter*, had little choice but to order withdrawal until the depleted air wing could be reinforced; especially after Japanese submarine *I-17* sank *Langley* (once designated CV 1, then redesignated AV 3, an aviation transport), ferrying replacement aircraft to *Yorktown*, on December 19. Nonetheless, the ABDA provided the only true victory for the Allies during the brief Pacific war.

Unless he chose to weaken his Fast Strike Force, Yamamoto lacked carriers to send against the American task force raiding through the Marshalls. Still, the fleet base at Truk, an obvious target for the Americans, offered an opportunity to attrit the USN. On December 9, Yamamoto dispatched a light force led by Rear Admiral Raizo Tanaka in the cruiser *Jintsu* to Truk. It included two additional cruisers, *Myoko* and *Nachi*, and eight destroyers. Tanaka had orders to attempt to develop a night action if the Americans approached the base.

Slowed by a boiler failure on the hastily commissioned *Washington*, TF4 did not enter strike range of Truk until December 22. Even then, Halsey hesitated to commit his dwindling air group against a possibly heavy Japanese air defense. Holding a cruiser and four destroyers back to defend *Enterprise*, the admiral ordered the remainder of the Task Force to close and bombard Truk under cover of darkness. Captain Tameichi Hara, skippering the destroyer *Amatsukaze*, describes what followed:

A seaplane reported two American battleships [*North Carolina* and *Washington*], two cruisers, and six destroyers steaming directly to Truk shortly before dark on December 22. Tanaka, perhaps the best in our navy at night actions by small ships, deployed us in parallel lines, an interior of three cruisers led by two destroyers, and an exterior of six destroyers. At 1123, [destroyer] *Kuroshio* spotted shapes approaching the front of our column at about 48°. A cloudy night, the Americans had approached to less then 3,000 yds before being spotted! Strangely, they seemed not to see us at all, until our division unleashed 48 torpedoes and turned quickly to port for reloading. At that instant star shells burst above the enemy battleships, and the leader, the *North Carolina* [actually the cruiser *Chicora*], was hit by concentrated fire from our cruisers. I was busy for the next few seconds as shell splashes swamped my frail vessel. The *Kuroshio* was not so lucky – at least one large caliber shell penetrated a magazine and it seemed to lift completely from the water. Seconds later, Murata [a spotter] screamed, 'Hits! Torpedo hits along the line!' My heart almost stopped before I realized that he meant the enemy line, and not ours ... By 0058, it seemed that the sea was covered in burning ships. A large American vessel, obviously out of control, bore down on us. I ordered our 5″ guns to open fire – a mistake as an enemy cruiser quickly hit us once the flashes revealed our position, our first damage of the engagement ... At 0153, *Jintsu*, burning and dead in the water, flashed a message to launch remaining torpedoes and disengage. It grieved us to so abandon our comrades, particularly my friend and mentor, Tanaka ...

Clearly, our success against the vastly superior American force resulted from our constant training in night combat actions and proper use of the torpedo, aspects of war neglected by the enemy. But given time, the USN could match the training, if not the warrior spirit, of the Imperial Navy. Thus the advantage of our grossly outnumbered ships would be fleeting – I prayed to my ancestors that it would last long enough for Yamamoto to crush the enemy's main battleline ...[17]

In the confused night action at Truk, both American battleships suffered severely. Each took two torpedoes, *Washington*'s already slow pace dropping to fifteen knots. All three USN cruisers sank before dawn, along with three destroyers. Halsey had little option except to return to Pearl – abandoning the damaged battlewagons to join Kimmel would result in their destruction. Even then, IJN submarine *I-221* managed to penetrate TF4's reduced ASW (anti-submarine warfare) screen and sink *Washington* on December 25.

Admiral Tanaka, his flagship reduced to a hulk by numerous large caliber hits, actually survived the battle, the vessel being towed to Truk the following day. The other Japanese cruisers and three destroyers were not as lucky. Tanaka shifted his flag to *Amatsukaze*, and having effectively stripped two battleships and a carrier from the American fleet, began moving his battered survivors to join Yamamoto off Luzon for the final showdown.

## What damn carriers?

TF1 reached the vicinity of Wake Island on December 19, shortly after Kimmel received a belated notification of *Yorktown*'s successful action against the Japanese light carriers. Though Kimmel should have been puzzled by the failure of the IJN to seize the lightly defended islands of Guam and Wake, he apparently wrote the matter off to Yamamoto's incompetence as a naval commander (perhaps understandably – Kimmel was operating under the delusion that Japan had lost as many as eight carriers). TF1 tarried but briefly in the vicinity of Wake, and then only because of a torpedo hit on the old battleship *Texas* (screening forces sank three IJN submarines in the area, of which only one managed a torpedo attack). The battlewagon's crew quickly fixed a temporary patch over the gaping hole in its bow, allowing it to remain with the task force when the latter turned for Guam on December 20.

As TF1 neared Guam, IJN submarine contacts increased. By December 26, when the APDs unloaded their marines as reinforcements for Guam's defenders, screening destroyers had defeated over a dozen attacks. Despite four confirmed kills, exhaustion took its toll, and *I-214* at last managed to hit *Nevada* with four torpedoes before being forced to the surface and rammed by destroyer *Manley*. Though valiant damage control efforts saved the battleship from sinking, its propellers and rudder had been smashed. When Kimmel began the last stage of his voyage on December 27, both *Nevada* and *Manley* remained at Guam. The APDs also stayed, to screen the damaged battleship.

Brown's TF2 and Fletcher's TF3 failed to find a single Japanese vessel in their rush across the Pacific, though *Lexington*'s air group bombed and strafed the small Japanese airfield on Saipan on December 24 and 25. War Plan Orange had called for the carrier task forces to close with TF1 on the final leg of its journey, but Kimmel, thinking the threat from enemy naval aircraft had been minimized, signaled Brown and Fletcher to unite their task forces on December 29, approximately 300 miles due west of Legaspi air-field on Luzon. They would then proceed, under Fletcher's command, to the Formosa–Luzon gap, fixing the position of the IJN Combined Fleet for Kimmel's rapidly approaching TF1.

Had the carriers united at 0800 December 29, as ordered, a thin chance existed that they could have survived the onslaught that overwhelmed them individually; but Fletcher, on December 28, had again slowed TF3 for refueling, despite the fact that the *Saratoga*'s tanks were well over half full. His first indication of a problem came at 0937 on the following day, while still eight full hours south of TF2. When given a radio message from *Lexington* which read, 'Under attack by large numbers of Japanese carrier planes. Where is TF3? All the world wonders', Fletcher could only exclaim, 'Carrier planes! What damn carriers can they still have?'[18] At last ordering the task force to full speed, Fletcher re-vectored his search planes and tried to contact Brown's force.

The world will never know exactly what happened to TF2. How did Vice Admiral Chuichi Nagumo's 'Ghost Fleet', the six carriers of the Fast Striking Force, manage to surprise Wilson? Why did Nagumo continue to pound the task force after *Lexington* sank? And why was no effort made to rescue the thousands of survivors abandoned in the shark-infested Pacific waters? What we do know is that a carrier, three cruisers, eight destroyers, and two fast oilers succumbed to eight hours of repeated air attack. The suffering of their crews, until taken by the sharks or succumbing to dehydration, is, perhaps, better left unimagined.

The death of *Saratoga* seems almost anti-climactic after the horrors experienced by TF2. At 1628 on December 29, one of Fletcher's scouts (before being destroyed) reported four Japanese heavy carriers approximately 250 miles west-north-west of TF3. Fletcher quickly launched a full strike, retaining only six fighters for CAP. While getting the strike into the air, *Saratoga*'s CAP killed a Japanese flying boat, but only after it had reported TF3's position. Though Nagumo's flyers were exhausted after destroying TF2, he nonetheless managed to deploy a small striking force of eight torpedo planes, twelve divebombers, and nine fighters (none would find their way home in the gathering darkness). These found *Saratoga* at 2010, quickly overwhelmed its CAP, and sank the carrier with three torpedo and at least four bomb hits. Fletcher died on his bridge. The remainder of TF3, crowded with *Saratoga*'s survivors, made full speed for Guam. As for the American air group, it reported sinking two carriers attempting to hide in a rapidly advancing storm front, then disappeared plane by plane as each exhausted its fuel. Though Nagumo reported 112 of his 497 available planes lost on December 29, he never mentioned an American attack on his force. Ironically, the two carriers reported destroyed by *Saratoga*'s air group may well have been the oilers attached to TF2.

## Der Tag

In the early hours of December 30, an exhausted Kimmel received word of the loss of *Saratoga*. With no word from TF2, and every indication that Yamamoto had more carrier strength than originally thought, Kimmel was caught in a dilemma. TF1 was only forty-eight hours from Luzon at top speed, and less than eighty hours from a presumed safe anchorage at Manila. To turn tail at this point not only admitted the failure of War Plan Orange, it certainly would not guarantee a safe return to Pearl for his battleline, which was mainly intact and certainly still outnumbered that of the Japanese. While standing on the bridgewing of *Arizona*, accompanied only by his aide, Zumwalt, Kimmel talked aloud as he worked through his options. 'First, Yamamoto will be waiting north of Luzon, guarding his

convoys. Second, he must have expended the last of his naval air today –
what's he got left, Zumwalt? A couple of escort carriers? Third – well, third,
I'll be damned if I want to be remembered as a Scheer! You know that story,
Ensign? From 1914 to 1916 the German navy waited for "Der Tag" – "The
Day", when it would challenge the British fleet in one last battle, to victory
or to the last ship. But the Germans never really had the advantage, and
when Scheer finally had his chance at Jutland, he turned and ran. I still have
the advantage, Ensign! This is the most powerful battleline afloat, and I just
can't see running away with it.'[19]

So Kimmel, wishing to avoid the condemnation of future naval historians, continued to Manila. Without air cover, however, he decided to use
the most direct route to his anchorage – via Surigao Strait. Unfortunately,
Kimmel and the remaining ships of TF1 – nine battleships, three cruisers,
and seventeen destroyers – already stood among the damned, thanks to the
American public, a faulty War Plan Orange, and the genius of Yamamoto.

## The gauntlet

On December 30, shortly after being advised of the sinking of the last
American carrier supporting Kimmel, Yamamoto ordered Nagumo to
slowly scout southward, find the USN's battlefleet, and drive it to Surigao
Strait. Nagumo did just that, using December 31 to rest and reorganize his
weary, but jubilant, air groups. At 1143 on January 1, 1942, his scouts
discovered the American fleet steaming at best speed for Luzon. Through
the remainder of the day, and amidst constantly deteriorating weather
conditions, Nagumo managed to launch only two waves of planes against
TF1. One of these never found Kimmel's fleet, the other sank the cruiser
*Vincennes* and two destroyers, disabled the aft turret on *New Mexico*, and
started severe fires on *Oklahoma* and *Tennessee*. As darkness fell, Nagumo
moved northwestward and counted his losses: an additional seventy-two
planes had fallen victim to heavy anti-aircraft fire or accident, bringing his
two-day losses to 184 of 497 original aircraft. Secure in the knowledge that
the fate of the American battleline now rested in the personal hands of his
brilliant boss, Nagumo sailed for a rendezvous with invasion forces to be
aimed at Guam and Wake Island.

With darkness more or less cloaking his battered TF1 (both *Oklahoma*
and *Tennessee* still flamed), Kimmel organized his fleet for a rapid advance
through the relatively narrow waters of Surigao Strait. Three destroyers
picketed his van of cruisers, *Chicago* and *Augusta*, followed closely by *Idaho*,
*New Mexico*, and *California*. About a thousand yards separated the van from
the remaining battleships led by Kimmel in *Arizona*, and trailed closely by
the two burning vessels, shepherded by four destroyers. The remaining two
destroyer divisions deployed 1,500 yards to port and starboard of the van.
By 0130 on January 2, it appeared that TF1, including the laggard

battlewagons whose exhausted crews were at last getting the best of fires fed by pre-war paint and furnishings, had negotiated the confined waters successfully.

Yamamoto had quietly gathered his Combined Fleet of six battleships – commanded by himself from the super-battleship *Yamato* – eight heavy cruisers, four light cruisers, and forty-two destroyers. Through the storms of January 1, his heavies, screened by a light cruiser and twelve destroyers, steamed back and forth across the west entrance to Surigao Strait. Closer to the entrance, three divisions of ten destroyers, each led by a light cruiser, waited to box the approaching task force. The weather had concerned Yamamoto, despite his commanding position and preponderance of light ships, but the front passed at midnight, and a float plane launched from the cruiser *Tone* reported the Americans steaming full tilt through the narrow waters with two burning vessels trailing the main force. At 0148 on January 2, sitting firmly across the American 'T' at a range of only 12,000 yards, Yamamoto flashed the code words, 'Tora! Tora! Tora!' This signaled his destroyers, stealthily advancing along the flanks of TF1, to launch their torpedoes at the enemy. The words of Captain Hara, whose *Amatsukaze* (still bearing the scars of the action at Truk) was in the division of destroyers some 4,000 yards to port of the American formation, capture the action:

> Tiger! Tiger! Tiger! The moonless night and the dark shore to our rear hid us from the enemy as our division alone launched over eighty Long Lances at the enemy line. I targeted the third and fourth battleships in their second echelon. Within seconds, and long before our torpedoes would reach their targets, water spouts began to erupt among the enemy van and second echelon. Hits came quickly, the two burning ships at the rear, *Oklahoma* and *Maryland* [actually *Tennessee*] outlined those vessels in front of them. The Americans appeared to panic, two destroyers colliding in their port division – confusion to which we added with my gun crews' rapid fire... Then the American battleline disappeared in a wall of water and flame! Apparently the torpedoes from both our port and starboard divisions arrived at the same time. As the mist and smoke cleared, one American battleship had simply disappeared [*West Virginia*], a second was turning turtle [*Maryland*], and a third, minus its bow to the first turret, was surrounded by burning oil and rapidly settling [*California*].
>
> Later I learned that every American battleship had been struck by at least one torpedo, and quite probably one cruiser and at least five destroyers had also been lost to our opening volley. Then and there I resolved never again to ship aboard a battlewagon. After this, my second night action, I knew that the Long Lance had ended their day of ruling the waves...[20]

What Hara had viewed as panic was, instead, the result of two large caliber shells, probably from *Haruna*, striking the bridge and flag bridge of *Arizona*. Every man on the bridge died immediately, and the flagship, helm untended, began a gentle turn to starboard. Though control of the rudder was restored in minutes, the damage had been done. The remaining vessels of the second echelon, as well as the destroyer division to port, apparently became confused as they tried to follow the unannounced maneuver.

Worse for TF1, the salvo had mortally wounded Husband Kimmel, who died within seconds, apparently after whispering his last commands to Ensign Zumwalt. Then, for the first time in history, an ensign took command of a modern battleship in combat. As flames raged through the superstructure of *Arizona*, Zumwalt, severely wounded himself, ordered a petty officer to send a message to the fleet ordering independent advance to Manila at best speed. Afterwards, he made his way, with two ratings, to the bridge. Discovering both wheel and intership communications intact, Zumwalt took control of the battleship, conning it through Yamamoto's line and to Manila Bay while in constant danger of being roasted alive or falling unconscious from loss of vital fluids. Nor did *Arizona* flee without drawing Japanese blood; its surviving guns turned the cruiser *Yubari* into a sinking mass of scrap, and Zumwalt actually managed to ram the destroyer *Shirakumo*, cutting it completely in half as *Arizona* escaped Yamamoto's trap.[21]

Along with the flagship of TF1, two destroyers and a miraculously undamaged *Augusta* escaped. *Texas*, closely following *Arizona*, also penetrated the Japanese battleline, but capsized an hour later when the patch that its crew had hastily installed off Wake Island gave way and added tons of water to that already taken in from two additional torpedo hits. Had it not been for the heroic efforts of the van battleships, *Idaho* and *New Mexico*, none of these vessels would have escaped. With *Idaho*'s speed reduced to half by flooded boilers, Captain Mark Smith turned his ship to parallel Yamamoto's battlewagons rather than attempt an escape. Captain Edward Coombs in *New Mexico*, despite a 14° list which prevented his remaining primary guns from firing, followed. For a vital half hour, the two vessels absorbed the fire of six Japanese battleships and their screen, while Smith pounded battleship *Mutsu* and Coombs' secondaries lashed at any enemy vessel in range. As *Mutsu* drifted out of control and sinking (the only Japanese capital ship lost in the action), *New Mexico* finally succumbed to its earlier torpedo hits and rolled onto its side at 0222. Less than a minute later, a shell from *Yamato* apparently penetrated the aft magazine of *Idaho*. It broke into two sections and sank in minutes.[22]

In the rear of TF1, *Oklahoma* and *Tennessee* had never recovered from the damage inflicted on the previous day by Nagumo's air strikes. With several magazines voluntarily flooded on January 1, numerous secondary casemates ravaged by fire, and additional flooding from the opening barrage of Japanese Long Lances, the battleships attempted to disengage to the west. After destroying the American van, Yamamoto pursued. By 0430, both battleships and their escorts had succumbed to a barrage of torpedoes and large caliber shells.

Dawn found the waters of Surigao Strait smothered with the detritus of battle – oil, lingering smoke, odd bits of wreckage, and sailors both living and dead. His victory won, Yamamoto counted his losses – one battleship, one cruiser, and fourteen destroyers – and then continued the war. The Japanese made only minimal efforts to rescue American survivors, though hundreds managed to drift ashore over the next four days. Most were immediately taken prisoner by the enemy, less than a hundred reaching the steadily diminishing territory controlled by MacArthur's now demoralized army.

For the four surviving vessels of TF1, Manila failed to provide the anticipated refuge. Their trial by fire continued. On January 4, a massive raid by Japanese land-based bombers resulted in a magazine explosion on *Arizona*. Sheathed in fire, it rapidly settled in the shallow mud of the harbor.[23] The following day, both destroyers fell prey to torpedo bombers. Somehow, *Augusta* again managed to survive the carnage unscathed, only to be scuttled by its crew on January 6, the day that MacArthur finally abandoned the port.

## A day that will live in infamy

On January 7, 1942, President Roosevelt authorized the release of information pertaining to the defeat of the American fleet in the Philippines. Panic swept through the United States, a nation which had never experienced sudden defeat on such a scale. Thousands upon thousands of American families wept for the fathers and sons feared lost to enemy action. Newspapers fed panic and fear with rumors of Japanese fleets off the Hawaiian Islands, and off the Pacific coast. Radio commentators listed the few vessels remaining in the Pacific fleet between their reports on Axis successes in Europe. And in Washington, Roosevelt and his advisors wrestled with one of the most difficult decisions ever faced by an American government.

They recognized that it would take months, if not years, to replace America's materiel losses. Even then, the loss of naval cadre would lead to difficulties in training recruits to man the new ships. In addition, in pre-war discussions with Great Britain, Roosevelt had already committed the United States to a 'Germany First' strategy. Moral issues (and many existed) aside, Fascist domination of Europe would hamstring the American economy, only just recovering from the Great Depression. The Philippines and American islands near Japan could not be defended without a strong navy; nor could the United States provide adequate aid to the struggling British Commonwealth in the Pacific Theater without ships. Could Japan successfully invade Hawaii? Probably. Could it invade the West Coast of the

United States with Hawaii secured as a fleet base? Probably not – but the IJN could eradicate American shipping in the Pacific, shipping which provided raw materials to much of the United States' industry. On the other hand, could Great Britain survive Germany's U-boats without the assistance of American shipping and the U.S. Navy? Possibly not. Would the American people fight? Could they rally from the fear and panic sweeping the nation? Absolutely! Ultimately, Roosevelt was left with one key question: could the United States successfully lead the effort to free Europe from Axis domination while simultaneously fighting a war against Japan, a war that threatened American shores, a naval war that would drain men, materiel, and national wealth at an abominable rate?

On January 12, 1942, after a final meeting with representatives of the British government, an exhausted President Roosevelt ordered MacArthur to seek a cease-fire and, in conjunction with British representatives in the Far East, to open negotiations with the Japanese government. One month later, in words now immortal, he addressed the American people: 'On February 12, 1942, a day that will live in infamy, General Douglas MacArthur and representatives of our European allies signed an armistice with Japan aboard the *Nevada* at Guam. This peace is necessary so that we may lead the struggle against Fascism in Europe; but we shall never forget Surigao!'[24]

War Plan Orange had failed. Japan claimed the Philippines as prize, though it allowed the United States to retain Guam and Wake Island (both demilitarized). Great Britain reluctantly agreed to a phased withdrawal from the Far East in exchange for trade concessions with India and guarantees that Australia and New Zealand would not suffer invasion. By the waning days of 1942, Japan managed to establish its Greater Asian Co-Prosperity Sphere, stretching from the Gilbert Islands to Indonesia, India, and China. With the collapse of Germany in early 1945, the world quickly polarized – Japan and its puppets arrayed against the rest of the world, led by the United States, Great Britain, and their uncomfortable communist bedfellow, the USSR. Winston Churchill's 1947 speech, in which he referred to a 'Bamboo curtain descending across Asia and the Pacific', is generally taken to mark the beginning of the brief East–West Cold War that culminated in the wave of internal revolutions led by such heroes as Mao, Gandhi, and Ho, and in the misnamed Sixty Minute War of 1953. But that, as the storyteller invariably says, is another story.[25]

## The reality

It is difficult to imagine any simple set of circumstances that would have allowed Japan to win any form of victory in World War II. Even Yamamoto, its premier naval strategist, knew that the industrial might of the

United States must prevail in the long run. For Yamamoto, Pearl Harbor seemed the best chance in a very desperate scenario. And Pearl Harbor was little more than a bee sting on the foot of a sleeping giant, awakening both an industrial power and personal commitments to victory among Americans that eventually doomed Japan while allowing the United States to support their allies in the destruction of European Fascism.

Only American military rashness of an improbable nature could have offered Japan an opportunity of victory. To tie that rashness to American politics seems more than reasonable in a nation where civilian guidance governs the ultimate deployment and strategy of its military forces (too often to the detriment of young, underpaid, and frequently unappreciated American servicemen). Everything following Roosevelt's decision to implement a long-abandoned and seriously flawed version of War Plan Orange is, of course, fiction. In reality, the United States closely followed its pre-war plan of a gradual erosion of Japanese power which would have culminated in the invasion of the home islands, had not the atomic bomb interfered. Fortunately, the discovery of the true industrial potential of the United States accelerated the course of the Pacific War – materiel was available to maintain Europe as first priority while still overwhelming Japan with ships, planes, and bombs.

A final idea (critical to this hypothetical victory) that must be addressed is the concept of civilian morale, or the 'national will' to continue a struggle. War has definite learning curves associated with it. We are familiar with those present on the field of battle; the techniques, for example, which once learned enhance individual survival. But civilians far removed from the field of battle seem to have a learning curve as well, a process of gradual inurement to increasingly long casualty lists as well as to individual material sacrifice. In reality, Pearl Harbor was a small shock that began a process of acclimatization to war. Without small shocks to prepare them for greater losses, could the American will to resist have been temporarily weakened by the horrific losses postulated in this alternative line of history? Quite possibly; at least, that will could have been weakened enough to accept a rapidly negotiated peace – which, in the end, was Japan's only real hope for victory in the Pacific.

## Bibliography

Edgerton, Robert B., *Warriors of the Rising Sun* (Harper and Row, New York, 1997).
Evans, David C., and Peattie, Mark R., *Kaigun: Strategy, Tactics, and Technology in the Imperial Japanese Navy, 1887–1941* (U.S. Naval Institute Press, Annapolis, 1997).
Miller, Edward S., *War Plan Orange: The U.S. Strategy to Defeat Japan, 1897–1945* (U.S. Naval Institute Press, Annapolis, 1991).
Spector, Ronald H., *Eagle Against the Sun: The American War with Japan* (Random House, New York, 1985).

## Notes

1. Aside from the IJN's institutional memory, the works of American Alfred Thayer Mahan were assigned reading for Japanese naval officers.

*2. For a brilliant indictment of the American voters' place in the Pacific debacle, see M. Palmer, *The True Price of Democracy* (Avalon Hill Press, 1992). The appended reading list offers several alternative histories that explore the absence of the Philippines Issue from the 1940 election.

*3. *New York Times*, October 18, 1940.

*4. Archives, *CBS*, New York.

*5. Yamamoto was not, as so many European historians have characterized him, a 'gambler'. Random elements are common to life, much less games; and it is the 'skilled' player – the person with the greatest knowledge of the game and an optimally implemented strategy – who manages to overcome that randomness and emerge victorious, whether shuffling cards or the fate of nations. See R. Snitzer, *Great Naval Leaders and 'The Game'* (Paper Wars, 1981).

*6. R. Gowan, *Kameto Kuroshima: The Man Behind Yamamoto* (ECU Press, 1973), p.110.

*7. *Ibid* pp.173–85. The name given to the operational plan accentuated its critical nature. At Tsushima, Togo had sent the famous Z signal to his fleet, 'ON THIS ONE BATTLE RESTS THE FATE OF OUR NATION. LET EVERY MAN DO HIS UTMOST.'

8. A surprise pact with the Soviets had secured the northern border for Japan, much to the consternation of Adolf Hitler.

*9. From the admiral's prepared notes, dated September 10, 1941; Yamamoto Papers, Harvard University.

*10. The secret formation of the ABDA naval command in October 1941 indicates an acknowledgment by the United States of the inevitability of war with Japan. See Admiral Karl Doorman's *The One Victorious Fleet* (Greenish Hill, 1967).

*11. *Official Transcript of the Court Martial of Admiral William F. Halsey* (U.S. Government, 1943), pp.99–100.

*12. Note that this reduced TFI to ten battleships: *Arizona, Nevada, Oklahoma, New Mexico, California, Tennessee, Maryland, West Virginia, Idaho*, and *Texas*.

*13. Letter to 'Dad' dated December 7, 1941; Zumwalt Presidential Papers, Annapolis. President Zumwalt was first in the accelerated Class of 1943 at the Naval Academy. In July 1941, the top ten percent of the class found themselves seconded to naval staffs as aides, releasing experienced officers for command slots.

*14. *JNI to Yamamoto, 12.8.41*, Yamamoto Papers, Harvard University. That civilian telegraph service still existed between Hawaii and Tokyo at 0645 on December 8 may seem shocking, but it should be remembered that the United States did not actually declare war on Japan until 1603 EST and that the civilian sector always reacts much slower to a declaration than does the military establishment.

*15. *Official Transcript of the Court Martial of General Douglas MacArthur* (U.S. Government, 1943), p.738.

*16. G. Bush, *Truk-ing with the Bull* (Yaquinto, 1988), p.111. Halsey's utterance was, of course, correct. The stalking horses sank splendidly, but *Ryujo* suffered only slight damage. In fact, though its planes contributed to the sinking of the *Indomitable*, the remaining British vessels had fallen prey to land-based aircraft.

*17. T. Hara, *Red Sun Rising: A Japanese Destroyer Captain Remembers* (GDW, 1961),

pp.58–71. Hara was correct. Training in night combat, with or without torpedoes, had been minimized by order of the Department of the Navy in order to
'prevent training accidents'. Such foolishness, along with the cost-cutting common to all peacetime navies, played a large part in the USN's performance in the
Pacific.

*18. J. Beeler, *All the World Wonders and Other Naval Blunders* (U.S. Press, 1998),
pp.31–2.

*19. H. Jones, *Zumwalt at the Helm: The Reason America Used Its Secret Atomic Arsenal*
(UA Press, 1999), p.53.

*20. Hara, *op cit* pp.126–53.

*21. *Shirakumo*'s captain, Sataru Tenabe, would become prime minister of Japan in
1951, in a great measure because of his ordeal after being rammed by *Arizona* and
given up for dead by the Japanese Navy. He heroically swam to shore with the
strap of his badly burned chief engineer's lifejacket clutched between his teeth,
having pulled him for twelve miles despite a severe injury to his own back. See H.
Shimizu, *Destroyer 109* (Gei Sha Publishers, 1947).

*22. Both Smith and Coombs, though seriously wounded, survived the action. John
Ford's 1942 movie, *The Gauntlet of Surigao* immortalized both men. The one-
armed Smith went on to write the Navy's official history of World War II, *The
One Ocean War*, while the tragic Coombs, victim of deep mental wounds, ended
his days as an alcoholic blues singer in New Orleans.

*23. In 1948, Japan dedicated the *Arizona Memorial*, actually built above the sunken
hull and inscribed with the names of the crewmen forever entombed therein as
well as the names of every Japanese sailor lost in the brief Pacific War.

*24. Archives, *CBS*, New York.

25. I would be remiss if I did not mention that storytellers (and writers) invariably
make this statement because we are compensated 'by the story'.

# 3
# PEARL HARBOR
## Irredeemable Defeat

Frank R. Shirer

December 7, 1941, is a day that has lived in infamy – not only because of the surprise attack of the Japanese on Oahu, but because America's sentinels were asleep at their posts in Hawaii. The well-planned attack was successful because the Americans feared sabotage by a 'fifth column' more than an aerial attack, an attack that the U.S. Navy had proved altogether possible in 1933. The thought pervading the command structure in Hawaii was that if Japan did move against the United States, the attack would come in the Philippines, to guard the left flank of its march on the oil fields in the Dutch East Indies.

Admiral Isoroku Yamamoto had been charged with leading the Japanese Navy's assault to seize the natural resources which Japan required. He realized that to get time to consolidate Japanese gains in the Indies, he would have to remove the U.S. Pacific Fleet as a threat. Commander Minoru Genda devised the plan that he used. It called for a fleet of six aircraft carriers, escorted by fast battleships, cruisers, destroyers and tankers, to sail north of the regular shipping lanes through the North Pacific to a point 200 miles northwest of Oahu. From there nearly 400 torpedo, dive, and level bombers and Zero fighters were to be launched in two waves against the American fleet on a quiet Sunday morning. The final approved order left open the possibility that there might also be follow-up strikes.[1]

The First Air Fleet, composed of the First (*Akagi* and *Kaga*), Second (*Soryu* and *Hiryu*), and Fourth (*Ryujo*) Carrier Divisions, was to be the centerpiece of the attack force. The *Ryujo* was detached during the summer of 1941 because she had older, Type 96 Claude fighters, and the Fifth Carrier Division (*Shokaku* and *Zuikaku*) was added. Selected to command this powerful carrier force was Vice-Admiral Chuichi Nagumo, who was unacquainted with naval aviation, but who specialized in torpedo attacks and large-scale surface warfare. He got the job because of his seniority.

Nagumo expressed his misgivings about the attack and enumerated the risks. It would be difficult, he said, to keep an exact timetable across over

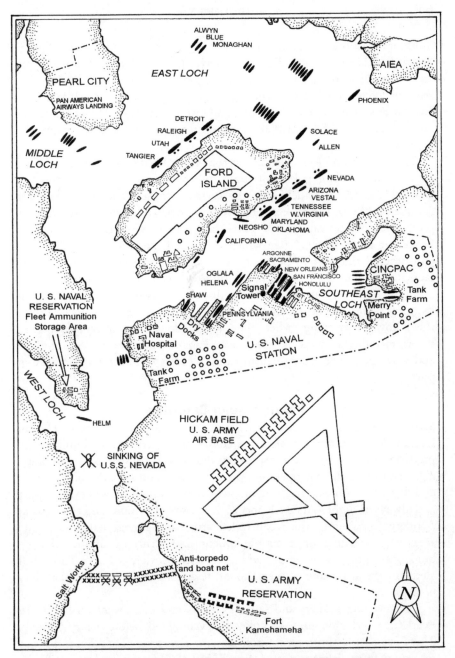

The Main Targets: Pearl Harbor and Hickam Field

3,000 miles of ocean, to refuel the escorting destroyers in the rough winter
North Pacific waters, and there was an ever present chance of discovery by
American submarines, aircraft carriers, or land based aircraft. Nagumo also
stressed the outcome of an August war game in which the attack force had
two carriers sunk and two damaged, and lost forty percent of its aircraft and
aircrew. However, he said that he would follow orders and command the
First Air Fleet.

For ten days the fleet sailed across the North Pacific, arriving undetected
at its final refueling point 600 miles north of Lanai Island at 0530 on
December 6. After refueling of the carriers, cruisers and destroyers was
completed (0830) the tankers departed for their December 13 rendezvous
point west of Midway Island. Three hours later, Vice Admiral Nagumo
broke out the famous 'Z' flag which Admiral Togo had used at Tushima,
and ordered the fleet to begin its final high speed (24 knot) run to the
launching point, 240 miles north of Pearl Harbor, at 0600 the next
morning. Still nervous about being discovered, Nagumo kept all of his
scouting planes out of the air that last day. None would be launched until
the following morning, when they would do a final reconnaissance to
determine whether the U.S. fleet was at Lahaina Roads or in Pearl Harbor,
and whether or not the American carriers *Lexington* and *Enterprise* were in
port.

## Pearl: A quiet Saturday

Saturday, December 6, saw American Army and Navy units in Hawaii
securing their equipment after a week of training. The battleships were
preparing for an 'Admiral's inspection' that would commence on Monday.
They had spent the day opening up entry hatches into the double bottoms
and dogging open watertight doors, which were usually closed even in port
and always at night. The 24th and 25th Infantry Divisions and the Coastal
Artillery Command, which controlled army anti-aircraft batteries in the
area, were cleaning up their equipment and returning ammunition to
bunkers for proper storage. It had been a week of Alert Number Three (full
alert) for the army troops, even though few among the local populace had
noticed.

That evening soldiers and sailors, officers and men, went on liberty to
Pearl City and Honolulu, to enjoy an evening off before a lazy Sunday.
There were still three task forces at sea. *Enterprise* (Task Force 8) was
returning from delivering a Marine F4F-2 (Wildcat) squadron to Wake
Island; after encountering heavy seas on the 5th, she got clear weather on
the 6th and expected to dock at Pearl by 0800 Sunday morning. *Lexington*
(Task Force 12) was en route to Midway Island to deliver a Marine dive-
bomber squadron. And Task Force 3, consisting of the cruiser *Indianapolis*
and five destroyers, was on patrol near Johnston Island.

Meanwhile, in San Francisco sixteen B-17 Flying Fortresses (eight C and eight E models with partial crews, no ammunition, and their machine guns still packed in cosmoline) had already taken off for a night flight to Hawaii. There they would refuel, get some crew rest, and then continue on to reinforce the Philippines. They were scheduled to arrive on Sunday morning at 0830 hours Hawaii Time.

In Washington, D.C., the Army and Navy departments were receiving a fourteen-part message that Tokyo was sending to its embassy. It was to be distributed to the President, Secretaries of War and Navy, Chief of Naval Operations Admiral Harold R. 'Betty' Stark, and Army Chief of Staff General George C. Marshall. It would not be until the following morning that decisions would be made that alerted the commanders in Hawaii, giving them just a couple hours' explicit warning that they might be attacked in force by the Japanese.

## December 7, last minute alert

Just after midnight, December 7, the fourteenth part of the message arrived in Washington, where it was decoded, then left until morning for trans-lation and delivery. Lieutenant Commander Alwin D. Kramer (Office of Naval Intelligence)[2] and Army Colonel Rufus S. Bratton (Army G-2), who shared the duties of distributing decoded messages from Japan, arrived at their office in the Navy Department by 0900 EST (0330 PH). They translated the fourteenth part and prepared copies for delivery. Admiral Stark was in his office already that morning, while General Marshall was out for his morning ride at Fort Myer, Virginia.

While the two intelligence officers were making their rounds with messages, the minesweeper *Condor* reported spotting a submarine in the Defensive Sea Area around Oahu. It notified a nearby destroyer, U.S.S. *Ward*, at 0342 (0912 EST). *Ward* searched fruitlessly until 0435, when she returned to her regular patrol route outside the harbor entrance. She did not detect the five I-class submarines that were lying in wait in a double arc outside the channel. They had already surfaced and launched their two-man mini-submarines, which would penetrate the harbor and assist in the coming attack.

## Stark alerts Kimmel

Lieutenant Commander Kramer walked down the corridor of the Navy building to the Chief of Naval Operations (CNO) office. He gave the messages to Commander Arthur H. McCollum, chief of the Office of Naval Intelligence's (ONI) Far Eastern Section, shortly after 1000 EST. Kramer pointed out to McCollum that 1300 EST was 0730 in Hawaii and 0200 in the Philippines. He then continued with his deliveries to the White House and the State Department. McCollum took the messages to Admiral Stark and ONI chief Captain Theodore S. Wilkinson. During the next few minutes the messages were read and re-read. Finally, Captain Wilkinson said: 'There is enough here to indicate that we can expect war.' Admiral Stark agreed. Then Wilkinson suggested: 'Why don't you call Kimmel?' Stark paused, then picked up his scrambler telephone. His call reached Admiral Kimmel at 0515 (1045 EST), awakening him. Stark briefly told Kimmel about the fourteen-part message that seemed to break diplomatic relations between the U.S. and Japan. He also informed him that the message ordered the Embassy to destroy all its codes and coding machines. Kimmel asked about the portent for Hawaii. Stark responded that he did not know, but that he feared that an attack might occur because the Japanese consulate in Honolulu had also been ordered to destroy all its codes and papers. Kimmel mentioned that Captain Layton had told him on Saturday that the consulate personnel were burning a lot of papers. When asked about the status of the fleet Kimmel said that it was safely in harbor and preparing for his inspection the following morning.

At that, Stark blew up in rage. 'Didn't you get our message of 27 November stating that "this is a war warning, execute defense deployment"?'

'Yes,' replied Kimmel, 'but I figured that you were talking about strategic defensive deployment, when I deploy the fleet to sea after the beginning of hostilities.'

'NO!' exclaimed Stark. 'I expected you to begin wartime defense measures, including defense against attack while the fleet is in the harbor. Don't you remember Admiral Schofield's 1933 war games? I thought you were there.'

'No, I wasn't out here then,' said Kimmel. 'I remember something about it. Didn't he strike Pearl with the carriers?'

'Yes, carriers striking from the north. Your first concern is to protect the fleet and that includes when it is in the harbor.'

'I've got the fleet at stage three,' said Kimmel, 'but I'm doing an inspection tomorrow. Most of the battleships are open for that. I've let Bloch and Short take care of the harbor defense.'

'You had better go to condition Zed on all your ships at once and recall all your people just in case,' advised Stark. 'Captain McCollum says that he thinks that the Japs will attack our fleet out there because it is a threat to them, even if they go for the Philippines.'

'I'll call Bloch and my chief of staff as soon as we finish and get the fleet to General Quarters,' replied Kimmel. 'It will take us two or three hours to get fully ready, and four hours to get up enough steam to take the fleet to sea. Hopefully we can get some PBYs up. I remember Ellis Zacharias telling me last May that he though the Japs would attack here with carriers and from the northwest. I'll have them search in that direction.'

'You may not have that long,' said Stark. 'But hopefully this will end up being a drill that will just cause the folks to grumble about having their weekend loused up.'

'Yes, Sir,' said Kimmel. 'Let me get off and call my people.'

'Good luck.'[3]

Kimmel called the commander of the 14th Naval District, Rear Admiral Claude C. Bloch, and ordered him to put the District on alert and to notify the commander of Patrol Wing Two, Rear Admiral Patrick N. L. Bellinger, to get PBYs (flying boats) into the air as quickly as possible. They were to search to the north, 60° either side of 0° north out to a distance of 700 miles. He closed by telling Bloch to meet him at his headquarters by 0600.

Bellinger's Patrol Wing 2 was at Condition B-5, which meant that fifty percent of the PBY-3s and -5s and their crews were on four-hours' notice. In reality they had less than two hours to avoid being caught on the ground at Ford Island and Kaneohe Bay Air Station. Kimmel rapidly dressed and was driven to his headquarters in the Submarine building. He had already forgotten about his 0800 golf outing with Lieutenant General Short, and about contacting him to cancel it.

As all of this activity was taking place in Hawaii, the Japanese were launching their aerial armada's first wave of 183 bombers and Zero fighters.

As the American fleet was being awakened and the battleship crews were rapidly closing up the inspection hatches and undoing the preparations for Admiral Kimmel's canceled inspection, the tug *Antares* sighted a submarine off the harbor entrance. She signaled U.S.S. *Ward*, which was still on patrol. Steaming to the *Antares*' assistance, *Ward* engaged the unidentified submarine with gunfire and depth charges and sank it in five minutes. At 0651 Lieutenant Outerbridge, *Ward*'s captain, reported: 'Depth-bombed sub operating in defensive sea area.' The 14th Naval District immediately relayed the message to Admirals Bloch and Kimmel.

At 0645 hours the first of U.S.S. *Enterprise*'s air complement of SBD-3 Dauntless dive-bombers and TBD Devastator torpedo-bombers began landing on Ford Island. Their arrival was the first notification for Admiral Kimmel that *Enterprise* was nearing the harbor after being delayed by a day due to heavy seas. Kimmel had ordered her to sail under radio silence and thus did not know her exact arrival date. He immediately notified her commander, Vice Admiral William F. Halsey, Jr., to keep his task force (TF8) south of Oahu, and go to general quarters. He also told Halsey that his planes would be fueled, armed, and returned to him. Throughout it all, he added, Halsey's force was to maintain radio silence.

## The Hawaiian Air Force

While Admiral Kimmel was putting the fleet on general alert, Lieutenant General Short continued to sleep, as did Major General Frederick L. Martin, the commander of the Hawaiian Air Force.[4] At 0645 Rear Admiral

Bellinger awakened Martin by phone to tell him about the warning from Washington and that he was launching his PBYs to scout the northern approaches to the Islands. He wanted to know if Army radar sites on the northern side of the island at Opana Point and Kaaawa were working that morning and if the Air Warning Center (AWC) was manned. Martin said that the three sites were scheduled to operate until 0700 but that there was only a skeleton shift on at the AWC. Bellinger said that he was sending the Navy's AWC liaison officer along with the Navy contingent responsible for coordinating with all Naval aviation units.

Earlier that year, Martin had worked with Bellinger to split the responsibilities for reconnaissance and aerial defense of the islands. The Navy would do the bulk of the reconnaissance, while the Army would provide air defense. Martin's B-17 force had been reduced from thirty-five in May to only a dozen when twenty-three were sent to the Far East Air Force in the Philippines in September. Six of the remaining twelve were non-operational hangar queens, providing replacement parts for other B-17s shuttling from the United States to the Philippines. Martin also had thirty-three obsolete B-18s (only twenty-one of them flyable) that could perform reconnaissance.[5] These forty-five aircraft were a far cry from the 180 B-17 or equivalent aircraft that an official study completed earlier in the year had said would be necessary to provide $360°$ coverage for the islands against a possible attack by six enemy aircraft carriers.[6]

The 14th Pursuit Wing had four interceptor and four fighter squadrons, all stationed at Wheeler Army Air Field. The Army fighter force had ninety-nine modern P-40Bs and Cs, and thirty-nine P-36As, although only sixty-four P-40s and twenty P-36s were operational that Sunday morning. Martin had two P-40 squadrons (twelve aircraft each) temporarily posted to the outlying Bellows Airfield (44th Pursuit Squadron [Interceptor]) and Haleiwa Airfield (47th Pursuit Squadron [Fighter]) for gunnery training. Major General Martin had been preparing for possible hostilities by having 120 revetments constructed at Wheeler Field for the pursuit aircraft.

Lieutenant General Short's Alert Number One was designed to protect against sabotage rather an air attack. It ordered Martin to group all of his fighters close together and in the open so that they could be easily guarded against sabotage with the minimum of personnel, instead of leaving them in their revetments, which required a larger guard force. Additional security measures included: the locking of the controls in each plane via a system of cables and locks, which normally required three to four minutes to undo; and the storage of all machine gun ammunition in hangar number three, with individual .30 and .50 caliber rounds stored separately from their belts.

The Hawaiian Air Force was also on a four-hour alert status for half of operational aircraft to get airborne. They would need every minute of it considering the need to recall pilots, belt the ammunition, and get to

altitude in the sectors where enemy aircraft could be expected. The planes at
Bellows were in particularly bad shape. After a week of gunnery training,
they had not only been parked on Saturday afternoon without having their
fuel tanks filled, but their machine guns had been removed so that the
armorers could give them a thorough cleaning on Sunday. The 47th
Squadron had its P-40Bs' fuel tanks full and machine guns on board, but in
their ammo dump they had only .30 caliber ammunition for the wing guns
and no .50 caliber ammunition twin-fifties in the fuselage.

### Late word to the Army

Back in Washington, General Marshall arrived at his War Department
office at 1130 EST (0600 Hawaii) and found Colonel Bratton waiting for
him with the fourteen part message. After reading it he wrote a warning
message to be radioed immediately to all Pacific commands. All were
notified except for the Army commander in Hawaii, Lieutenant General
Short, because the radio circuits were down. Bratton decided not to send via
RCA (Radio Corporation of America) and urged Marshall to telephone
Short with the warning. Marshall hesitated, noting that the Army suspected
the Japanese had tapped the transoceanic cable and could decode scrambled
telephone conversations. Bratton said that he thought the chance had to be
taken, and reminded Marshall that he could use the 1300 meeting between
Secretary Hull and Ambassadors Nomura and Kurusu as the reason for the
call, to check on their alert status. At 0650 (1220 EST) Marshall telephoned
Short, awakening him.

General Marshall inquired what alert status the Hawaiian Army was on.
Short replied, 'Alert Number One.' Marshall was relieved, because Alert
One meant all troops were on full alert, with anti-aircraft artillery in
defensive positions and the air force on thirty minute take-off status.

'I'm glad you're on full alert,' said Marshall, 'that's what's needed. I don't
see sabotage as the major threat this morning.'

Short replied: 'Alert One is anti-sabotage. I changed the numbering last
summer after I arrived, so folks out here wouldn't be alarmed.'

Shocked at this revelation, Marshall was furious. 'You know the Army
standard is for Alert One to be full alert. Did you pass that change on to
War Plans here? If you had, I would have denied permission for it! You need
to get your folks up and deployed right now! It may be nothing, but I don't
think this is the time for worrying if the local civilians are "alarmed".'

Short was startled. 'We just came off of a week's full alert yesterday
morning, but OK. I'll call everyone out now.'

'Let's hope that nothing happens,' replied Marshall, 'because that is what
you bet your stars on when you changed the alert procedure. I didn't expect
you to be asleep on guard duty out there.'[7]

As Short hung up his phone rang again. This time it was Major General

Martin, calling to inform him of Rear Admiral Bellinger's call and of the
Navy's full alert status. Short told Martin to put the Hawaiian Air Force on
full alert as well. The island defense plan was to go into effect. PBY patrols
were to be reinforced, and fighters were to be manned and ready. Short
called Colonel Walter C. Phillips, his Chief of Staff, and repeated the
instructions to him. The time was now 0715 hours.

### The first wave strikes

The Opana Point radar site was slated to close down at 0700 hours. Since
the morning chow truck had not arrived, however, its operators, Privates
Joseph L. Lockard and George E. Elliot, decided to keep the set on and to
get more training. At 0702 hours a large blip appeared on the radar screen.
They estimated it included at least fifty aircraft on a heading of $3°$ east of
north at a range of 130 miles. They continued to track the southward-
moving target for thirteen minutes before they called the AWC to report
that the target was now eighty-eight miles from Opana Point on an
inbound bearing. Only a single telephone operator and the duty officer,
First Lieutenant Kermit A. Tyler, were in the AWC when the report came
in. Tyler concluded that the sighting involved Major Landon's flight of
sixteen B-17s, due in that morning from San Francisco.

The Japanese cruiser *Tone*'s floatplane spotted *Enterprise* and the rest of
TF8 at 0733 hours and reported it to Commander Fuchida. Two minutes
later, *Chikuma*'s Pete reported that there were no aircraft carriers in Pearl
Harbor but that there were many carrier planes landing and taking off from
Ford Island and that ships seemed to be getting up steam. Commander
Fuchida faced a decision about how to exploit this new and unexpected
information. He quickly decided to split his attack force between Pearl
Harbor and TF8. He ordered the torpedo-bomber and fighter squadrons
from *Akagi* and *Soryu* (twenty Kates and eighteen Zeros), along with two of
*Zuikkaku*'s dive-bomber squadrons (eighteen Vals), to find and sink
*Enterprise* along with her escorting cruisers. The remainder of the force
would attack Pearl Harbor as planned. At 0745 he fired double red dragon
flares to signal 'surprise lost' to the half of the force that was to attack
Pearl.[8]

Simultaneous with the Japanese scout plane reports came the arrival of
Commander William E.G. Taylor and the Navy's four-man contingent at
the AWC. Tyler received a call from Major Kenneth P. Bergquist, the
AWC's second-in-command, asking if any radar sites were still operating
and if any recent targets had been reported? Tyler told him of Opana Point's
report. Bergquist ordered him to call Opana Point to see if they were still
tracking it. While Tyler was making his call, Major Bergquist phoned
Major General Martin about the blip. Martin said that it could not be the B-
17s because it was coming in from the wrong direction. Martin then called

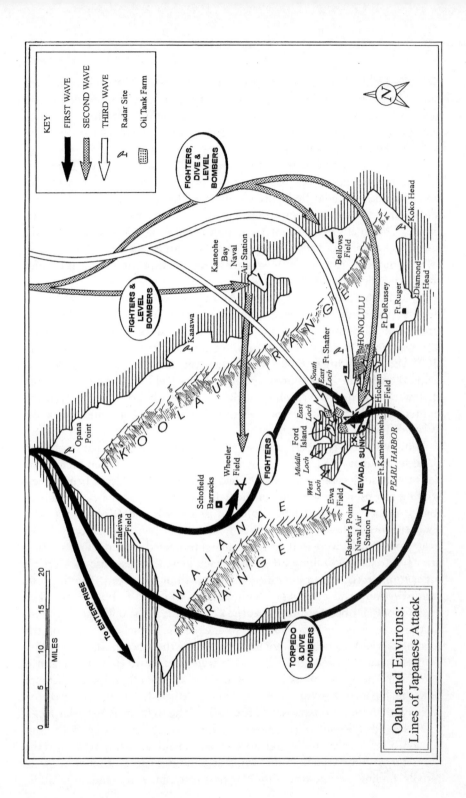

Oahu and Environs:
Lines of Japanese Attack

Wheeler Field and told them to get every P-40 and P-36 they had airborne
and to intercept a possible enemy force to the north of Oahu. Bergquist had
Army plotters recalled from breakfast to put the AWC into full operation.
He also ordered the crews of the sites at Kaaawa on the northeast coast and
at Koko Head to resume operation.

The resources and expertise of Commander Taylor and Major Bergquist
had been squandered because of inter-service non-cooperation, a lack of
understanding of radar by Lieutenant General Short and Admiral Kimmel,
and the lack of central Army control over the Air Warning System and its
radar.[9] The final Opana Point radar plot came in at 0739, when Lockard
and Elliot reported contact being lost as the target entered a 'dead space'
twenty miles to the north. It was just after disappearing from the radar
screen that Fuchida split his force.

By then the crews at the various American airfields were scrambling to
disperse and ready their fighters, bombers and PBYs for combat. Dragged
from their all-night poker game, Second Lieutenants Kenneth M. Taylor
and George S. Welch were among the pilots sent from the Wheeler Field
BOQ (Bachelor Officer Quarters) to their planes at Haleiwa and Bellows
fields. The Japanese were unaware of Haleiwa Field and had not targeted
Bellows in the first wave. The splitting of the strike force had halved the
fighters and had reduced to nine the dive-bombers allocated to strike
Wheeler Field.

Nine Val dive-bombers and six Zero fighters began their strike on
Wheeler Field at 0752. The Vals struck the fuel dump and then each of the
hangers in succession, just as they had practiced. The Zeros began their
strafing run from the west end of the field. However, they found not a neat
row of planes as expected but only a dozen P-40s and P-36s along with
another fourteen obsolete P-26s sitting out in the open. The majority of the
P-40 Tomahawks were in their revetments, protected from the first strafing
attack, but six were taking off as the attack began, in response to Martin's
order to intercept the unidentified target north of the island. Two of these
were shot down as they were pulling their wheels off the runway. The
leading four climbed for altitude as the Zeros went in the opposite direction.
Within moments the Zeros zoomed to engage the Tomahawks, leaving the
strafing to the Vals, which were ill equipped for the mission. In the swirling
dogfight that followed all of the P-40s were shot down, but they claimed
one Zero. The Army pilots had been caught at take off and knew little of
how the Japanese flew and fought. Their sacrifice, however, had depleted
the Zeros' ammunition and saved the bulk of the fighters at Wheeler Field.

Meanwhile, Second Lieutenants Taylor and Welch, along with four
squadron mates, were taking off from Haleiwa field and heading toward the
'large target' near Opana Point, while at Bellows Field ground crews were
rapidly fueling and re-installing the hastily cleaned .50 and .30 caliber

machine-guns aboard the dozen P-40Cs. Of the major airfields, Kanoehe Naval Air Station was the most fortunate, being spared attack because the fighters and dive-bombers designated for it were searching for TF8 instead.

Zero fighters from *Kaga* opened the attack over Pearl Harbor by shooting down six of *Enterprise*'s Devastator (TBD) torpedo-bombers as they climbed southward from Ford Island. The Zeros then pounced on and destroyed four more TBDs and three Dauntless (SBD) dive-bombers on the Ford Island runway. Victorious over Ford Island, they winged their way to Ewa field and destroyed the few Marine fighters and dive-bombers that had not been sent to Wake and the Midway Islands. At 0755 twenty-seven Vals from *Akagi* and *Kaga* began their dives on Hickam Field, destroying the majority of the B-17s and B-18s that were parked in the open. The twenty remaining torpedo-carrying Kates began their run toward Battleship Row from the southeast, flying over Fort Kamehameha and down the Southeast Loch.

Despite the warning, both Hickam and Wheeler Fields were defenseless. The anti-aircraft artillery units assigned to defend them were still in their motor pools at Schofield Barracks preparing to deploy. The Kate torpedo-bombers nonetheless ran into a barrage of .50 and 1.1 inch caliber machine-gun and 3- and 5-inch anti-aircraft gunfire from the ships in Pearl Harbor. This fire was not as withering as it would become later in the war, when each cruiser and battleship carried dozens of 20 and 40 mm anti-aircraft guns.[10]

U.S.S. *Oklahoma* was the target of seven Kates. Her crew splashed two, but the modified torpedoes from the remaining five ripped out her port side. Rapid counter-flooding prevented her from capsizing, although she settled at a 30° list. *West Virginia* also received four torpedoes to her port side; however, her hits were more evenly spaced and she settled on an even keel. The three remaining Kates began their run on *Nevada*, but two were shot down and the third's torpedo missed. *California* and the ships anchored on the western side of Ford Island escaped attack entirely, because the force scheduled to attack them was another of those heading south to intercept TF8.

Minutes after the torpedo-bombers struck, the level bombers began their run over Pearl. They carried armor-piercing bombs modified from 14-inch battleship shells. Their targets were the inboard battleships *Maryland*, *Tennessee*, and *Arizona*. Long hours of practice paid off. They made repeated hits on the battleships. At 0820, *Soryu*'s Petty Officer Noboru Kanai placed a bomb through *Arizona*'s forecastle and into her forward powder magazine. The explosion that followed not only destroyed the battleship, but its concussion knocked sailors to the deck on all the surrounding ships. Admiral Kimmel watched in shock from his headquarters next to Southeast Loch, as the pride of his fleet sank into the forty-foot waters of Pearl Harbor – forty feet of water that was thought to have been too shallow for a torpedo attack.

### *Enterprise* is discovered

The ad hoc strike group under the command of Lieutenant Commander Shigeharu Murata separated from the main force at 0745 to seek out TF8. They found their prey at 0830, steaming south at 30 knots. On *Enterprise* and her escorts all hands stood at their battle stations. They had long since heard the radio message 'Air raid Pearl Harbor. This is no drill.' Circling at 20,000 feet was their combat air patrol of ten Wildcats. *Enterprise*'s thirty SBDs and six remaining TBDs were circling over the island of Maui, sent out of harm's way by Halsey. His plan was to recall, refuel, and arm them to strike the Japanese fleet, once he had an idea of its location.

Commander Murata ordered his veteran torpedo pilots to split their force in half, his element engaging *Enterprise* while the others hit her escorts. The Vals were to strike after the Kates had made their run. Murata's ten Kates began their runs at both sides of *Enterprise,* charging through a hail of anti-aircraft fire much heavier than what their comrades were facing at Pearl. Three went down before launching their fish, but the remaining planes successfully loosed their torpedoes. Three hit *Enterprise* on her starboard side in quick succession, followed by another two on her port. She began to slow. Her advanced damage control design matched the effects of the five massive torpedo holes, but once the modified battleship shells dropped by the Vals exploded within her hull, destroying her watertight integrity, she began to settle slowly to the bottom of the Pacific.

Meanwhile her Wildcats had been engaged by the Zeros as they dove to attack the Kates. In a whirlwind fight, seven Wildcats went down, taking with them three Zeros and two Kates. The remaining Kates and Vals made their runs on the cruisers *Northampton, Chester,* and *Salt Lake City.* Swerving wildly and putting up a dense canopy of triple A, *Chester* and *Salt Lake City* took repeated hits and were soon ablaze and sinking. Of the nine escorting destroyers, *Blach, Dunlap,* and *Benham* were sunk. *Northampton,* flagship of Rear Admiral Raymond A. Spruance, escaped with one torpedo hit and one bomb strike.

His job done, with *Enterprise* sinking, Murata led his strike force – less eight Kates, seven Vals, and three Zeros – back to its home carriers. The remaining U.S. destroyers rescued the survivors of TF8, Vice Admiral Halsey among them.[11]

### The lull between strikes

The destroyer *Helm,* which had gotten underway before the attack, cleared the harbor entrance at Pearl at 0817. She was followed by the destroyer *Monaghan* a few minutes later. Both had escaped being attacked during the initial assault. At 0825, coinciding with the end of the first wave's attack, the light cruiser *Phoenix* slipped her moorings and sailed through the harbor. She was not noticed, for all eyes were on

*Nevada*. Taking advantage of *Nevada*'s standard practice of having one boiler on line when in harbor, Ensign Joseph K. Taussig, the officer of the deck that morning, ordered her remaining boilers fired up when general quarters were sounded. It was his order that enabled *Nevada* to be the only battleship ready to sortie. With an ensign navigating, Chief Quartermaster Robert Sedberry piloted her down battleship row and into the main channel by 0855. This was a masterful feat of seamanship, but one that would be for naught.

At 0830 the Opana Point radar site reported another 'fifty plus' blip approaching Oahu on a southward heading. Kaaawa Station, now on the air, reported it too. Both stations also reported smaller blips that were departing to the north-northeast. Major Bergquist relayed the new targets to Wheeler Field control so that it could direct the P-40s that had taken off to intercept them. Koko Head station began reporting a scattered group of targets, approaching from the east. These were Major Landon's twelve B-17s just arriving from the mainland; four had turned back because of mechanical problems. Major Landon, who had heard the attack over the radio, contacted Hickam control for landing instructions. He was ordered to divert his flight to alternate airfields on Maui and Hawaii and to await orders to return to Hickam.

Commander Taylor relayed the information about the incoming Japanese flights to Rear Admiral Bellinger and Patrol Wing Two at Kaneohe Naval Air Station. Their presence confirmed the wisdom of Bellinger's earlier decision to send the PBYs scouting to the north in search of the Japanese fleet. So far the eighteen PBYs which had gotten airborne had not yet encountered any Japanese aircraft.

The Haleiwa Field P-40s landed at Wheeler to refuel and rearm. They then took off with orders to patrol over Bellows field, since the planes there were still not airborne. Twelve P-36s stayed over Wheeler Field as well, to serve as local air defense, but the thirty P-40s which had taken off from there after the initial attack were directed to intercept the inbound second wave. They spotted 150 Japanese planes flying below them at 0840. Exploiting their altitude, they shot down two Zeros and half a dozen Vals and Kates as they dove through the surprised formation. Climbing back up to re-engage the enemy, however, they made the fatal mistake of engaging the nimble Zeros with classical dog-fighting techniques. As a result, twenty of their number never made it home. The remainder escaped after running out of ammunition. Many were damaged. The thirty-four remaining Zeros regrouped and raced ahead of the bombers splitting to attack Bellows, Kaneohe, and Hickam airfields.

Fifty Vals arrived over Pearl at 0855. Commander Fuchida ordered them to concentrate their attack on *Nevada*, which had just entered the main channel. The battleship's anti-aircraft guns opened fire but were too few to deter the attack. Having to steam straight and slow in the channel, the ship was racked from stem to stern with repeated bomb hits, some of which ripped through her armored decks and exploded in her interior, starting fires and knocking out her main electrical system. Minutes after being hit by the first bomb, she also took two torpedoes in the stern from one of the mini-submarines that had penetrated the harbor earlier that morning. The first hit destroyed her rudder and screws, while the second tore a forty-foot hole in her stern. Losing headway, she slowed to a stop in the narrowest part of the channel, where she blew up fifteen minutes later at 0910, breaking her back.

With *Nevada* gone, the level bombers and remaining dive-bombers shifted their attention to the battleships *California* and *Pennsylvania*, and the cruisers still at anchor. *California* took three torpedoes from lurking mini-submarines during this assault, which caused her to settle to the bottom of the harbor. The destroyer *Alwyn* sank one of the mini-subs with gunfire when it broached the surface after firing its torpedoes. A total of fifteen Vals and Kates fell to anti-aircraft fire and the guns of the Marine Corps Wildcats that had arrived over the harbor from Ewa Field.

Bombers also struck Hickam again, destroying the few hangars not hit in the first strike and leveling the machine shops. The runway escaped damage, even though more of the planes there were damaged.

Second Lieutenants Taylor and Welch led the Haleiwa contingent of P-40s against the twenty plus Vals and Zeros that began their raid on Bellows Field at 0900. Their aerial offensive broke up the attack and sent a half dozen Vals crashing to the ground. Having experienced the abilities of the Zeros earlier, these pilots refrained from dog-fighting but instead dove to the attack and then zoomed away to gain altitude before re-engaging. Five of them drifted over Kaneohe Naval Air Station and into the midst of the attack there, where they surprised the Vals and Zeros in mid-attack. Several of the enemy went down. Meanwhile, the Zeros and Vals that had been interrupted in their attack on Bellows switched to secondary targets at Wheeler Field. After climbing to altitude, the Zeros swept down on the defending P-36s, effecting a near slaughter of the obsolescent aircraft. Even so, the P-36s kept the Zeros from strafing the field, restricting the damage there to a dozen bomb hits from the Vals, several of which hit the ball field, which had been planned originally as the location of underground gasoline storage tanks.

By 0930 the second attack had ended, and the attackers had disappeared over the horizon. Radar tracked them to the north until they went out of range at 130 miles. En route home, the formation intercepted and shot down two of Patrol Wing Two's PBYs, but not before one got off a location report that confirmed the continued flight north beyond radar range.

## The third wave

Nagumo's carriers began recovering the first wave at 1000 hours. At 1030 the Admiral met with his staff to discuss initial attack reports and information radioed by Fuchida on the success of the second wave, which was still an hour out. Captain Genda proposed that Nagumo execute a planned third strike. The targets would be Pearl's oil storage farm, submarine docks, headquarters, and maintenance shops. Nagumo was reluctant to risk his fleet by staying in the area for another strike. Genda countered that the sinking of *Enterprise* left only *Lexington* unaccounted for. Meanwhile the sinking of *Nevada* prevented the surviving cruisers and submarines from exiting the harbor, so there was no real surface threat to worry about.

Since Nagumo continued to fret, Genda suggested that he send scout planes to search to the west and south – the location of *Lexington* by his guess, since Midway Island was in that direction. Nagumo agreed that it was time to use the scouting force, ordering it launched. He delayed his decision on the third attack, however, until Fuchida returned and reported on the damage he had seen.

Commander Fuchida landed on *Akagi* at noon. He reported the attack results to Vice Admiral Nagumo, emphasizing that the channel was closed and that what was left of the U.S. Pacific Fleet was trapped inside Pearl Harbor. He recommended the launch of a third strike immediately to take out the port's oil tank farms and machine shops. There were also a number of submarines that had largely gone unscathed. The Zeros, he added, had shot down over sixty American planes and had left the remainder burning on the ground, eliminating any threat from that direction. After taking all of this in, Nagumo decided to launch the strike, but he emphasized that it would be the last and that the fleet would withdraw as soon as it returned. At 1300 hours fifty-four Zeros, thirty-six Vals, and forty-four bombers took off.

## Recovery and search

The shock and devastation of the first two strikes had by then begun to sink in. Admiral Kimmel surveyed the burning and sunken hulks that had been the main battleline of the Pacific Fleet. He was further saddened by a report from Rear Admiral Spruance that *Enterprise*, two heavy cruisers, and three destroyers had also been lost. He found no solace in the fact that thirty of *Enterprise*'s SBDs had survived and would soon land at Ford Island. Most distressing of all was his realization that Pearl Harbor was useless, plugged by the wreckage of *Nevada*. His chief salvage officer had informed him that it would take several months to clear her, especially if she could not be re-floated. It might, indeed, be easier to dig a new channel if equipment to do the job could be brought in from the west coast.

Lieutenant General Short had less damage to deal with. Forts Shafter,

Debussy, and Kamehameha had largely escaped attack, and Schofield barracks had received only minor damage. His anti-aircraft batteries were now deploying to positions around Pearl Harbor and the two main airfields. Meanwhile, both of his infantry divisions were intact and moving to man beach defenses. Even so, Major General Martin's Hawaiian Air Force was shattered. Martin had lost four of his six serviceable B-17s. Out of thirty-six obsolete B-18s only eleven survived, and his fighter strength was reduced to twenty-five P-40s and sixteen P-36s. On the positive side, nine A-20 light attack bombers had escaped destruction,[12] and the safe arrival of Major Landon's twelve Flying Fortresses had given him a small but valuable heavy bomber force. Martin decided to get the B-17s back to Hickam Field and to prepare to attack the Japanese fleet if it could be located.

Commander Taylor informed Rear Admiral Bellinger that Army radar was tracking the Japanese planes as they returned to their carriers. Bellinger relayed this and the PBY report to Admiral Kimmel, who ordered the information to be relayed to *Lexington* along with orders for it to seek out and engage the Japanese fleet. He also ordered the SBDs to be recalled and readied for launch once the fleet was located.

### The final strike

At 1345, one of Patrol Wing Two's PBYs found the Japanese fleet steaming on a north-northeasterly course, 170 miles north of Oahu. It had just missed seeing Nagumo's third wave head south to strike Pearl. Receiving word of the discovery, Rear Admiral Bellinger notified Admiral Kimmel and Major General Martin. Martin ordered his B-17s to take off immediately, and Kimmel told Bellinger to send *Enterprise*'s thirty Dauntlesses. They would be striking at maximum range, but he would chance that. Neither group had a fighter escort.

The Air Warning Center had received a month's worth of training that morning and was functioning better than Major Bergquist had hoped. Again it was Lockard and Elliot at Opana Point that picked up the first track of incoming Japanese aircraft at 120 miles. Bergquist called Major General Martin, who ordered the twenty-five flyable P-40s to take off and orbit at 20,000 feet over Wheeler until they received instructions to intercept the attack. Meanwhile, the leader of the incoming Japanese, Commander Murata, split his sixty fighters, ordering half of them to range ahead to clear the skies of enemy interceptors. The other half would fly escort.

Martin's radars detected the splitting up of the Japanese force and the AWC relayed both locations to the orbiting Tomahawks. Captain James O. Beckwith, commander of the 72nd Pursuit Squadron, led his fighters against the larger formation, the melee beginning at 1435 hours, twenty miles northeast of Kaneohe Bay. Again the P-40s had an altitude advantage over their prey. They dove through the Japanese formation, shooting down six to ten Vals and Kates, but were then pursued by the Zero escort. During the next twenty minutes the Zeros shot down half of them.

For the first time that day, Army anti-aircraft greeted the attackers when they arrived over Pearl Harbor. The leading Zeros had already strafed Hickam Field and the ships in the harbor to divert attention from the bombers. Eighteen Vals dived on the tank farms at either end of the naval station between Hickam Field and the Southeast Loch. Carrying conventional 550 kg bombs, they ripped a number of fuel tanks open, starting massive fires. The remaining eighteen dive-bombers hit eight submarines moored side by side in Southeast Loch, next to the Submarine Headquarters building. They also hit the cruisers *Honolulu*, *San Francisco*, and *New Orleans*, all of which had escaped serious damage during the first two attacks.[13]

Unknown to the Japanese, Admiral Kimmel had established his Pacific Fleet headquarters in the Submarine Headquarters Building the previous summer. The Admiral preferred to operate from ashore in order to free his flagship for full duty with the fleet. When the headquarters was struck by three thousand pound bombs, Admiral Kimmel and many of his staff were killed. Unintended as it was, Kimmel's death would provide America with her first hero of the war and her first winner of the Navy Cross. Kimmel had, after all, gone down with his ships. Performing as level bombers, the Kates next rained bombs on machine shops near a dry dock that held the Pacific Fleet's flagship, U.S.S. *Pennsylvania*.

Having destroyed the fleet's fuel reserves and her heavy repair shops, Murata led his force back to their carriers. However, Kimmel's death did not go unavenged. At the very moment when Murata was completing his mission and turning his force homeward, the Flying Fortresses found the Japanese fleet and launched their attack.

Major Landon's Flying Fortresses justified their name that afternoon by fending off the attacks of the twenty-four Zeros defending the fleet and absorbing intense anti-aircraft fire from below. However, his hopes of sinking the carriers with the six 600-pound bombs each plane carried came to nothing. Dropped from 25,000 feet, they failed to score a single hit.

The Zeros were still swarming around Landon's B-17s when *Enterprise*'s SBDs arrived and began slow but deadly dives on the enemy below. The ill-advised decision of the captains of *Zuikauku* and *Soryu* to cease evasive maneuvers and launch more Zeros attracted the attention of both Scouting Six and Bombing Six. These walked their bombs the length of both carrier decks, ripping open their vitals and setting off gasoline, torpedoes and bombs aboard planes being held in readiness to strike *Lexington*. The price was high for the Americans though, only eight of their aircraft making it back to Ford Island. Several more had survived the encounter with the

Japanese fleet, but fell prey to the Zeros of Murata's returning strike force when their paths crossed.

The four intact carriers, *Akagi*, *Kaga*, *Hiryu*, and *Shokaku*, recovered the returning planes at 1700, taking aboard the orphans from *Zuikaku* and *Soryu*. After the recovery was completed, Vice Admiral Nagumo ordered the fleet to head north-northwest and back to Japan. He had been right in his worries. The August war game had correctly predicted the loss of a third of their planes and two carriers. He left behind two cruisers and four destroyers to rescue the survivors of the sinking carriers.

The destruction of *Zuikaku* and *Soryu* was a bittersweet victory for the Americans, for the Pacific Fleet had ceased to exist as a battle force. One carrier and seven battleships had been sunk, the harbor entrance at Pearl was blocked, the machine shops were destroyed, and the fuel reserves were gone. Although there remained twenty-five PBYs and fourteen B-17s, only a dozen P-40s were left that were serviceable. The Hawaiian Islands lay open to another aerial assault. The remainder of TF8 steamed into Honolulu harbor the next morning, but the port was too small to serve as more than a temporary shelter for the Pacific Fleet's cruisers and destroyers. It could not hold a fleet. *Lexington*'s TF12 arrived on the 9th. Vice Admiral Halsey, who had assumed command of the Pacific Fleet, ordered the carrier to Long Beach, California, taking the damaged *Northampton* with it. With the closing of Pearl Harbor, America's defenses shrank back to the West Coast, leaving the U.S. with the terrible dilemma of fighting a war in the Atlantic at the same time as it tried to rebuild its Pacific Fleet. Pearl Harbor would not be reopened until April 1942.[14] Unfortunately, that was exactly when Yamamoto arrived with the Japanese Combined Fleet.

### The reality

The warning phone calls by Stark and Marshall were never made. It was later discovered that the transoceanic cable had been tapped by the Japanese.[15] U.S.S. *Enterprise* was delayed by two days of bad weather which resulted in her being 200 miles west of Oahu on the morning of the attack. The state of the Hawaiian Air Force was as presented, including both the Navy and the Army aircraft being on four hour alert. However, the unintentional benefit of this was that while most of the aircraft were lost, the pilots survived the day. *Nevada* was ordered not to sortie and grounded herself at Hospital Point, where she sank.

Pearl Harbor survived as a forward striking base for the Pacific Fleet, which, stripped of its old battleships, was reformed around fast carrier groups. The alternatives played out here show that only the changing of the mindset of the Army and Navy commanders, both in Hawaii and in Washington, could have changed the historical outcome of December 7, 1941.

## Bibliography

Arakaki, Leatrice R., and Kuborn, John R., *7 December 1941: The Air Force Story* (Pacific Air Forces, Office of History, Hickam Air Force Base, Hawaii, 1991).

Clausen, Henry C., and Lee, Bruce, *Pearl Harbor: Final Judgement* (Crown Publishers, New York, 1992).

Cressman, Robert J., and Wenger, J. Michael, *Steady Nerves and Stout Hearts: The Enterprise (CV6) Air Group and Pearl Harbor, 7 December 1941* (Pictorial Histories Publishing Co, Missoula, 1989).

Goldstein, Donald M., and Dillon, Katherine V. (eds.), *The Pearl Harbor Papers: Inside the Japanese Plans* (Brassey's [U.S.], Washington, D.C., 1993).

Lord, Walter, *Day of Infamy* (Henry Holt, New York, 1957).

Prange, Gordon W.; Goldstein, Donald M.; and Dillon, Katherine V., *December 7, 1941: The Day the Japanese Attacked Pearl Harbor* (McGraw-Hill, New York, 1988).

Prange, Gordon W.; Goldstein, Donald M.; and Dillon, Katherine V., *At Dawn We Slept: The Untold Story of Pearl Harbor* (McGraw-Hill, New York, 1981).

Taussig, Captain Joseph K., Jr., 'A Tactical View of Pearl Harbor', in Stillwell, Paul (ed.), *Air Raid Pearl Harbor: Recollections of a Day of Infamy* (U.S. Naval Institute Press, Annapolis, 1981).

## Notes

1. Donald M. Goldstein and Katherine V. Dillon (eds.), *The Pearl Harbor Papers: Inside the Japanese Plans* (Brassey's [U.S.], Washington, D.C., 1993), pp.100–1.

2. Lieutenant Commander Kramer was assigned to ONI with duty at the translation section, Communications Division. They were responsible for the decoding and translating of the Japanese Purple code. Gordon Prange, Donald M. Goldstein and Katherine V. Dillon, *At Dawn We Slept: The Untold Story of Pearl Harbor* (McGraw-Hill, New York, 1981), p.19.

3. Admiral Harold R. Stark, *Commanding the Fleet* (Navy Press, Annapolis, 1953), pp.140–2.

4. I have adopted Arakaki and Kuborn's term 'Hawaiian Air Force' to refer to those Army Air Force units under the command of Major General Martin, and to differentiate them from Army Air Force, Army Air Corps, and Air Force Combat Command units that were either under Lieutenant General Short's Hawaiian Department or were in transit from the mainland to the Philippines. Leatrice R. Arakaki and John R. Kuborn, *7 December 1941: The Air Force Story* (Pacific Air Forces, Office of History, Hickam Air Force Base, Hawaii), p.viii.

5. *Ibid* p.151.

6. Prange, Goldstein and Dillon, *op.cit.* p.187.

*7. Colonel Rufus S. Bratton, 'Too Late the Warning', *Journal of Military History* vol.19, no.1, January 1955, pp.107–8.

*8. Admiral Mitsuo Fuchida, *The Emperor's Samurai* (Bobbs-Merrill, Indianapolis, 1975), p.89.

9. U.S. Army, Annex A, 'Lessons of the Pearl Harbor Attack', *Army Field Manual FM 100-5, Operations*, August 1949.

10. The battleships of the Pacific Fleet were in the midst of receiving additional anti-aircraft guns when the Japanese attacked. The fleet modernization program called for the adding of four quadruple mounts of either sixteen 1.1-inch machine guns or sixteen 3-inch anti-aircraft guns (depending upon their availability) to

the battleships. On December 7 the *Pennsylvania* was having hers installed and the *Arizona* was to receive hers in early 1942. Norman Friedman (ed.), *USS Arizona (BB-39)* (Leeward Publications, Annapolis, 1978).

*11. John P. Ryan, *The Fighting Sailor: The Biography of Admiral William F. Halsey* (Navy Press, Annapolis, 1987), pp.87–9.

12. In April 1941 the 58th Bombardment Squadron received its first twelve A-20 light bombers to replace the obsolete B-18 Bolos it was flying. The arrival of these new aircraft was the reason the squadron was transferred from Bellows to Hickam Air Field. Arakaki and Kuborn, *op.cit.* pp.51 and 151.

*13. Francis G. Cavendish, *The History of the Pacific War* (Triangle Press, Columbus, Ohio, 1968), pp.200–4.

*14. The *Nevada* was fully loaded with ammunition and fuel for a week of maneuvers scheduled to begin on December 8. Because her back was broken and the shell and powder was on board, Navy salvagers had to cut her apart and remove the ammunition round by round. It was determined that to blow her up would cause massive collateral damage in the harbor. In addition she sank in the narrowest part of the channel between the outer entrance and the entrance to West Loch. The Fleet's main ammunition depot was located a half mile away at West Loch. Ensign Taussig later wrote that 'thousands of 14-inch and 16-inch projectiles, each with two bags ... of powder, were out there in plain sight. The *Nevada,* alone, had 1,440 14-inch shells at West Loch ... and 2,800 seventy-pound bags of smokeless powder. The explosion [of this] would have rattled the windows in Topeka, Kansas, but, more importantly for the Japanese, it would have been the kind of solar plexus punch that would have guaranteed that the stunned U.S. Navy would not quickly be back on its feet.' It was therefore too dangerous to attempt clear the channel by blowing up the *Nevada* and risking the accidental detonation of the ammunition dump. The four-month recovery effort proved to be the greatest challenge faced by Navy salvagers during the war. Captain Joseph K. Taussig, Jr., 'A Tactical View of Pearl Harbor', in Paul Stillwell (ed.), *Air Raid Pearl Harbor: Recollections of a Day of Infamy* (Naval Institute Press, Annapolis, 1981), p.140.

15. Henry C. Clausen and Bruce Lee, *Pearl Harbor: Final Judgement* (Crown Publishers, New York, 1992), pp.135–6.

# 4
# CORAL AND PURPLE
# The Lost Advantage

James R. Arnold

## Station Hypo, Honolulu, April 17, 1942

'This is different, Joe,' said fleet intelligence officer Lieutenant Commander Edwin Layton. 'King himself wants your analysis, and he wants it fast.'

'Sweet Jesus,' replied Lieutenant Commander Joseph Rochefort, 'I didn't realize he was aware of our existence. I'll put together a report right away.'

Layton hung up the phone. He recalled the instructions issued by Admiral Chester Nimitz during the darkest days following Pearl Harbor. Nimitz told Layton to 'be the Admiral Nagumo of my staff.' Nimitz elaborated that Layton was to analyze the war from the Japanese viewpoint and to advise him about enemy strategy and objectives. Nimitz knew that the U.S. Pacific Fleet would suffer from numerical inferiority throughout 1942. To compensate, he wanted superior intelligence.

It was a tall order, yet Layton possessed unique attributes suiting him to the task. He had served as a naval attaché in Tokyo. Numerous bridge sessions with Admiral Isoroku Yamamoto and his staff gave Layton useful insight into the character of key Japanese officers. But it was the information provided by Station Hypo's traffic analysts, combined with the station's increasingly successful decrypts of the Japanese Naval Code, JN-25B, that gave Layton the ability to try to predict Japanese naval strategy. By dint of prolonged painstaking labor, the traffic analysts sorted through intercepted Japanese radio chatter and learned the call numbers for Japanese bases and ships. Thus they could identify a concentration of enemy strength at a specific location and thereby forecast a pending Japanese operation. Better yet, after just three months of war, Rochefort and his team were intercepting and breaking significant portions of the Japanese operational radio traffic.

At the beginning of April, Rochefort's radio intelligence briefs said that the Japanese were preparing to resume operations in the southwest Pacific for what the Japanese called an 'RZP' campaign. Rochefort tentatively identified 'RZP' as Port Moresby. In fact, it was the Japanese designation for

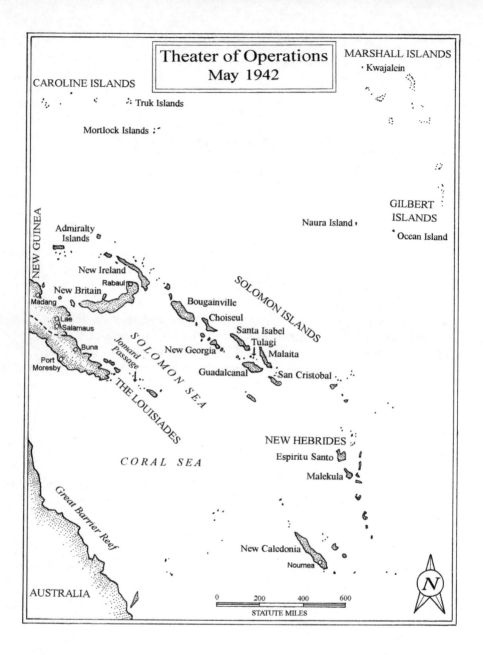

**Theater of Operations May 1942**

MARSHALL ISLANDS
· Kwajalein

CAROLINE ISLANDS

Truk Islands

Mortlock Islands

GILBERT ISLANDS

Naura Island

Ocean Island

NEW GUINEA

Admiralty Islands

New Ireland

Rabaul

New Britain

Madang

Lae

Salamaus

Buna

Port Moresby

Bougainville

Choiseul

SOLOMON ISLANDS

Santa Isabel

New Georgia

Tulagi

Malaita

Guadalcanal

San Cristobal

SOLOMON SEA

Jomard Passage

THE LOUISIADES

CORAL SEA

NEW HEBRIDES

Espiritu Santo

Malekula

Great Barrier Reef

New Caledonia

Noumea

AUSTRALIA

0    200    400    600

STATUTE MILES

N

Tulagi in the Solomon Islands, and Tulagi merely represented a supporting prong of a multi-prong Japanese offensive. However, Rochefort correctly added that a buildup at Rabaul suggested that it was to serve as the Japanese base for a campaign into the Coral Sea. By April 7 Rochefort reported that repairs on the carrier *Kaga* were being rushed ahead so it could participate. Shortly thereafter, Nimitz received Australian reports of intensifying air raids against Port Moresby. These raids were consistent with Rochefort's prediction.

Nimitz's mandate from the commander in chief of the U.S. Fleet, Admiral Ernest King, included maintaining the sea lanes to Australia. Consequently, Nimitz resolved to oppose the Japanese offensive into the Coral Sea. Yet his available forces were few. The carriers *Enterprise* and *Hornet* were committed to Doolittle's raid against Japan. *Lexington* was in dry-dock at Pearl Harbor. Only *Yorktown* was on the scene. Nimitz knew that if he was going to take action to prevent a southward Japanese advance he would have to move quickly. His sense of urgency increased on April 15 when Layton presented a British decrypt indicating that the Japanese striking forces were completing operations in the Indian Ocean and that Carrier Division Five would proceed to Truk, 'arriving about 28 April'. At the great natural harbor in Truk lagoon, Carrier Division Five could refit. Thereafter it would be well poised to begin a campaign to the south. Accordingly, Nimitz ordered *Lexington* to sail south to join *Yorktown*. It was a high risk decision involving half of the available American carrier strength, and it was based on intelligence estimates that the senior American staff knew were far from perfect. Because of the gravity of the decision, Nimitz had felt compelled to inform King that it was possible that the American carriers would be outnumbered two to one in a battle for the Coral Sea.

It was a measure of King's concern that he took the unprecedented step of directly requesting Station Hypo's analysis. Six hours after Layton conferred with Rochefort, the reply was on its way. There were five main points: 1) the Japanese had now concluded their Indian Ocean operation; 2) there was an offensive planned for eastern New Guinea, to be combined with 3) an offensive into the Coral Sea; 4) there was no evidence of preparations to invade Australia; 5) there was another Japanese operation in preparation but its objective was not yet clear. Later that same day, Rochefort's team discovered that a Japanese light carrier and a cruiser division was being assigned to cover the buildup at Rabaul. This unwelcome intelligence meant that the American carriers would confront ever more difficult odds. Still, Nimitz and King did not waver. Nimitz calculated that Station Hypo's priceless intelligence would allow his carriers to ambush the unsuspecting Japanese and that surprise would even the odds.

Had Station Hypo been privy to the activities of its enemy counterpart, its analysts would have realized that successful traffic analysis was a two way street. Unbeknownst to the Americans, their own high-frequency, ship-to-air radio transmissions were not limited to the horizon, as experts asserted. Instead, they bounced up and down from the Heaviside layer and skipped across the Pacific to Japan. The Japanese radio intelligence center at Owada detected increased radio activity at Pearl Harbor on April 15. When *Lexington* landed its complement of planes amidst a great deal of radio chatter, analysts at Owada correctly deduced that a carrier was preparing to sortie. Accordingly, Owada issued an alert that a carrier task force was departing Pearl Harbor.

### *Yamato*, fleet anchorage, Hashirajima roads, April 18

The thud of gunfire announced that the battleships had renewed their target practice. These vessels, which the aviators dismissively labeled the 'rest and reserve fleet', hoped that their turn would come soon when the commander of the Combined Fleet, Admiral Yamamoto, led them out to fight the decisive fleet action. In preparation, day after day, they trained very hard.

Aboard the giant battleship *Yamato*, Yamamoto re-read the Imperial General Headquarters' war plan with distaste: after 'a strategic situation of long-term invincibility' had been established by consolidating Japan's island defense system in the Pacific, the ambitious plan called for the 'capture of Hawaii and the outlying islands, attack on the United States, Canada, Panama Canal, as well as against Central America until the United States loses its fighting spirit and the war can be brought to a conclusion.' The plan's first phase – a surprise attack on Pearl Harbor to cover the capture of the Philippines, Malaya, and the Dutch East Indies – was almost fulfilled. So far the Imperial Japanese Navy had reigned supreme. The surpassing issue was what to do next. What should be the second phase objective?

Yamamoto keenly felt the crushing progress of time. He well knew that Japan could not endure a protracted war of attrition with the American colossus. Only a short decisive war would do, and this required bringing the U.S. fleet to battle. Consequently he doubted the wisdom of taking time to consolidate gains before launching a decisive offensive. Yet this was precisely what many Japanese strategists at Imperial General Headquarters were advocating. Yamamoto called it a 'wait in ambush' policy, with the prey being the American fleet. It was entirely too passive. Indeed, in his view recent American carrier raids and cruiser bombardments against Japanese bases demonstrated the futility of a passive defense. It made far more sense to take the fight to the enemy. He had wanted to eliminate Allied bases in northern and eastern Australia by direct invasion.

Yamamoto sighed. Those army blockheads. All they could think about was China and Russia. Everything else was secondary. The army had vehemently opposed the Australian plan because it would require vast resources of troops and shipping. The two services had reached a compromise: Australia would be isolated by severing its lines of communication with Hawaii. Yet when Yamamoto and his Combined Fleet staff proposed opening the second phase with the capture of Ceylon, New Guinea, and Port Darwin, the army had refused to yield on the Australian invasion. Finally, Imperial General Headquarters authorized the Combined Fleet to initiate Operation 'MO', featuring the assault on and occupation of, as soon as possible, two bases in New Guinea, Lae and Salamaua. Army aircraft stationed there would begin to soften up Port Moresby. Then Tulagi in the Solomon Islands, code-designated RZP, would be captured to provide a base to support floatplane reconnaissance on the flank of an amphibious assault against Port Moresby.

By the time Operation MO had been approved, Yamamoto had conceived something far grander. After much wrangling within the high command, he won permission to attack Midway Island in order to entice the enemy's carriers into action. The MO campaign in the Coral Sea would serve as a satisfactory preliminary, but it would have to adhere to a tight schedule so as not to take resources away from the thrust into the central Pacific.

Then came a shocking surprise, as Doolittle's B-25s appeared in the skies over Tokyo. It caused a tremendous loss of face among Japanese strategists. Frantic air and sea searches failed to yield a single clue about the size or direction of the American task force. Consequently not one blow could be struck in retribution. Yamamoto observed that the affair 'provides a regrettably graphic illustration of the saying that a bungling attack is better than the most skillful defense.' His chief of staff, Admiral Matome Ugaki, added, 'This brings up the necessity for fundamental changes, from now on, in our plans and countermeasures.' Referring to previous American raids, Ugaki continued, 'Some day, when he has launched his planes and closed in for gun bombardment, the golden opportunity to get him will surely come.'

A long silence ensued. Then Yamamoto said, 'In war, one must make one's own opportunities.'

## MacArthur's Headquarters, Melbourne, April 19

Rachel Bray steadied herself with an effort. 'God, hurry, just please finish', she thought as MacArthur's spokesman continued with his tedious recital of the day's events. Rachel well knew that once he ended, the newspaper scribes would ask innumerable questions and thus prolong the session. She wondered if she could endure.

An anxious air pervaded the headquarters of MacArthur's Southwest Pacific Area (SWPA) command. To date, each day had seemed to bring yet another report of Allied setback and disaster. Yet MacArthur's arrival in Australia and his establishment of a large headquarters in Melbourne had been a bracing tonic for a worried people. Reporters flocked to his headquarters, both because MacArthur's big personality provided colorful news and because his spokesmen offered interesting tidbits about SWPA operations that censors at other headquarters seemed to restrict.

Rachel Bray had used an old university connection to obtain a press pass that allowed her to attend the briefings. Her shapely legs and ample bosom had helped her overcome the only obstacle, an officious censor who had questioned her reporter's qualifications. In truth, a few journalism classes and a handful of published articles were the extent of her experience. During her second year at university she had largely abandoned her journalistic studies to focus on what at first had seemed a harmless diversion and then had become something far more. Seeing the pencil in her hand shaking, Rachel willed herself to ignore the accelerating pace of her craving and tried to listen to the briefer. After all, Mr Long would expect something better than she had provided last week.

'So,' the spokesman continued, 'the Japs are starting to appear at Port Moresby, but our pilots are ready. We have some experienced men there and they are achieving some striking results. But I have to tell you, boys, we think this is just a hint of things to come. We think something big is coming, but rest assured the General has duly taken every precaution. We are ready this time. This time,' the spokesman paused for dramatic emphasis, 'this time we are going to hit back very hard. Now, I have time for one or two questions.'

'Does General MacArthur think the men on Corregidor can be relieved.'

The spokesman scowled. His boss had told him that the General wanted him to bolster the spirits of the Australian people. This day was supposed to be about what MacArthur and SWPA was going to do to the Japs, not about those poor unfortunates back in the Philippines.

'Dick, as you know, the garrison at Corregidor is fighting very hard. General MacArthur personally selected General Wainwright to conduct the defense and he has every confidence in him. Yes, young lady.'

After carefully selecting the question on her list that had yet to be addressed she asked, 'Sir, many of my readers are not what you might call worldly. Like me and my family, they live in some pretty isolated places,' a few titters interrupted, as those that knew Rachel knew about her legendary parties at and after university, and that she had long ago dissociated herself from her farming family, 'and they worry, are the Japs going to invade?'

She locked her green eyes with those of the officer conducting the briefing, flashed her most provocative smile, and then demurely looked away.

The officer smiled in return. 'No ma'am, the General particularly wants me to have everyone reassure readers that there is nothing to worry about on that score. There may still be an occasional air raid, or the odd sub firing a few rounds from somewhere offshore, but nothing indicates an attempt against Australia.'

'Sir, if I may...' Rachel fixed his gaze again.

'Yes?' the officer nodded and smiled.

'This is really not for my readers, it's for me. I have a dear uncle living outside of Port Moresby. Is he in danger?'

'Ah,' the officer hesitated. Well, his boss did say he wanted to reassure the public while making sure that it was MacArthur and the army, not the goddamned navy, that got the proper credit. 'The General thinks that the Japs just might have a go at New Guinea. As we have been describing, they like to get their air strips established first, and then move their troop convoys under the air umbrella. But we are quite sure that our Kittyhawks at Port Moresby are going to deny him that cover. You can tell your uncle that General MacArthur says we are ready for whatever the Japs send our way.'

Agent T, known to Rachel Bray as 'Mr Long', waited for her weekly report. Japanese agents had found that they were best absorbed into their target countries by passing as fishermen, porters, or agricultural workers. This had worked particularly well in Hawaii and Mexico. Because it lacked a significant Japanese population, Australia presented a special challenge for the Japanese intelligence service. But beginning with its intervention in Shantung in the late 1920s, the service had been on the lookout for Chinese recruits. The usual mix of bribery and blackmail had produced a handful of candidates. Among them, Agent T had emerged at the top of his class. His handlers were confident that Agent T would perform well. After all, his family's fate back in Shantung depended on it.

Agent T, in turn, had correctly anticipated that once war began, Australian coastal surveillance would be too intense to maintain a cover as a fisherman. He had no interest in menial labor. He found that his mathematical skills – the same ones that had impressed his trainers when they taught him about codes – suited him to gambling. This was the avenue he used to enter Melbourne's small, shapeless Asian community. Soon he was running his own gambling room in a building he shared with a Chinese-run opium den. At that time, back in 1940, he had encountered a desperate young woman who said that she had mistakenly left most of her money at home (Agent T had often heard that time-worn story before) but really badly wanted some cash just now so she could meet up with her friends at a party down the street. She had just enough for one or two bets at the roulette wheel. Agent T had seen her type before. He lent her money for her habit and thereby recruited his most promising agent. She provided him with information from the SWPA briefings as well as loose gossip from the officers' bars.

Hating herself, but having no choice, Rachel told herself that, after all, she was just telling this man stuff that everyone else was going to read tomorrow.

Agent T heard her out and then passed over the precious envelope. Reviewing her information, he decided that it was not important enough to justify sending a radio report.

### Pacific Fleet Headquarters, Honolulu, April 20

Nimitz met again with his staff to discuss how to confront the impending Japanese offensive into the Coral Sea. Station Hypo was more confident than ever about its prediction. Independent corroboration came from an Australian naval intelligence report of intensification of enemy air surveillance in the Coral Sea. The British reported that a cruiser division and a carrier with a name ending in 'kaku' were due in Truk by April 25. This confirmed previous decrypts predicting that Carrier Division Five, comprising the carriers *Zuikaku* and *Shokaku*, was bound for Truk. There was one ominous development. A decrypt from Australia alerted Station Hypo that the Japanese intended to introduce a new operational code on May 1. This was sure evidence that a major operation was to follow. It also meant that Allied intelligence would be blinded for weeks until analysts cracked the new code.

Layton summarized the intelligence picture: 'There are many indications that the enemy will launch an offensive in the New Guinea–New Britain–Solomon area.'[1] The offensive would enjoy superior carrier strength and land-based airpower and it would 'start very soon'. Layton said that the Japanese might deploy as many as five carriers. However, intelligence had confirmed the participation of only three. Nimitz considered. He could count on radio intelligence to reveal Japanese direction and deployment. While it was well and good to know his foe's intentions, Nimitz realized he might not have enough strength to stop the Japanese. *Enterprise* and *Hornet* were due back at Pearl in three days. The Coral Sea was a ten-day trip, thus the outcome would probably be decided before they could participate. So, he had only two carriers, supported by MacArthur's planes based in northeast Australia and New Guinea, to confront three to five Japanese carriers. Nimitz made the momentous decision: 'We should be able to accept odds in battle if necessary.'[2] He issued orders for *Lexington* and *Yorktown* to unite to stop the Japanese thrust.

### Fourth Fleet Headquarters, the light cruiser *Kashimi*, Rabaul Harbor, April 22

Vice Admiral Shigeyoshi Inoue read his orders with dismay. Yamamoto was giving him only until the second week in May to capture Port Moresby. This neither provided enough time for fleet carrier *Kaga* to be repaired nor allowed time for the deployment of sufficient land-based air cover in New Guinea. Reviewing his orders, Inoue reflected that at least the impatient fools in Tokyo had not been so foolish as to go ahead with the planned code change. There was simply not enough time to distribute the new code books to all the widely dispersed commands. So the change was postponed until May 27.

Inoue, like all Japanese strategists, was reluctant to send transports into waters where they did not enjoy a comfortable air superiority. Thus, control of the airspace off the east coast of New Guinea was crucial to the success of Operation MO. Although the 25th Air Fleet would contribute its Rabaul-based forces, air superiority depended upon the Striking Force fleet carriers *Zuikaku* and *Shokaku* and the light carrier *Shoho*. Inoue's assignment required striking at multiple dispersed objectives, but intelligence anticipated that he would face only one enemy carrier. Once he established seaplane bases at Tulagi and the Louisiades, the flying boats would provide early warning of any American task force steaming to intercept the Port Moresby invasion force. Then his carriers and the superb heavy cruiser squadron should be ample to accomplish the job.

If the Japanese landing group forced the Jomard Passage and reached Port Moresby, there could be no doubt about the outcome. The base could support only a single brigade group. Its garrison was comprised of low-quality reserve formations, deficient in equipment and morale. Two months of frequent air attack and a sense of having been written off did not improve their outlook. They could not match veteran Japanese ground troops. Thus, from an Allied perspective, everything depended upon the ability of fewer than 150 carrier planes to check the Japanese invasion force.

### Yorktown, the Coral Sea, May 2

Rear Admiral Frank J. Fletcher commanded the American carrier task forces. His orders required him to 'destroy enemy ships, shipping and aircraft at favorable opportunities in order to assist in checking further advances in the New Guinea–Solomons area.'[3] Toward this end Fletcher resolved to operate about 700 miles south of Rabaul in an area outside of expected Japanese reconnaissance. Once he received specific intelligence of the Japanese southward advance he planned to counterattack into the exposed Japanese flank.

While steaming to the projected strike position, a Dauntless anti-submarine patrol plane from *Yorktown* sighted a surfaced submarine about thirty miles from Fletcher's task force. It was the *I-21*, one of the units in the Japanese patrol group. Three SBDs sortied to attack the sub. They drove *I-21* down, but the critical question was whether it had radioed a sighting report. Fletcher summoned Lieutenant Forrest Biard, a junior lieutenant who was one of Station Hypo's skilled Japanese linguists. Biard had been assigned to *Yorktown*'s radio intelligence unit (RIU) with the job of providing tactical intelligence. Fletcher was an admiral of the old school and had little use for junior lieutenants in general and RIU officers in particular.

'Did the Jap sub report our position?' he demanded. 'Sir, I don't know,' replied Biard. Fletcher dismissed him with disdain.

Later that day, Fletcher's specialist in carrier operations, Admiral Aubrey Fitch, flew to *Yorktown* for a conference. He came with the news that *Lexington*'s RIU officer had heard the submarine signaling. Irate, Fletcher summoned Biard again and chewed him out for his failure. A few hours later a message from Pearl alerted Fletcher that the Japanese operation was 'now under way'. The admiral assumed that his foe knew his position because of the submarine report. In fact, *I-21*'s transmission had never reached Rabaul. Consequently the American carrier task forces managed to get behind the Japanese I-boat screen without detection.

At 0800 the next morning the Tulagi Invasion Group began landing. Three seaplanes and *Shoho*'s ten Zekes provided air cover, but since the invasion was unopposed they were not needed. Because the Japanese did not expect any Allied reaction for several days, the Covering Force then steamed west to get in position to protect the Port Moresby Invasion Force.

Nine hours later Fletcher received news that Japanese vessels had been sighted in the sound between Guadalcanal and Tulagi. It was just the kind of opportunity he had been waiting for. Rather than break radio silence, he sent the destroyer *Sims* and the oiler *Neosho* to meet Fitch and instruct him to head for a new rendezvous point 300 miles south of Guadalcanal. Meanwhile, Fletcher steered north at 24 knots to attack the Tulagi Group.

## Carrier Division Five, off the coast of Rabaul, May 3

Encumbered by orders to deliver nine Zeke reinforcements to Rabaul, plagued by poor weather, Carrier Division Five was some 340 miles north of Tulagi. It annoyed the commander of the Carrier Striking Force, Vice Admiral Takeo Takagi, that his two carriers were not yet in position to provide air cover for Tulagi. But, he ruefully reflected, if a sailor allowed himself to be overly bothered by weather delays, then he had chosen the wrong profession. Besides, the American carrier that intelligence had alerted him about could hardly be on station yet. Takagi ordered his carriers to spend the next day refueling in preparation for the coming battle.[4]

Far to the north, a staff officer carried the day's news to Yamamoto. The admiral was involved in his nightly round of chess with Ugake. The staffer told them that Operation MO was proceeding smoothly and that Tulagi was secure.

Ugake lifted his head from the board and asked, 'I imagine we captured the garrison.'

'Actually no, sir, the Australians abandoned the base before we arrived.'

'That's surprising,' said Ugake.

Yamamoto uttered a characteristic grunt and the men returned to their game.

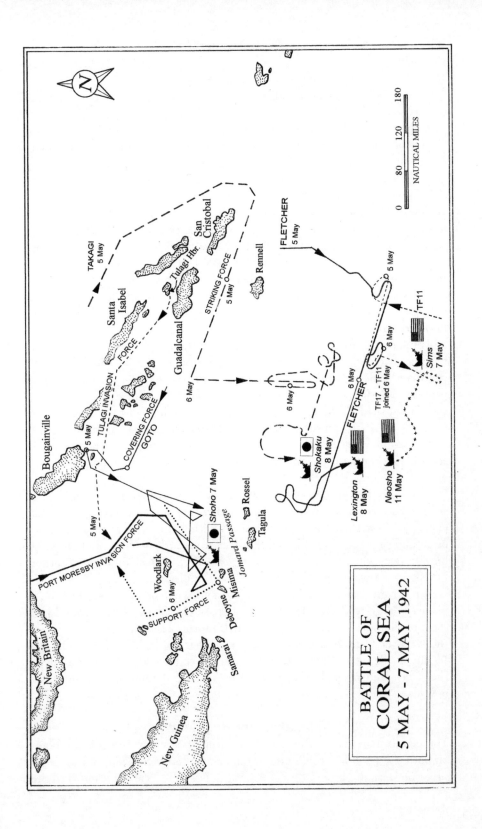

BATTLE OF
CORAL SEA
5 MAY - 7 MAY 1942

## The Coral Sea, May 4–6

Ten minutes before sunrise, May 4, twelve Devastator torpedo planes and twenty-eight Dauntless dive-bombers launched from *Yorktown*. They lifted into an overcast sky laden with rain squalls. The northern edge of a hundred-mile-wide cold front had now reached the north coast of Guadalcanal. It was poor flying weather until the strike force neared the target. During the ensuing action, the American pilots committed the mistake – typical of both sides – of overestimating what they confronted and what they achieved. Thus, when pilots returned they claimed that they had damaged a light cruiser, a seaplane tender, and numerous transports. During the day two additional attacks went in. By 1632 the 'Battle of Tulagi' was over and the American task force was jubilant. As *Yorktown* steamed south for a rendezvous with Fitch, pilots compiled their claims: two destroyers sunk, along with a freighter and four gunboats; a light cruiser driven aground; and numerous other vessels damaged. That same day Fifth Air Force B-26s bombed Rabaul while P-39s escorted a B-17 strike force against Lae.

The Japanese forces were far less active on May 4. Not until noon had the first report of American planes over Tulagi come to Takagi. He ordered his command's best speed southeast to engage the enemy. It was a futile gesture. On May 5, by the time his carriers arrived within striking distance, the enemy had disappeared. Later in the morning, when a four-engine seaplane failed to return to Rabaul following its dawn search, Inoue correctly assumed that it had been shot down by the American carrier. Since he still did not know the enemy's location, he ordered Takagi to send his planes on a raid against Port Moresby.

Although the Americans possessed excellent operational intelligence, such is the nature of naval warfare, with small ships operating in a vast expanse of water, that Fletcher remained blithely unaware of the proximity of Takagi's carriers. He believed that they were at least 400 miles ahead of him. In fact, when *Yorktown* and *Lexington* united at dusk on May 5, Carrier Division Five was astern, less than 250 miles distant.

What some called the friction of war and what others called luck now played a large role. On May 6 Fletcher's search planes turned around just short of the Japanese carriers during their morning search. In the afternoon, the weather front brought overcast skies that concealed Takagi. On the Japanese side, a land-based search plane correctly reported the location of the American carriers but Takagi did not receive the information until the next day.

## *Zuikaku*, morning, May 7

The penultimate day of the Coral Sea Campaign began with senior officers on both sides still laboring under significant misapprehensions of the actual situation. Lacking knowledge of American positions, Takagi listened to the advice of his carrier specialist, Rear Admiral Tadaichi Hara, and ordered a thorough search southward in order to make certain that there was no carrier behind him. Once he knew that his rear was clear, he intended to press westward to provide air cover for the Port Moresby Invasion Group. At 0600 the search went out. When a cruiser's floatplane reported the sighting of a U.S. carrier force, Takagi complimented Hara for his sage advice. Hara immediately ordered a full scale, seventy-six plane attack. The target turned out to be the destroyer *Sims* and the fleet oiler *Neosho*, the latter having been misidentified as a carrier. The overwhelming aerial assault sank *Sims* and left *Neosho* a floating hulk.

Five minutes after the strike set out, Takagi received another sighting report. A patrol plane had spotted an American task force 350 miles to the west. Hard on the heels of this unsettling news came yet another report of a force on the same bearing but only 200 miles away. When the Japanese strike force radioed that the presumed carrier target was in fact an oiler, Takagi and Hara realized that they had committed a potentially disastrous blunder. With Takagi's approval, Hara ordered *Zuikaku* to radio an urgent recall signal to the strike force.

### *Yorktown*, morning, May 7

Dawn found *Yorktown* also sending out a search force. Ten scout planes fanned out into the northeast skies where Fletcher expected to find the Japanese. At 0815 a scout reported that he had shot down an enemy floatplane about 250 miles away, on the edge of the Jomard Passage. Station Hypo had predicted that the invasion group would use this passage en route to Port Moresby. The shoot-down confirmed that the Japanese were out looking for the American carriers and reinforced Fletcher's notion that the hostile carriers were ahead of him. Thirty minutes later came another contact report: two carriers and two cruisers off Misima on the New Guinea coast, heading south.

Fletcher reacted in the same overly credulous manner that had characterized Hara's decision. He too ordered an all-out strike. At 1015, ninety-three planes roared off of the American flight decks and flew northwest. Then the young pilot who had reported the Japanese carriers landed on *Yorktown* and hastened to the bridge. He anxiously informed Fletcher that he had made a coding error. What he had actually seen were two cruisers and two destroyers!

'Young man, do you know what you have done? You have just cost the United States two carriers!' shouted Fletcher. While Fletcher and his staff debated sending out a recall order, Lieutenant Biard, *Yorktown*'s RIU officer, went to the radio shack to listen, with dread, for any Japanese pilot making a sighting report of the American carriers.

Instead, at 1022 came a relay from MacArthur's headquarters. A B-17 had sighted a Japanese carrier north of Misima! Fletcher's despondency changed to elation. It was all going to work out. He ordered the strike redirected thirty miles to the new target. Minutes later came a new alarm. From 300 miles astern, *Neosho* radioed that she was under aerial attack. A quick glance at the charts revealed that *Neosho* was outside of land-based attack range. Fletcher realized that he was boxed in with Japanese carriers ahead and astern.

Then Biard picked up *Zuikaku*'s repeated homing signal with the course '280° speed 20 knots'. This meant that the Japanese carriers were closing fast. But Fletcher distrusted Biard's competency. After all, five days ago Biard had been unable to inform him whether the enemy sub had made a contact report, something his counterpart aboard *Lexington* had easily accomplished. A signaler from *Lexington* interpreted *Zuikaku*'s signal as 'enemy course and speed as 280° 20 knots'.[5] Fletcher had no doubt who to believe. In his mind, Biard had already proven ridiculously fallible. He accepted the interpretation given by *Lexington*'s RIU officer, even though the American task force had not recently been steaming on a course anything like 280°. In fact, *Lexington*'s RIU officer had mistranslated the Japanese.

Next came the splendid report that American planes were attacking a Japanese carrier. It was *Shoho*, the light carrier assigned to cover directly the Port Moresby invasion force. *Shoho* had entered service in early 1942. Compared to the superb veterans aboard Carrier Divisions One and Two, her pilots were inexperienced. The overwhelming U.S. strike force easily brushed aside the handful of Zekes flying combat air patrol. A barrage of bombs and torpedoes sent the hapless ship to the bottom. In anxious radio rooms aboard *Yorktown* and *Lexington*, a strong, sharp voice pierced the static: 'Scratch one flattop! Dixon to Carrier, Scratch one flattop!'[6]

By 1338 the strike force was safely back aboard the carriers. Fletcher now turned his attention to finding and fighting Carrier Division Five. He continued to ignore Biard's ongoing plot of their location. With the curtain of heavy weather closing in, he decided that 'there was insufficient daylight for an attack following an extensive search.' He decided to keep all of his planes available to repel a Japanese strike. He did not know that his counterparts had come to a similar conclusion.

### *Zuikaku*, afternoon, May 7

Carrier Division Five recovered its strike planes and prepared for another mission. By mid-afternoon, Hara asserted that 'there is no possibility for an attack today'. Then, at 1600, a floatplane provided a contact report indicating that the American carriers just might be within range before nightfall. Had he commanded more experienced pilots, Hara might have launched a massive strike. Instead, he called for volunteers from among his

A senior Japanese naval delegation presents a wreath at the World War I Tomb of the Unknown Soldier, Arlington National Cemetery, Virginia, c. 1927. The junior officer on the right of the Japanese group is Captain Isoroku Yamamoto, the Japanese naval attaché in Washington at the time. *Courtesy U.S. Naval Historical Center.*

The Japanese battle line gathers near Surigao Strait on the afternoon of January 1, 1942. *Ise* leads, followed by *Fuso*, *Haruna*, and *Mutsu*.

Captain Tameichi Hara, present at both Truk and Surigao, felt that destroyers such as his *Amatsukaze*, and their Long Lance torpedoes, spelled the end of the battleship. They certainly contributed to the destruction of the American battleships attempting to implement War Plan Orange.

(*Above left*) Command of the First Area Army gave General Yamashita the opportunity to make use of the lessons on armored warfare he had observed on his recent visit to Germany. He combined four tank regiments, motorized infantry, and artillery into an ad-hoc tank corps. Here a Japanese tank from the 6th Regiment (rebuilt after its destruction at Nomonhan in 1939) attacks on the drive to Voroshilov. *Courtesy U.S. Naval Historical Center.*

(*Left*) Japanese troops of General Homma's Seventh Army celebrate the fall of Vladivostok in one of the surrendered coastal defense batteries defending the port. Despite being hopelessly cut off after Yamashita's breakthrough on the Ussuri front, the garrison of Vladivostok held out tenaciously, earning Homma an Imperial rebuke as the siege dragged on. *Courtesy U.S. Naval Historical Center.*

Smoke rises from the first bombs dropped in the Pearl Harbor oil farm by the Japanese third wave attack. The fire in the center is from the still burning U.S.S. *Arizona*, next to Ford Island. The shipboard anti-aircraft fire has been reinforced by the Army anti-aircraft batteries which had deployed to their positions around Pearl Harbor and Hickam Air Field during the lull between the second and third attacks. *U.S. National Archives.*

(*Left*) An aerial view of Pearl Harbor on November 30, 1941. Ford Island Naval Air Station is in the center, with Battleship Row on its left. Left and upper left of center are the oil farms, Admiral Kimmel's headquarters and Hickam Air Field. Bombs from the Japanese third wave attack that missed the oil tanks hit the headquarters building, killing Admiral Kimmel and many of his staff. The U.S.S. *Nevada* sank where the channel narrows just before the entrance from the sea at the top of the photo. *U.S. National Archives.*

A catastrophic explosion rips apart the U.S.S. *Lexington*. Seeping avgas caused huge explosions on both the Japanese *Shokaku* and the *Lexington* that day. For *Shokaku*, it was the only major wound. For *Lexington*, the explosion was to prove one injury too many after a succession of torpedo hits.

An SBD Dauntless dive bomber on the U.S.S. *Enterprise*. This aircraft was a powerful instrument of war, armed with a 500- or 1,000-pound bomb capable of sinking an enemy carrier if it got a hit. This 'if' was to lose the Battle of Midway for the United States. *Courtesy U.S. Marine Corps University Archives.*

(*Left*) The Japanese light carrier, *Shoho*, under attack by torpedo bombers and dive bombers from the American carriers *Lexington* and *Yorktown*, shows the mortal hits that would soon take her to the bottom. 'Scratch one flattop!' was the famous signal sent from the U.S. aircraft.

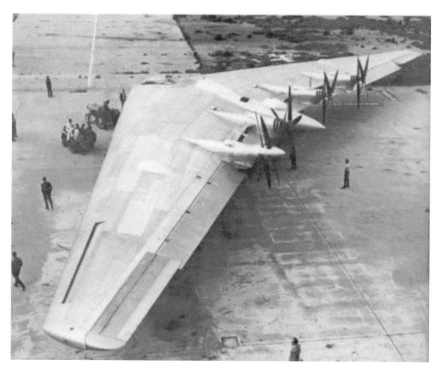

The XB-35, Jack Northrop's flying-wing bomber. After the loss of most of the Pacific Fleet's carriers at Midway and the retreat to the West Coast, a desperate U.S. government placed an immediate contract for the XB-35, which could reach Japan non-stop from the United States.

(*Right*) A Japanese 70mm battalion howitzer used in action by the 51st Division in the drive towards Mount Garnet, during which the Australian 14th Brigade received some rough handling. Despite its appearance, the Model 92 (1932) provided effective fire support at the tactical level. It was light but could fire a powerful round at effective ranges from 110 to 3,000 yards. *Courtesy U.S. Naval Historical Center.*

The TBF Avenger torpedo bomber. Squadrons from Long Beach, Seal Beach and Los Alamitos Naval Air Stations joined General Hap Arnold's counter-strike on Nagumo's carriers when these attacked military bases and industrial facilities in San Diego and Los Angeles. *Courtesy U.S. Marine Corps University Archives.*

Japanese medium tanks of the newly raised 2nd Tank Division after unloading in Townsville on the eastern coast of Australia. The 2nd Tank Division achieved a brief moment of glory as it punched through the U.S. I Corps in Yamashita's September offensive, making a deep penetration. The Malayan triumph seemed about to repeat itself. *Courtesy U.S. Naval Historical Center.*

Mitsubishi A5M 'Claude.' Despite its outdated design, it was still able to exact a heavy toll of Allied fighters in Southeast Asia and over Burma in the opening days of the war. *James V. Crow*.

Mitsubishi G3M 'Nell.' The bombardment of Calcutta by such aircraft had a psychological effect far greater than the physical military damage. *James V. Crow*.

Yokosuka D4Y1 'Judy' carrier-based dive-bomber. Designed to replace the older Aichi D3A 'Val' dive-bomber, the 'Judy' was an improved version of a German design, the He-118. It first went into service as a high-speed reconnaissance aircraft in 1942 (two were at Midway on the *Soryu*) but it was mid-1944 before significant numbers were in service as dive-bombers. *James V. Crow*.

Admiral William F. Halsey, an aggressive commander whose strength was unrelenting tenacity in combat. He would find an opponent equally determined and far luckier in Admiral Takeo Kurita in the Philippines. *Courtesy U.S. Naval Historical Center.*

Admiral Takeo Kurita held the destiny of the empire in his hands when he was given the most critical arm of the *Sho-1* Plan to execute. He would command the last strong surface element of the once mighty Combined Fleet in a desperate gamble against the overwhelming numbers of the U.S. Navy, led by brilliant enemies who had developed a taste for victory. *Courtesy U.S. Naval Historical Center.*

(*Top left*) H.M.A.S. *Canberra* sinks off Guadalcanal following the battle of Savo Island. U.S.S. *Blue*, alongside *Canberra*'s bow, removes survivors, while U.S.S. *Patterson* approaches the sinking ship's stern. *U.S. National Archives.*

(*Left*) Five smashed Japanese tanks, destroyed by U.S. Marine artillery, lie on a sand spit across the mouth of the Matanikau River, Guadalcanal Island. Savo Island is in the background. *U.S. National Archives.*

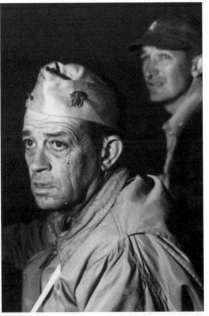

Rear Admiral Clifton A.F. Sprague commanded Taffy 1, the only force – a handful of jeep carriers and destroyers – left behind by Admiral Halsey to guard the huge collection of transports and merchant ships that supported General Krueger's Sixth Army in the desperate battle for Leyte Island. *U.S. National Archives*.

*(Left)* Japan, December 12, 1945. Fires rage aboard the U.S.S. *Antietam* after a Japanese suicider careened into aircraft refueling near the stern. The resulting explosions destroyed additional aircraft on the hangar deck below, but swift action by other crew saved the ship and kept casualties below 600, including 146 killed. Minutes after this photograph was taken, another suicider struck just below the bridge of the U.S.S. *Midway* cruising one mile to starboard.

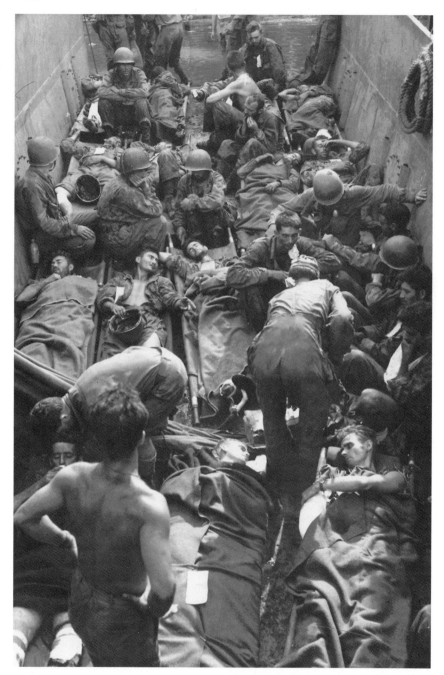

Mainland Japan, December 7, 1945. Casualties from U.S. operations in Japan wait on a landing craft at the beach after the hospital ship they were to be transported to, U.S.S. *Consolation*, was set afire from repeated strikes by suicide aircraft and towed from the invasion area.

best aircrews. Twelve Val dive-bombers and fifteen Kate torpedo planes launched and flew south into the thick squall line. They clawed their way westward through frightful conditions but failed to penetrate the front. Two hours later they were turning back when disaster struck. *Yorktown*'s radar had detected them and vectored its Wildcats to intercept.

The Vals unloaded their bombs to be more maneuverable and nimbly evaded the Wildcats. The Kates lacked agility and could not escape. At the cost of three American fighters, seven Kates and one Val were shot down. The scattered survivors struggled home through poor conditions. Amazingly, some overflew the American carriers, briefly mistaking them for their own until flak started bursting around them. They managed to locate their own flight decks only because Hara turned on his searchlights to help his pilots locate and land. Displaying superb skill, eighteen planes successfully completed a nocturnal landing. Only one Kate splashed during the recovery. So the abortive strike subtracted nine of the best naval aircrews from the Japanese order of battle, and for the first time the Japanese learned that they confronted two American carriers in the Coral Sea.

## Battleship *Yamato*, Hashirajima anchorage, May 7

During this time Ugake had been monitoring reports. When the Americans had launched their May 4 surprise attack against Tulagi, he wrote in his diary, 'The enemy seems to have attacked after detecting our situation fairly well.' Still, he and his staff remained confident. The Owada Radio intercept analysts had enjoyed good success identifying the American call signs. Once Fletcher's task force broke radio silence they correctly reported that two U.S. carriers were in action in the Coral Sea. Judging from their reported positions, Ugake expected good news. He noted in his diary that the carrier closest to Hara's 'can be wiped out with one blow'[7] while the other carrier 'will be nice bait for the medium torpedo bombers from New Guinea.' Instead came distressing news of the loss of *Shoho*.

## The carrier exchange, May 8

Allied intelligence had contributed all that it could. May 8 would involve hard pounding as history's first carrier versus carrier battle took place. Success would go to whichever side could hit the hardest. The tactical factors were nicely balanced. The weather front that had plagued the Japanese carriers the evening before gave them valuable concealment. In contrast, the American carriers operated under good visibility. However, the Americans deployed 121 aircraft while the depleted Japanese had ninety-five operational planes. Each American carrier possessed sixty percent more anti-aircraft guns than its counterparts. Coupled with their slightly larger escort screen, the Americans thus had a more powerful defensive capacity. Lastly, unlike *Shokaku* and *Zuikaku*, *Lexington* and *Yorktown* possessed radar.

Each side knew the approximate location of its opponent and sent out searches at first light. At 0820, Lieutenant J.G. Smith radioed a sighting report. Two minutes later, Flight Warrant Officer Kenzo Kanno did the same. Thus neither side was able to achieve the all important first contact while remaining unseen itself. The Americans launched eighty-two planes – forty-six dive-bombers, twenty-one torpedo planes, and fifteen escorting fighters – against the enemy. Seventeen Wildcats remained to protect the carriers. Sixty-nine Japanese aircraft – eighteen Zekes, eighteen Kates, and thirty-three Vals – launched in turn against the Americans. Nineteen Zekes remained for combat air patrol.

The Americans proved less adept at formation flying than the Japanese. Consequently, their attacks went in piecemeal and lacked coordination. The Devastator torpedo planes launched at overly long ranges and were easily evaded. The Dauntlesses pressed their bombing runs through the Zeke screen, suffering losses in the process, and hit *Shokaku* three times. Lieutenant Joseph Powers delivered the most serious blow. Exhibiting courage for which he earned a posthumous Medal of Honor, Powers held his flak-stricken Dauntless in a dive from which he could not escape. His 1,000-pound bomb penetrated well forward in the anchor windlass room, where it ignited a huge aviation gasoline fire. The force of the explosion vented upward through the flight deck, rendering *Shokaku* incapable of flight operations.

Meanwhile, Japanese aviators attacked *Yorktown* and *Lexington* with greater coordination than the Americans. Nonetheless, *Yorktown* displayed expert ship handling while steaming at 32 knots and managed to move inside the path of enemy torpedoes. *Lexington* was some eighty feet longer than *Yorktown*, had twice her full-load displacement, and thus had a turning circle almost double. After she had evaded numerous torpedoes, two hit home. In addition, at least two Vals struck her. Although she developed a list, it appeared that the rugged vessel would survive. Instead, a generator left running when the crew abandoned the room ignited seeping aviation gasoline. The ensuing explosion gave *Lexington* a mortal wound. One dive-bomber hit *Yorktown* fifteen feet inside her island. The bomb penetrated three decks and exploded within an aviation store room. Damage control crews quickly brought the ensuing blaze under control.

So the battle ended. Neither side had prior experience in defensive carrier warfare. Moreover, damage control practices were in their infancy. The battle's results showed the vulnerability of vessels laden with aviation gasoline and explosives. One American carrier was sunk and one damaged. On the Japanese side, one carrier was disabled. But it was the *Shokaku's* inability to land planes that proved decisive. Carrier Division Five had already lost thirty-seven percent of its aircraft in the past twenty-four hours. The need for *Zuikaku* to throw nine bombers and three fighters overboard in order to land returning strike planes changed the losses from serious to prohibitive. Of the total of seventy-two operational planes that began the battle that morning, only twenty-seven remained fit to fly.

Aboard the light cruiser *Kashima*, swinging at anchor in Rabaul harbor, Admiral Inoue digested the day's horrifying intelligence. His first instinct was to order all his surface fighting elements to close on the enemy and seek battle. Then he thought about his vulnerable transports. The knowledge that enemy cruisers were patrolling the Jomard Passage and that the American carriers were between the transports and Carrier Division Five unnerved him. He ordered the transports to turn away rather than enter the Jomard Passage. The four heavy cruisers belonging to the Covering Force would protect their retirement. Takagi was also anxious about his position. The losses among his most experienced aircrews made him feel cautious. After an exchange of messages with Inoue, he too decided to withdraw. That evening Inoue completed the disagreeable task of sending a dispatch to Yamamoto. After blaming Hara's loss of confidence for his decision, Inoue concluded, 'Port Moresby attack will be postponed to a later date. Your approval is requested.'

### Battleship *Yamato*, Hashirajima anchorage, May 8

Chief of Staff Ugake completed his briefing and asked Yamamoto how to respond to Inoue's request for a withdrawal.

A long silence ensued. 'Something is wrong out there, my friend', Yamamoto said. 'Since the war's beginning we have been trying to engage the American carriers. Finally we find them and what happens? Hara or Inoue or both lose their nerve.'

'There is an opponent in a war,' replied Ugake, 'so one cannot progress just as one wishes.'

'Things progressed pretty damn well for the Americans,' responded Yamamoto testily. 'They evacuate their base at Tulagi just before we get there. They strike our ships at anchorage when they are without air cover. They bomb Rabaul and New Guinea while we are trying to mass our strength. Then they appear to block our passage through the Jomard and sink the *Shoho* in the bargain. What is wrong out there?'

Ugake answered, 'I think in part it's due to the insufficiency of air reconnaissance. We should keep this in mind.'

'Hmm,' grunted Yamamoto. 'I want our best men to study this closely. But nothing must interfere with the operation against Midway.'

### A pawn is sacrificed, May 10

Agent T read Rachel Bray's summary of the daily briefings from MacArthur's headquarters. It appeared that the just concluded action in the Coral Sea had involved losses on both sides. However, just as had occurred pre-

viously, the spokesman seemed clearly to be saying that the Allies had
advance information about Imperial plans. Once might be a mere boast.
Twice could be something else. Could there be an enemy agent or even a
traitor somewhere in the Japanese chain of command? Agent T thought it
unlikely, but still . . .

He resolved to break his radio silence and send his first message since the
brief signal announcing his safe arrival in Australia. It would require a long
transmission. He had to anticipate that Allied listening posts would detect
his presence. If they were skilled enough with radio directional finding he
would have to move to a safe house while covering his tracks.

Rachel interrupted his silent musings. She anxiously inquired, 'It's good
enough, isn't it? Can I please have my packet?'

During his training at Owada, Agent T had been strictly enjoined never
to allow affection for a recruit to interfere with pragmatic judgement. His
instructor had quickly realized that this would not be a problem for Agent
T.

He reached beneath his desk. Instead of the envelope in the right-hand
drawer he extracted the envelope from the left. With a hint of a smile, he
passed the packet. 'Good work. Here's a special reward.'

## Battleship *Yamato*, Hashirajima anchorage, May 12

Two days later, a senior staff officer requested an audience with Yamamoto
and his senior Combined Fleet staff. He ushered in a young officer who
seemed extremely nervous to be in the admiral's august presence.

'Sir, this is Lieutenant Ichiki with Oswada radio intelligence. He has
something I think you would want to know.'

Yamamoto fixed a harried gaze at the trembling lieutenant. 'Yes?'

'Sir, we have received a relay from a listening post in New Guinea. It's
from an agent in Australia.' His voice wavered and trailed off.

'Go on,' said Yamamoto.

'Well, sir, this agent had instructions not to transmit unless he had
something extraordinary. In fact, sir, we had not heard from him since the
war began and we had written him off. His message is a bit garbled, but in
essence he reports that the Americans knew we were coming. They knew
when and where.'

'Impossible!' snorted Ugaki.

Yamamoto looked at the lieutenant more kindly. 'Proceed.'

'Sir, if the department had not been reviewing security to fulfill its part in
the general analysis you ordered, I don't know how much credence we
would have placed in this report. But, sir, coupled with Tulagi . . .'

Yamamoto interrupted. 'The resistance at Port Moresby, the *Shoho*, the
cruisers at the Jomard Passage, the carriers in ambush for Takagi. Yes?'

'We think the Americans are reading our signals.'

The Combined Fleet intelligence officer sputtered. 'Impossible! We use a double-coded polyalphabetic superencipherment...'

'Enough!' barked Yamamoto. 'How often have I told you not to underestimate the Americans? We will put it to a test. Ugake, is Inoue proceeding with Operation RY against Ocean and Nauru?'

The chief of staff replied, 'Yes, sir.'

'Surely the American carriers cannot anticipate that as well,' continued Yamamoto. 'Inform Inoue to proceed. But if he encounters the American carriers he is to cancel the operation. And Ugake, send this order by courier. Send this young man here.'

## End game, May 13

In Washington, D.C., Major General Dwight Eisenhower drafted a secret memorandum to MacArthur regarding SWPA's release of information to the Australian press and presented it to General Marshall. It read: 'Publicity purporting to emanate from your headquarters gives important details of recent naval action in the south Pacific. The Commander-in-Chief of the Pacific Fleet considers that this imposes definite risks upon participating forces.' Here Marshall inserted a handwritten phrase, 'and jeopardizes the successful continuation of fleet task force operations.' The message continued: 'Information concerning action by land, sea, and air forces under the control of CINCPAC will be released through the Navy Department only.' It concluded by asking MacArthur to work with Australian authorities to put an end to SWPA's loose censorship practices. The criticism angered MacArthur, as both Eisenhower and Marshall knew it would, but, with another major Japanese offensive pending, they also understood the absolute necessity of protecting the secret of the Allied radio intelligence coup.[8]

On May 15 a Japanese flying boat based at Tulagi sighted *Enterprise* and *Hornet* in position to attack an invasion force operating against Ocean and Nauru. Dutifully, Inoue canceled Operation RY.

For the next twelve days, driven by the suddenly demanding Chief of Staff Ugake, the Combined Fleet staff worked furiously. Yamamoto never considered canceling the offensive against Midway. Instead, the near certitude that it would entice the American carriers into battle rekindled his energy. His revised strategy involved operational planning along parallel paths. One path involved the radio dispatch of orders to continue the operation against Midway as planned. The second, true, path involved detailed, hand-delivered instructions that revised the plan entirely. While the Aleutian task force continued as originally planned, two cruisers were to utilize the radio call signs of the light carriers *Ryujo* and *Junyo*. Meanwhile, those carriers joined the Midway-bound carrier striking force. A similar radio deception ploy concealed the reassignment of the light carriers *Zuiho* and *Hosho*. These measures added some 120 naval aircraft to the strength of the Carrier Striking Force and compensated for the absence of the damaged Carrier Division Five. In addition, Yamamoto shuffled his other surface units to strengthen the carriers' anti-aircraft screen. Last, he demanded that the submarines belonging to the Advance Expeditionary Force be in position no later than June 1 to detect the arrival of the American task force off Midway.

Having been ordered to concentrate all resources on the Midway threat, Station Hypo decrypted much of the voluminous Japanese radio traffic. It gave Nimitz a comprehensive, detailed, and accurate picture of the Japanese order of battle, its division of forces, and its routes of approach to the Aleutians and Midway. On May 27 Nimitz convened a final strategy session designed to place the American carriers in position to ambush the dispersed Japanese forces.

That day, the light cruiser *Nagara* led the massed carrier and battle strength of the Combined Fleet out from the Hashirajima anchorage on a course east toward Midway. From the bridge of his flagship Admiral Yamamoto studied his mighty fleet with a sense of great complacency. The battle's outcome could hardly be in doubt. It would be a case of the biter bit.

## The reality

So delicate was the balance of forces during the Coral Sea–Midway period – for example, had the bomb that hit *Yorktown* during the Coral Sea battle struck twenty feet toward her centerline, thereby damaging her flight deck instead of penetrating the comparatively unused lee of her island, she would have been disabled for Midway – that it is not hard to suggest 'alternative' outcomes. In the event, Allied radio intelligence, the combination of traffic analysis and decryption, was absolutely central to all that took place. Everything in the story occurred through the May 8 carrier exchange. Thereafter, in reality Nimitz circumvented King's orders and covertly instructed Halsey to allow Japanese recon to find his carriers. Nimitz correctly anticipated that this would be enough to abort the Japanese drive against Ocean and Nauru. Unlike King, Nimitz desperately wanted to bring the carriers back to Hawaii to prepare for the Midway Campaign. Rachel Bray did not exist. But authorities in Washington were intensely concerned about the possibility of revealing their golden source of intelligence. Indicative of this concern is Marshall's rebuke to MacArthur, which is verbatim and found with the kind assistance of the George Marshall Museum. Fortunately, in spite of MacArthur's indiscretion and the similar folly of the *Chicago Tribune* after Midway, the Japanese never suspected that their codes had been compromised until too late.

## Bibliography

Bergerud, Eric, *Fire in the Sky: The Air War in the South Pacific* (Westview Press, Boulder, 2000).

Dull, Paul S., *A Battle History of the Imperial Japanese Navy (1941–1945)* (U.S. Naval Institute Press, Annapolis, 1978).

Goldstein, Donald M., and Dillon, Katherine V. (eds.), *Fading Victory: The Diary of Admiral Matome Ugaki, 1941–45* (University of Pittsburgh Press, Pittsburgh, 1991).

James, D. Clayton, *The Years of MacArthur, vol.II: 1941–1945* (Houghton Mifflin, Boston, 1975).

Layton, Edwin T., *'And I Was There': Pearl Harbor and Midway Breaking the Secrets* (W. Morrow, New York, 1985).

Lundstrom, John B., *The First South Pacific Campaign: Pacific Fleet Strategy December 1941–June 1942* (U.S. Naval Institute Press, Annapolis, 1976).

Morison, Samuel Eliot, *History of United States Naval Operations in World War II, vol.IV: Coral Sea, Midway and Submarine Actions* (Little, Brown, Boston, 1949).

Willmott, H.P., *The Barrier and the Javelin: Japanese and Allied Pacific Strategies February to June 1942* (U.S. Naval Institute Press, Annapolis, 1983).

## Notes

1. Edwin T. Layton, *'And I Was There': Pearl Harbor and Midway Breaking the Secrets* (W. Morrow, New York, 1985), p.390.
2. John B. Lundstrom, *The First South Pacific Campaign: Pacific Fleet Strategy December 1941–June 1942* (U.S. Naval Institute Press, Annapolis, 1976), p.86.
3. *Ibid* p.100.
4. For a complete discussion of this important delay (an example of how small matters can have large consequences), see H.P. Willmott, *The Barrier and the Javelin: Japanese and Allied Pacific Strategies February to June 1942* (U.S. Naval Institute Press, Annapolis, 1983), pp.207–8.
5. Layton, *op.cit.* p.399.
6. Samuel Eliot Morison, *History of the United States Naval Operations in World War II, vol.IV: Coral Sea, Midway and Submarine Actions* (Little, Brown, Boston, 1949), p.42.
7. Donald M. Goldstein and Katherine V. Dillon (eds.), *Fading Victory: The Diary of Admiral Matome Ugaki, 1941–45* (University of Pittsburgh Press, Pittsburgh, 1991), p.121.
8. Marshall's telegram, complete with his handwritten annotations, is in the archives of the George C. Marshall Museum, Lexington, Virginia. Marshall's attitude towards MacArthur's loose censorship practices at this time is discussed in D. Clayton James, *The Years of MacArthur, vol.II: 1941–1945* (Houghton Mifflin, Boston, 1975), pp.164–6.

# 5
# NAGUMO'S LUCK
# The Battles of Midway and California

Forrest R. Lindsey

## Decisions

Commander C. 'Wade' McCluskey USN stared out over a seemingly endless expanse of the Pacific Ocean. He was leading a striking force of carrier dive-bombers in search of the four Japanese carriers that were the most important part of a huge enemy force heading for Midway Island. Other American aircraft flying from Midway and his carriers earlier that morning had been sent out to find them and attack; but he didn't have any news from them and didn't know how successful they'd been. His and thirty-two more Navy SBD Dauntless dive-bombers were a powerful instrument. They each carried a 500- or 1,000-pound bomb which would be more than enough to wreck a carrier if they could get close enough for a hit. SBDs were slow and lightly armed, but they were accurate and rugged and in the hands of a good pilot could deliver a bomb within a few feet of an aim point. His pilots were good, but most were inexperienced. Once they got to the target he'd lead the first run in himself, to make sure they'd know the best way to get in and get a hit.

The weather was clear and the visibility was almost unlimited, but instead of seeing the telltale streaks of white that would denote the wakes of Japanese carriers and their escorts there was only the smooth and trackless ocean from horizon to horizon. He was following the course they'd predicted would intercept the Japanese fleet at their last estimated speed and course but there was no sign of them. The original plan covered in his morning briefings was for careful precision: the torpedo-bombers would arrive at the target at the same time as the dive-bombers, while the fighters kept the Zeros off of them. With the torpedo-bombers hitting the carriers low and the dive-bombers coming from high above, the enemy would have little chance of stopping them. This was the 'old one-two punch' that would overwhelm the Japanese defenses for the critical seconds they needed. Even though they had delayed their SBDs after takeoff to allow the slower Devastator torpedo-bombers to get ahead of them, they lost sight of each

120

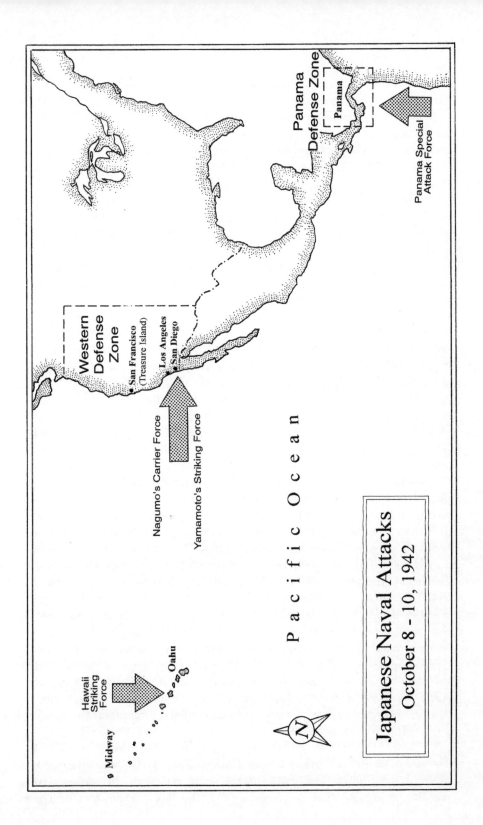

Japanese Naval Attacks
October 8 - 10, 1942

other almost from the beginning. Worse, he'd used a lot of fuel doing that. Trusting that they would find the Japanese and the rest of the strike force, they had flown steadily towards that spot in the ocean towards which the enemy was moving.

Where were the Japanese? He had heard some scraps of radio traffic from the pilots of Torpedo 8 from *Hornet* as they apparently ran into the Japanese task force, but no indication of where the Japanese were located now. Fuel was critical: they had flown almost 155 miles so far and this was added to the fuel used to get to their present altitude and the fuel used to circle his planes over the carriers while waiting for the torpedo-bombers to get going.

He had two choices. He could backtrack to the right (northwest) on the guess that the Japanese had made a major turn towards the U.S. carriers. Or he could turn left (southeast) towards Midway Island on the possibility that the Japanese carriers had moved faster than estimated and were continuing their attacks on that island's defenses. A left turn had another advantage: if the enemy wasn't there, he could land his dive-bombers on Midway, refuel, get an updated position for the Japanese and then go after them from there.

Looking balefully at his fuel gauges and then back to a clear, empty ocean, McCluskey tossed the mental coin and turned left towards Midway.[1]

At that moment, Admiral Chuichi Nagumo, Commander of the Japanese Carrier Striking Force, had what had been a very tough morning end with a piece of luck. None of the morning's attacks by American land-based bombers or carrier torpedo-bombers had even touched any of the ships of his powerful carrier force. The presence of enemy carriers had been a shock – the Americans were supposed to be near Pearl Harbor – but, tardily, a scout plane had located the position of the U.S. carriers, a surprising 200 kilometers to the northeast. His aircraft had finally been recovered from the morning strikes against Midway Island and his fighter pilots were getting a break after flying interception that morning. There wasn't enough time to arm all of his aircraft with the optimum mix of torpedoes and armor-piercing bombs for an anti-ship strike, but he was satisfied that his pilots would be able to successfully destroy the American carriers with the weapons they had. The American attacks were over and the confusion and the repeated rearming of aircraft was finished. The attack, the decisive battle against the last strength of the enemy fleet, was what mattered now. At last, signals were flashed from the air fleets aboard his four carriers that they were ready to launch. Twenty-eight minutes after the last of the American torpedo-bombers had sunk to the bottom of the deep Pacific, Admiral Nagumo ordered his aircraft to take off and form up for the attack on the American carriers.

The situation on the carriers *Hornet*, *Enterprise*, and *Yorktown* wasn't good. Most of the fighters available had been sent out with the strikes that morning, gambling that they would catch the Japanese flat-footed. The carefully planned attacks of the morning had come apart when the torpedo planes, bombers, and fighters had arrived at different times and the Japanese had been able to deal with them piecemeal as they arrived. Many hadn't even found the Japanese and many had landed on Midway Island or had ditched at sea. Only short unintelligible scraps of radio messages had gotten through to the Combat Information Centers and most of these seemed to point to confusion and desperation, not success. A few planes made it back to the carriers, badly shot up with only fumes remaining in their fuel tanks. By midmorning on June 4, 1942, the main striking power of the American carriers was scattered far away or down in the ocean and no help to them.

Two Japanese aircraft had located the American fleets by now and were using the bits of available cloud cover to keep hidden while maintaining contact. They were sending navigation information to the oncoming Japanese strike force of bombers and fighters and would guide them to their targets with the minimum loss of time. Shortly after 1100 local time, U.S. air search radars detected the first wave of over 200 Japanese aircraft closing on the sparsely defended carriers. There were only a handful of F4F Wildcat fighters available to deal with the attacking planes and they weren't enough. The battle was over very quickly. Within less than thirty minutes, all three carriers were burning and the attacking Japanese turned on the escorting cruisers and destroyers. When the attacks ended *Enterprise* and *Yorktown* were afloat but abandoned except for damage control parties. *Hornet* had gone down quickly and destroyers moved as quickly as they could to recover survivors. Despite desperate efforts to restore power and to get the carriers under way, time became an issue. No one doubted that new air attacks would be coming soon, and not long after that they would be in range of the guns of Japanese battleships. After every crewman that could be evacuated was removed, destroyers moved alongside and fired torpedoes into the hulks. Now two more of America's carriers joined their pilots and aircraft two miles down under the deep Pacific. The surviving vessels, overloaded with the men that they could find and rescue, moved as quickly as they could north and east to escape.

Not long after, the Japanese Invasion Force, covered by the heavy fire of the Support Force's battleships and cruisers, began landings on Midway. After a short and brutal battle, the island's defenders were overrun and the Rising Sun was raised once more over what had been American territory.[2]

News of the loss of the three carriers and Midway itself struck Washington like a hammer. The news couldn't be kept from the American people; there were too many stories in the newspapers and on the radio about a major naval battle taking place. Once the news hit in full force, there were loud and emotional calls for accountability from the government. Emergency meetings were conducted between the President and his staff, General Marshall, the Department of War, the service Secretaries, and ranking members of Congress. When the shock of the losses began to sink in, blame for the disaster was swiftly attributed to Admiral Chester Nimitz's foolhardy gamble with almost all of America's remaining sea power in the Pacific. Why was *Yorktown* risked, even though it had sustained serious damage just days before in the battle of the Coral Sea? With all the warnings Nimitz had received, why had the air attacks on the Japanese carriers failed? When Admiral Halsey had been hospitalized, why had Nimitz picked Spruance, a cruiser admiral of all people, with no experience in carrier operations, to lead these critical carrier strikes against the Japanese?

Naturally, an investigation was initiated, but the new and difficult situation facing the U.S. and her Allies had first to be understood and confronted. This was more than another major defeat in the Pacific. This was a crippling loss; what little initiative the U.S. and Allied forces could have had before Midway in the form of raids or campaigns seemed impossible now. Australia and all of the Southwestern Pacific lay vulnerable against a virtually unscathed Imperial Japanese army and navy. *Wasp* and *Saratoga* were the only remaining American carriers in the Pacific, compared to ten fleet carriers and five light carriers of the Imperial Japanese Navy. There weren't any battleships available in the Pacific Fleet since Pearl Harbor, which meant that the Japanese were essentially unopposed from the Indian Ocean to the California coast. Recriminations abounded but solutions seemed elusive.

Now, the Japanese felt, His Highness the Emperor was safe from any further danger from Doolittle-style attacks and, most importantly, the United States would be forced to recognize Japan's supremacy and to accept peace on their terms. This had been the foundation of Japan's war plans since the beginning. First cripple the American fleet, then isolate and defeat America's garrisons, then lure the remainder into an all-out decisive battle at sea. Everything had fallen into place, as it should have. All that remained was to ensure America's acceptance of the Japanese terms and Japan could concentrate on the development and solidification of her Empire. When the celebrations in Tokyo were in full swing, only Admiral Isoroku Yamamoto stayed at his headquarters with his top staff. There was no time to be lost, even with the enemy apparently prostrate. His mind was working on his and the Navy's proposals for the next phase of operations to ensure that the initiative would stay with Japan. Armistice proposals were being drafted, to be passed to the Allies through the good offices of Sweden and Switzerland, and almost every member of the Japanese senior leadership believed or hoped that the U.S. government would see no choice but to agree their terms. Yamamoto wasn't one of those leaders. His experience as a naval attaché in Washington had taught him that while Americans were fractious and uncultured, they could also be stubborn and determined. The courage of those American torpedo-bombers, fruitlessly boring in against his carriers, had impressed his officers. All of the American pilots had stayed committed to the attack, flying at a ridiculous 120 kph as his much faster Zero fighters shot each of them down in turn. They died like true warriors, his officers had said. That thought sobered him as worked over the next phase of operations in his mind.

Strategically, the near-term courses of action were:

1) Seize New Guinea and Australia: Resume the campaign that was prematurely ended by the Battle of the Coral Sea and expand the Empire to the south. This was near and dear to senior Japanese leaders and particularly the Army, since it would solidify Japanese control of the entire southwestern Pacific and the entrances to the Indian Ocean. Control of these seas guaranteed unobstructed access to fuel and raw materials and a firm road to the seizure of India. Japan, it was thought, would be unassailable. The problem with this course of action was that it would require all of his Combined Fleet's resources, and once Australia and the Straits of Malacca were secured, large land, sea, and air defensive forces would be pinned in place to keep that area secure. This course of action was an all-or-nothing option, for at least the next nine months to a year.

2) Reinforce the forces at Midway and seize Oahu and the Hawaiian chain: A logical and easily achievable objective: Oahu was the last remaining outpost of American power in the Pacific. Its great natural anchorage at Pearl Harbor, its fleet and army air force bases, and its large fuel stores, were a threat to Japanese forces operating at Midway and a potential springboard if the Americans still had the will to counterattack. Seizure of the Hawaiian chain and the reduction of American military forces and facilities on Oahu would guarantee the safety of the home islands and provide Japan with an insurmountable water barrier against any future American offensive. Full supremacy at sea would facilitate the movement and support of the landing forces and it was in hand now, but this situation would be fleeting. Any decision to commit forces for operations to seize the Hawaiian Islands would have to be done quickly. It went without saying that the foothold in the Aleutians on Attu and Kiska would have to be reinforced and enlarged, with any remaining American power within range eliminated.

3) Strike the US mainland: Japan's enormous striking power could reach and severely damage the cities, factories, transportation, and fuel reserves on America's west coast. Strong enough attacks would also convince America's leaders that continued war against Japan was impossible. The Combined Fleet was the perfect weapon to strike a large part of the enemy's critical design and production capabilities. The major American aircraft companies were well within carrier-based aircraft range and some were even within range of his battleship's guns from fire support areas along the Pacific coast. Sudden and powerful strikes would emphasize Japan's new position in the Pacific, damage the American citizens' morale and their support of their government, and would give a gift of revenge to His Majesty for the insult of Doolittle's raid against His Person. Given the impotence of land-based

bomber attacks against his fleet during the Midway battle, Yamamoto was sure that he could operate close to the U.S. coastline without fear. He was concerned about low-altitude attacks by torpedo-bombers, but the swift Zero fighters could make short work of these assaults, as they had before. Such combatant vessels as were available to the Americans would have no chance against him. Besides aircraft production assets, there were oil production and refining facilities, power stations, shipbuilding yards, and many other critical targets within the reach of his unbeaten fleet. America had 2,200 kilometers of coast to defend and no way of knowing where and when the Japanese could choose to attack.

4) Answer the forceful German requests to strike the Soviet Union: Some influential members of the Japanese government and the Army urged immediate attack on the Soviet southeastern flank from Manchukuo, to support the Nazis in bringing about the collapse of the USSR. This possible course of action was attractive. It would solidify the Manchukuo frontier, with the possibility of securing all of the northern Pacific area, including the Sea of Okhotsk, the port of Vladivostok, and the riches of Siberia. This would almost certainly guarantee an Axis victory against the USSR, since it was still reeling from Germany's blitzkrieg towards Moscow and the Caucasus. A second front by the Japanese would divert a large part of Stalin's forces and ease Germany's path in the west. This would be an expensive option in manpower and logistics and would be another all-or-nothing proposition. The Russians and the Japanese had been adversaries before and the combination of rugged terrain and weather, long distances, and tough troops would mean that this course of action could not be undertaken lightly. As with option (1), it assumed that the United States would not become a threat in the near future and could be held in place with minimal effort.

5) A combination of all these courses of action: U.S. forces were incapable of offensive operations but were not yet negligible. The key remaining capability available to America was its submarine force, which was being operated from Pearl Harbor and Australia. While its submarines were few in number and their torpedoes were poor, no Japanese skipper could ignore the threat they posed. American aircraft were a problem too, and U.S. bombers had already conducted strikes against his forces consolidating on Midway. Radio interception units had also detected reinforcement of the aircraft on Oahu. His own staff's recommendation was for course of action (2), the isolation or seizure of Hawaii, in order to permanently seal the Pacific from the U.S. Navy and to continue the objectives of the Midway operation. However, his discussions with the Army General Staff showed that Army remained committed to course of action (1), offensive action against New Guinea and Australia.

Yamamoto, as usual, had different ideas. To maintain the momentum gained by the victory at Midway, he would recommend a multiple set of objectives in the short term, to obtain what they all wanted in the long-term. He would isolate the American forces on Hawaii, and damage or destroy the ports, facilities, and production capabilities on the West Coast of the United States, using carrier air power and the guns of his battleships. The gains made so far put Japan in the right position to threaten the mainland of the United States and Yamamoto knew that nothing less than the direct threat of attack could push the Americans into giving in to Japan's demands. Then they could turn their attention to the southwest Pacific and complete control of their empire.

He knew that the enormous tactical advantage Japan now enjoyed would still prove temporary if the unmatched resources of the United States were allowed to come into their own. He was also sure that new American carriers were being rushed into service, with many more pilots being trained to fly from them. He considered the possibility of locating the shipyards where the new carriers were being built and attacking them. That would give Japan some extra time with their well-won advantage in naval air forces. However, his naval intelligence service had located the carriers in yards on the East Coast of the United States in New Jersey and Virginia and a long way out of reach. It would be helpful to coordinate attacks with their German allies, but other than recommendations that could be accepted or rejected, the Germans had not as yet shown any inclination for more aggressive support of Japanese forces. The key to preventing rapid rein-forcement of the Pacific and parity, then, lay in interdicting the Panama Canal and cordoning the gap between South America and Antarctica with submarines. He also had to consider the possibility of operations by the two remaining U.S. carriers. That thought made him smile. If he could find them quickly, the Japanese victory would be absolute. What chance would two carriers have against all of his?

Once he had made up his mind to concentrate his naval forces against the U.S. mainland, Yamamoto brought in his most trusted planners under Captain Genda[3] to put the operation together. In his view, Japan had won six months to a full year of freedom of movement to utilize against America before the latter either capitulated or was sufficiently restored to strength to become a threat again. There was the usual resistance by the Army and the General Staff to his plans, but his prestige and force of personality made sure that they would be accepted. The Emperor had issued an Imperial Rescript for his victory over the American Pacific Fleet at Midway and he had little trouble convincing his opponents to allow him to go ahead. His plans promised to close the lid on a formerly formidable enemy and would allow the Army to begin pursuing its own agenda very soon. Most of all, his plan appealed to the view now held by most Japanese: why push for an armistice when complete victory was within reach? After all, the Japanese forces were undefeated! He had work to do.

## MacArthur reacts

The Secretary of War opened the Emergency War Plans Conference at the Pentagon immediately after conferring with the President and General Douglas MacArthur. The latter had been brought home from Australia to accept command of the Pacific Theater, with overall command of all Army, Army air forces, and naval forces. Despite many voices against this decision, the President was sure that MacArthur was the right man to take charge of this situation and get the nation back on the road to victory. MacArthur made it very clear that he would accept only if he would have all available forces under his command and if the additional materiel and supplies that he deemed necessary would be provided. Panic was just below the surface as the Emergency War Plans Conference opened, as briefing officer after briefing officer laid out the losses, the forces available to the enemy, and the vulnerability of U.S. positions on the Pacific coast and Hawaii.

After the briefings were completed, General MacArthur was introduced as the Commander-in-Chief, Pacific, and the members of the conference listened in silence as he laid out his plans to assemble, train, and set America's combat power in motion against the Japanese. The original belief that the war could be conducted by holding the Japanese at bay while concentrating on the Germans alongside America's European allies was dead. The defeats that had started at Pearl Harbor and been followed by the surrender of 20,000 troops in the Philippines had now been capped by the loss of nearly 10,000 airmen, soldiers, sailors and Marines dead or missing near Midway. Hawaii was universally believed to be untenable. No air force could maintain the lines of communication and support for U.S. forces there, and no sea force could be assembled any time soon to defend it against attack and invasion. Japanese air attacks from Midway and from carrier raids were common occurrences now and the morale of its civilians was visibly and understandably poor. Anyone that could get transportation away from Hawaii packed their possessions and left. It was apparent to everyone that it was only a question of time before the Hawaiian Islands fell. The Pacific Fleet headquarters and other command centers on Oahu were evacuated back to San Francisco, where MacArthur was building his command center at the Treasure Island naval facility.

To America's leadership, the threat to the West Coast was obvious. For the first time, American cities lay open to the kinds of devastation that Europe and West Asia had already seen. The first priority was to reinforce air power for the full length of the Pacific coast, stretching from San Diego to Seattle, to provide reconnaissance as well as fighter and bomber forces. Critical industries and facilities would have to be moved, hidden, or protected from attack, and much of the noncritical civilian population would have to be relocated further from the coast.

Politically, the situation was in turmoil. The Republican leadership in

Congress was incensed that the Roosevelt government had been so inept, so unprepared. Some even called for Roosevelt's resignation or impeachment and for a new national leadership. This movement surged and then ebbed as the Democratic members of Congress rallied to the President. Once the situation stabilized, the timing was right to issue the Secretary of War's recommendations for the redirection of the war effort:

First, the agreement with Churchill that the Germans and the war in Europe would be the United States' first priority was rescinded; the war against the Japanese would take precedence. The British, the Soviets, and Occupied Europe would be essentially on their own again for a while. The plans for Operation Torch – an amphibious operation by U.S. and British forces in French North Africa – was cancelled. Forces previously allocated for that operation were sent to San Diego to prepare against any attempt to land on the Pacific coast and to be ready for future operations against the Japanese. Radar installations and communications relays were hurriedly engineered and constructed at intervals along the coast with the aim of completing a chain to detect air and surface targets well out to sea. Aircraft, artillery, tanks, ammunition, trucks, and in particular anti-aircraft guns, were sent to California, Oregon, and Washington instead of Britain and the Soviet Union. The only direct response to the Germans that would be continued would be operations against U-boats along the Atlantic Coast and in the Caribbean. They were directly threatening U.S. operations and could not be ignored.

Second, air forces earmarked for movement to Britain were sent to airfields all along the West Coast to begin preparation and training for anti-ship strikes against the Japanese. Some of the best-trained fighter squadrons were sent to Panama to reinforce its defenses. The only question was whether they had enough time left for the complex job of assembling the necessary aircraft, support facilities, crews, munitions, fuel, and spare parts to face the Japanese when they arrived. Construction and training became a round-the-clock activity both in Panama and all along the West Coast.

Third, the aircraft carrier *Ranger* would be sent to join the Pacific Fleet immediately. All submarines available in the Atlantic and the Caribbean would also move to the Pacific for use as scouts and to ambush Japanese vessels in key sea lanes and choke points.

Fourth, training camps throughout the United States began intensive and abbreviated preparations to ready infantry, artillery, anti-aircraft and armor forces for duty at West Coast staging areas.

Fifth, the Army Corps of Engineers, under the direction of MacArthur's headquarters, would have the responsibility for emergency construction of airfields up and down the Pacific coast. The Corps would also be responsible for coordinating and directing the building of coastal fortifications. They had already begun site surveys and the necessary materials had priority over all rail traffic except for the movement of troops and arms.

Sixth, the aircraft factories for Consolidated Vultee (San Diego), Lockheed (Burbank), Douglas (Los Angeles), North American Aviation (Los Angeles), and Boeing (Seattle) would be dismantled and moved inland from the West Coast, to Colorado, Arizona, and New Mexico. It was anticipated that full operation could be restored in about one year. Only Northrop, Martin, Bell, Chance Vought, Republic, Grumman, and Curtiss would remain where they were and continue design and production unabated. In the offices that were hurriedly emptied, drawing boards were cleared of blue prints, drawings were packed in cardboard tubes, and tools, jigs, and wind tunnel models were sealed into sturdy wood crates. This would have an incalculable effect on some types of aircraft. The P-51A Mustang would not receive a proposed re-engine to the Packard Merlin 61, and the P-38F Lightning would continue to suffer from unresolved compressibility effect problems. B-17s and B-24s would have to restart production in Kansas City and Wichita and would be available in reduced numbers for a while. The Boeing Model 345 or XB-29 and the Consolidated Vultee B-32 and B-36 designs would stay in their storage tubes for more than six months as facilities to continue design and production were completed. Only the B-26 Marauder could increase production, and the facilities at Glenn Martin's Baltimore Maryland factory expanded quickly. The Republic P-47 fighter would become the premier interceptor and escort fighter and other aircraft companies would be tasked to retool to build them. Contracts for a very long-range bomber, necessary to strike the Japanese home islands, were let to Jack Northrop to accelerate development of his strange flying wing bomber, the XB-35.

Seventh, key facilities and personnel in the Hawaiian Islands would be evacuated back to the U.S. mainland. Only those personnel needed for the support of the remaining fleet operations and the defense of the Hawaiian Islands would remain. The residents of Hawaii were given the option of remaining where they were, transportation to the mainland to temporary resettlement camps, or movement to Hawaii, Molokai, Kawai, Niihau, or Maui, away from the anticipated center of Japanese attacks on Oahu.

MacArthur agreed that these steps were inevitable but he was not the man to allow the United States to be cornered into a defensive fight. He had seen at close hand how the Japanese could move inexorably towards their objectives and he had also seen the fate of his men and women, American and Filipino, at Corregidor. The Bataan Death March was something tangible and living to him and his whole being focused on the problem of how to turn America's situation round into a war-winning offensive. He had disagreed with Admirals Nimitz and King about the gamble at Midway and he was grimly vindicated by the results. Now he had the full cooperation of the Navy to concentrate on the forces at hand, the forces that could soon be brought to bear to reverse the tide and turn it against the enemy.

One of his biggest problems was that his window into his enemy's mind had been closed: Station Hypo, the code-breaking and radio traffic analysis facility in Hawaii, had been closed down and sent to California. It would be weeks before any useful material came from them. To add to that loss, the Japanese must have guessed that the Americans were reading some of their messages and had changed all of their principal military codes immediately after Midway. JN-25b, as the new Japanese naval code was called, had the Americans starting all over again in the intelligence arena at the worst possible time.[4]

Although MacArthur was busy, a call from the Secretary of the Navy made him interrupt his schedule to meet with scientists from the Naval Weapons Center at Dahlgren, Virginia, and Johns Hopkins University in Baltimore. They briefed him about a new weapon development and its capabilities that they felt could be crucial. Their breakthrough was top secret and phenomenal. They had developed and successfully tested an artillery fuze that used a radio signal to sense its proximity to aircraft and detonated the projectile at the closest point to the plane. They called it the VT Proximity Fuze and it could revolutionize artillery effectiveness against aircraft. They showed MacArthur a film of the first live shots fired at drone aircraft and the results were better than they had described. The test plane was literally blown apart with a single shot. MacArthur called for its immediate production and issue to anti-aircraft crews as fast as possible.[5]

MacArthur could easily see the directions the Japanese could go. They had the free run of the Pacific and if they were true to form, America could expect very bold and aggressive offensive strikes, and soon. He agreed with intelligence estimates that the Japanese would probably attack Hawaii and the West Coast, but he didn't agree that the Japanese would win. He had one or two ideas of how to sting the enemy and force them off guard. In MacArthur's view, Japan's apparent supremacy over the Pacific could work against them. They were getting almost predictable at this point: they would overrule the peace seekers in their government and would continue the offensive somewhere. The only real options available were Southeast Asia and Australia or, continuing in the direction indicated by their victory at Midway, Oahu. The possibility of attacks on the West Coast was nevertheless real, and he knew that reinforcement of the Pacific Fleet depended on keeping the Panama Canal open and functioning. He also knew that if the Japanese chose to bypass Oahu and the American mainland to go after Australia, they would be using nearly all of their offensive power a long way from the American military and industrial centers, allowing America to get back on its feet. Conversely, if the Japanese chose to attack Hawaii and the West Coast, they would be placing their principal striking arm, the Combined Fleet, close to American air power and a long way from their own logistic bases. The Japanese would be at the extreme limit of their range and too far away to support. The trick would be to lure them close enough to take advantage of this weakness.

The key became clear just a few short days later: American reconnaissance aircraft spotted a new Japanese airfield under construction in the Solomon Islands, on an island called Guadalcanal.

## Western Pacific Operations: the Battle of California

Admiral Yamamoto's flagship *Yamato* had just cleared Truk Lagoon when the astonishing news reached him: an American force had been sighted in Tulagi harbor in the Solomons and American forces were landing in unknown numbers on Tulagi and Guadalcanal islands.

None of the intelligence services – not least his own staff intelligence officers – had given the slightest warning that the Americans were even capable of attempting something like this. How could they? They had only two carriers in the Pacific and the supporting forces couldn't amount to more than a light force of cruisers and destroyers. Transports leaving the West Coast ports had been spotted by his submarine reconnaissance, but that had been believed to be a movement to evacuate Hawaii. What were the Americans up to? How could they hope to sustain their invasion, much less win?

At that moment, Yamamoto's massive operation was just beginning. A Striking Force centered on the super-battleships *Yamato* and *Musashi* was forming at sea to the east of Truk for movement to the California coast. Like an intricate watch, the other parts of Yamamoto's machine, made up of a six-carrier task force and a cruiser-destroyer group under the command of Admiral Nagumo, moved directly east towards California. Simultaneously, another Striking Force headed for the waters north of Hawaii, and a third headed for the west coast of Panama. A Diversion Force with the carrier *Ryujo* was approaching the Coral Sea for a feint towards Port Moresby and would be close enough to begin executing their portion of the operation by morning. As the Diversion Force conducted attacks on the Allied forces in New Guinea, Yamamoto's Striking Force would link with Nagumo's Carrier Force 300 nautical miles west of San Clemente Island. From there, they would move to launch points for a series of carrier and naval gunfire strikes against the ports and facilities of San Diego and Los Angeles.

Careful night reconnaissance flights by submarine-launched aircraft had pinpointed critical targets with an emphasis on military and civil airfields, military bases, port facilities, and shipping and shore battery emplacements. Any naval forces or shipping within range would be engaged directly and the southwest coast of the United States would have its first view of Japan's warships enveloped in flame and smoke as they sent thousands of shells inland. Carrier aircraft would engage any remaining enemy air forces and conduct deep strikes against targets as far as 200 kilometers inland. Much of this striking range wasn't necessary, since the Americans had obligingly located the majority of their most important facilities very close to the coast. Privately, though, Yamamoto had one concern. Admiral Nagumo was his only choice for command of the critical Carrier Force, because of his apparent success in the operations against Pearl Harbor and Midway; but Yamamoto didn't trust him. He had turned away from finishing the job at Pearl Harbor, and with his inadequate air reconnaissance at Midway it had been just good luck that the Americans had missed his carriers.

The Hawaii Striking Force, arriving off Oahu at the same moment as the California Striking Force off California, would finish off any remaining military capability. This time the attacks would be relentless, destroying any dock, pier, barracks, warehouse, hangar, fuel farm or ammunition depot that they could find. Supported by the Army bombers from Midway, this force had enough aircraft and ammunition to stay in place for as long as it took. The objective wasn't to seize Hawaii; it was to nullify its usefulness. Yamamoto had realized that a Hawaiian landing operation would take more of his available strength than he was willing to allocate in the short time available. This operation would allow him to blunt the thorn in his side while still pinning U.S. forces uselessly on the island. Neutralizing and bypassing Hawaii achieved all of his short-term tactical goals. They could come back for the rest later.

The Panama Striking Force would launch aircraft from the carrier *Zuiho* to bomb and torpedo the Pedro Miguel and Gatun Locks while commando teams of the Naval Special Landing Force would conduct demolition operations against pump stations and port facilities in Balboa. The main attack would be pressed against the Miraflores Locks using the destroyer *Mutsuki* as a Special Attack ship with a volunteer crew that would race into the lock entrance area under the cover of suppressing aircraft and naval gunfire, to drive itself at full speed into the lock itself. At the moment of furthest entry into the lock, the volunteer crew would detonate over 500 tons of explosives and wreck the Pacific entry to the Panama Canal. With the canal sealed, it would be several more critical weeks or months before the Americans could attempt to reinforce their Pacific naval forces.

The only problem was that the Americans weren't just waiting for them on their West Coast. They were in Japan's area of operations, threatening their flank with some unknown operation. In an urgent message to Yamamoto from Rabaul, American aircraft were reported to be above Guadalcanal and it was only a matter of time until the key base at Rabaul would be threatened. This could not be allowed; they had to be dealt with. Orders were transmitted to Rabaul to reassign the Diversion Force from the Port Moresby Operation and to add a counter-landing force under Colonel Kiyaoano Ichiki, 28th Infantry Regiment, 35th Brigade, 17th Army. This new force would eradicate the Americans on Guadalcanal.

In Washington, the Emergency Council met again to discuss MacArthur's latest recommendations – though with the General's personality and style, 'recommendations' were always much stronger than that. They had

begrudgingly approved the landing at Guadalcanal, partially because
Admiral King had agreed with MacArthur, a rare enough occurrence, and
partly because Admiral Bill Halsey had been given overall command of the
operation. It had still been a difficult and contentious decision. It involved
the risk of America's only remaining Pacific theater carriers and four scarce
cruisers to support the landings until the airfield on Guadalcanal could be
made ready for air operations. Those same fleet units were desperately
needed to support Oahu and the West Coast, but a deal was made to move
the carriers back quickly once the landing force became self-sufficient and
the airfield there was ready to accept its own air units. Unknown to the
Japanese, the aircraft carrier *Ranger* was just leaving the Panama Canal and
entering the Pacific, and the launching and preparations for sea trials of the
new carriers *Essex* and *Independence* had been accelerated by round-the-clock
operations. The Council members were comforted by the first news out of
Guadalcanal, that the landing force – the First Marine Division under
General Vandegrift – had seized the island's airfield against light opposition
and was rapidly solidifying its position.[6]

The President had more to worry about. His British allies were angry
and increasingly desperate. Rommel continued to hold out in North
Africa despite Montgomery's victories against him and the Axis whittled
away at British and ANZAC troops in a back-and-forth bloodletting of
attrition warfare. The Nazis had stepped up U-boat operations in the
mid-Atlantic, just out of reach of the Coastal Command's aircraft, and
large and well-coordinated 'wolfpacks' of enemy submarines savaged convoy operations. America was helping as much as it could, but every surface combatant down to the size of minesweeper was being used to
protect its two coasts. FDR couldn't spare anything more at sea or in the
air. Britain's Bomber Command was pushed to the limit to carry on
attacks against Germany and German targets in Holland and France. It
had tried daylight bombing against industrial targets but the attrition
was too high and now it had adopted mass night attacks. These were
considerably less accurate but carried the war to the enemy nonetheless.

FDR's Soviet allies were also getting more strident. The Nazis were at
Moscow's gates and had seized the center of Stalingrad on the Volga after
desperate fighting. America said that it couldn't spare anything more to
support the Soviets and Stalin was getting more and more convinced that
America was double-dealing them. They desperately needed a second front
to divert the full force of the Wehrmacht away from them.

As bad as things were with his allies, FDR knew that the next few months
were critical to America's survival. While most intelligence estimates held
that Japan could not invade the U.S. at this point, any more reverses in the
Pacific would keep America further away from helping in the European
theater of operations and even more focused on defense against Japan. His
own political position was deeply threatened. The November elections were

just two months away and his re-election was in doubt. His leadership was more and more suspect to the American people and even his own Party was beginning to openly question his judgement, even talking about having 'someone new and fresh' to run for President. As much as MacArthur was a strong dose of salts to take, he had the faith of the American people so far. Now they would see whether his strategic plan would work or not.

MacArthur himself was worried, even if he didn't show it. While maintaining a public confidence – even arrogance – he knew how bad things could be. Intelligence from the Australian listening posts had determined that large Japanese forces were on the move. A submarine posted at the entrance of Truk Lagoon confirmed that major enemy fleet units had put to sea and were gathering for movements east. He had moved as many forces west as he could get, but he concentrated on air forces. His only real means of defense for the West Coast and Panama were attack bombers and submarines, and he and Admiral King had allocated all of the Army and Navy assets available to prepare for in-depth reconnaissance, attrition, and then destruction of enemy units. The key was to keep the enemy strength off balance and to delay their blows until American forces could be brought up to offensive parity. The Navy was training new carrier crews feverishly and the best estimates had *Essex* and *Independence* available for combat as early as January–February 1943 but not arriving in the Pacific until April or May. That was if the Panama Canal stayed open.

All along the West Coast and around Oahu and along the Central American coasts, patrol aircraft and radars and radio intercept stations and submarines searched for signs of the approaching Japanese. They didn't have long to wait. At 0330 Pacific Time, October 8, 1942, a PBY from the North Island Naval Air Station flying to the west of San Diego spotted a large formation of enemy ships, reported their location, and then was quickly shot down. Yamamoto and the Combined Fleet had arrived.

Air raid sirens all over San Diego and Los Angeles began their wails and hundreds of thousands of residents went to shelters or took to the roads out of the cities. Just as the sun came up over the hills, swarms of Japanese carrier fighters began strafing airfields in and around San Diego and searching for any aircraft that might be up and waiting. There were. Swarms of P-40s and P-38s from Brown Field and Lindbergh Field and F4F Wildcats from North Island Naval Air Station poured down on the Zeros from high above. Soon there were swirling trails of aircraft mixed in with each other, some racing after one another down to the red tile roofs of the homes in San Diego's hills. Close behind the fighters, nearly 200 Kate level bombers and Val dive-bombers poured in over the coast from six carriers to attack targets in the Naval Base, the airfields, and the Consolidated Vultee aircraft factory. More American fighters dove in to fall in behind the bombers and smoke trails intersected the blue skies of California. Anti-aircraft fire was sporadic and inaccurate at first, but as the gunners began to get more accustomed to the mayhem and their own weapons more aircraft began falling. Bombs were landing all over the city. Some hit their target but many didn't. Badly aimed or jettisoned bombs, downed aircraft, and falling anti-aircraft shells began fires which spread a pall of smoke that carried over the city and out over the harbor to the sea. San Diego was burning and the battle had just begun.[7]

MacArthur's Command Center went to full alert as soon as the first contact report came in. Direct telephone lines to the San Diego and Los Angeles area command centers relayed radar data and orders to launch strikes against the Japanese. Bombers from dispersed strips all over Southern California gained altitude and took headings based on radar bearings from the attacking Japanese aircraft, which helped them locate the Japanese fleet. The training and tactics that had been rethought and amended following the debacle at Midway began to tell: while high-level B-17s began runs from several directions, the wildly twisting Japanese ships had dozens of separate bombers to watch and avoid all at once. A lookout aboard the carrier *Shokaku* spotted twin-engined bombers approaching from wavetop height from the east. Scores of B-26 Marauders carrying torpedoes and B-25 Mitchells carrying bombs raced in to strike the flanks of the wildly maneuvering ships. The Zeros, which had been climbing to meet the B-17s, were forced to break off and dive to try to catch the medium bombers speeding towards their ships. Navy F4F fighters joined the fray from Long Beach Naval Air Station and headed to intercept the Zeros. The first bombs to strike were aimed at *Yamato* and there seemed to be little damage, but smoke from her after quarters showed that aviation gasoline for the spotter planes had been hit. The cruisers *Mogami* and *Mikuma* were hit then hit again, with *Mikuma* stopping dead in the water.

Nagumo, watching from the flag bridge, saw a bomber going directly for *Hiryu*. He held his breath as the medium bomber, hotly chased by Zero fighters into their own anti-aircraft fire, dropped a torpedo at point-blank range. The Marauder burst into flames and rolled, right wing first, into the sea. Then its torpedo hit *Hiryu*, dead center.

The anti-aircraft fire, which had been ferocious, littered the water with wrecked planes, but once the attacking aircraft had scored hits the anti-aircraft fire lessened as damage control parties had to fight the resultant fires. More aircraft arrived on the horizon from two directions: Navy TBF Avenger torpedo-bombers from Long Beach, Seal Beach, and Los Alamitos Naval Air Station. MacArthur's Air Forces Commander at Treasure Island, General 'Hap' Arnold, directed more and more aircraft into the battle from outlying areas. Other aircraft and crews were being vectored to Los Angeles, and from there control was passed to the Aviation Control Center at Los Alamitos NAS, south of Los Angeles. There, Army and Navy staff officers

monitored scout reports and battle progress while controlling and posi-
tioning new units for their attacks. When an element of aircraft returned
from strikes, they were directed to dispersed airfields to be refueled and
rearmed. In the short months that MacArthur had to prepare, his air officers
had devised a web of Air Control Centers to mass and coordinate air
combat.[8]

Yamamoto went from surprised to stunned: how could the Americans be
so effective? The assumptions based on their performance at Midway were
clearly wrong. The Americans had learned to conduct coordinated attacks,
and one of his carriers and several of his bombardment units were taking the
worst of it. He wanted to get in close enough to begin the shore bombardment program with his battleships, but the air attacks were already
beginning to achieve results, only thirty minutes into the battle and 200
nautical miles from his planned gunfire support areas offshore. He had
hoped for more surprise but the Americans had demonstrated a remarkable
ability to predict his moves. He knew that it was only a matter of time
before more of his carriers were hit and he decided to order his task force
south and west, to get more sea room out of reach of the air attacks. He
would evaluate the next step from there, based on his aircraft crews' reports
on the effectiveness of their own attacks and some post-attack reconnaissance photos. The battle was developing badly so far. He knew that he
could not afford to give the Americans a victory.

The President was awakened at 0710, Washington time, when the PBY's
contact report was relayed to the Department of War Operations Center.
The confrontation he had been dreading had arrived just as had been
predicted and now it was up to MacArthur's boys to stop them. The reports
of training and preparations for defense had been encouraging but he knew
all too well what effect another major defeat would have on the country and
on his political leadership. Recent communication with his allies had been
very rough: Churchill was adamant that the British needed help immediately and that the situation in Europe was grave. Nighttime bombing was
proving to be ineffective, with rapidly increasing losses as the Germans
improved their nightfighter defenses. North Africa was a steady drain as the
Germans stubbornly held out against Montgomery, and nightly German
terror raids against Britain's cities increased as reprisals for attacks against
Germany. The situation at sea was the worst. The U-boat 'wolfpacks',
sometimes as large as twenty boats, destroyed vital shipping in staggering
quantities. Russia had gone beyond desperate. The Nazis were close to
Moscow and Stalingrad had fallen after a desperate and heroic defense.
With only minor raids from the west and no chance of a Second Front
opening, Hitler was confident, and applied ever larger proportions of the
forces and assets available to him to increase his offensive against the

Soviets. Stalin was hinting darkly at potential options to reach a separate arrangement with the Germans if the Allies didn't help him soon.

FDR stayed close to the phone and sent messengers to the Pentagon to get the most current reports of the battle taking place over California.

Five time zones away, Oahu sustained heavy air attacks by land-based bombers from Midway, and, for the first time since Pearl Harbor, carrier aircraft. This time, though, the defenses were warned and prepared. As in California, American Army and Navy fighters were up and on station slashing through the fighter cover to get at the Japanese bombers. New radars had been pushed through to Oahu during the months since Midway and submarine and seaplane patrols had stretched Hawaii's 'eyes' further out to sea. When masses of aircraft were seen on radar this time, they were believed, and the Americans were ready. Anti-aircraft fire was much more effective too. For some reason the gunners were finding the range more quickly, and in some cases Japanese aircraft were exploding from single large-caliber hits almost as soon as they were within range. Despite the careful preparations, the high morale and fighting spirit of the Japanese aircraft crews, and the preparatory raids that had been taking place for months, their casualties were much higher than expected. The Americans were surprisingly better than before. Nevertheless, despite the improved defenses fires were raging all over Oahu and virtually nowhere was unscathed.

Before the sun rose in the south-central Pacific that morning, the Panama Canal Striking Force had arrived at its launch point and was warming its aircraft engines while *Zuiho* turned into the wind. The aircraft had been staged and armed with heavy bombs and torpedoes for the attack. Then a surprised lookout on *Zuiho* called out a warning of torpedo tracks in the water. The fast carrier turned radically to starboard to clear the torpedoes' paths, but it was too late. Two explosions rocked *Zuiho* and fire began to spread. Escorts began frantic depth charge attacks on the submarine responsible, but that only provided an opening for two more subs closing on their port quarter, which fired more torpedoes at the stricken carrier. At least two of these connected with *Zuiho*, increasing its list to over 30° and effectively sealing its fate. One more torpedo from the same spread kept going and connected with *Mutsuki*. The massive explosion where the Special Attack destroyer had been only an instant before formed a giant mushroom cloud, rising quickly into the sky.[9]

By midday the reports reaching Washington were grim, with news of substantial damage and casualties, but a first inkling that the tide was turning in America's favor was beginning to emerge. MacArthur was masterful at his headquarters, directing the counterattacks against the three

Japanese forces without let up. Where one series of blows ended another began, until suddenly the Japanese withdrew further out to sea and out of reach of U.S. aircraft. The California attacks had badly damaged San Diego's port and Santa Monica's piers and warehouses. Fires darkened the sky with thick smoke and military and civilian casualties were severe. Ambulance sirens could be heard all over the city, mixed with the sounds of explosions. However, none of the damage had put San Diego or Los Angeles out of action for very long; wreckage could be cleared, fires could be put out, and many of the casualties would heal. The Japanese had never got close enough to use naval gunfire, while on the ground and in the sea over two hundred of their aircraft were reported to be downed, with several more observed to be trailing smoke as they flew back to their carriers.

The attacks on Oahu were even worse, but had a similar outcome: Most, if not all, of the damaged American facilities could be restored soon or replaced with others. Aircraft losses for the Japanese had been particularly severe, much worse than their most sanguine predictions, and the Japanese did not know why.

It was a busy morning too for the Panama Canal defense forces. American submarines had attacked a Japanese force, and long-range bombers were now out searching for them to continue the attack. Other than that, the morning had been a beautiful one, as anti-aircraft crews, PT Boat crews and fighter pilots awaited the Japanese.

Yamamoto stayed at his Command Center on *Yamato* as reports were brought to him. Casualties had been high and *Hiryu* was lost. Struck by torpedoes and bombs and swept by fire, it could not be salvaged, and torpedoes from his own destroyers finished off the doomed carrier after the last of its crew had been evacuated. Three destroyers were also lost, and most of his ships had some damage to report. *Mikuma* was reportedly taken under tow and would be able to rejoin the task force. Damage aboard *Yamato* had been light after the debris had been cleared, but the effect of being attacked had been distracting and the battle had not gone well. The loss of so many aircraft and their experienced crews was the worst blow. Carriers without aircraft were just soft-skinned targets and task forces without sufficient air cover were as good as lost. His intelligence reports gave strong hints that the carriers *Saratoga* and *Wasp* could be nearby soon. Earlier that morning that would have been excellent news, but now, with over half of his aircraft gone, the Americans would have the advantage. Coded reports of the Oahu and Panama attacks were distressing, with heavier than predicted losses to his aircraft and less damage than had been hoped-for on Oahu. The Panama Striking Force was withdrawing after losing *Zuiho* and the Special Attack ship *Mutsuki* to submarines. With a few lucky shots, the enemy had destroyed the heart of the Panama Striking Force and there was little left for them to do.

He considered attacking again, perhaps to the north, but he knew that the effect he was trying to achieve with this offensive was lost. Nagumo, true to form, had opened up the distance between his carriers and the battle area until they were not only safe from land-based attack but also ineffective to cover his naval gunfire attacks. The American fighting spirit was increasing, not decreasing, and any hope of a dictated peace had disappeared. He resolved to accept the blame for this failure and to apologize to the Emperor himself. This war was going to be a long one after all.

Meanwhile, contact with Colonel Ichiki was lost after the appointed time to attack the American forces on Guadalcanal. When he had last reported, he had been planning to attack the American forces at Alligator Creek just before dawn. Now there was only silence. This was troubling.

## Epilog

In late December 1942, the carriers *Essex* and *Independence* slid from their ways to the waiting Atlantic. They would go through an accelerated fitting-out and shakedown schedule as their new aircraft crews went through intense training. Within only six weeks, both carriers were ready for combat and were traversing the Panama Canal for the Pacific. The Japanese had positioned subs to catch them as they emerged from the Canal, but aggressive patrolling preserved the new carriers intact to join the Pacific Fleet. Within a very short time more and more of these new fleet carriers moved to that theater, and the balance of forces began to swing in America's favor. Guadalcanal had been held and then secured and enemy forces all over the Solomons and New Britain were under increasing American attack.

Finally FDR directed that more of America's strength be directed at the Germans. Despite the reverses of the last seven months, the Germans could be beaten and America had promises to keep. American convoy escorts now took charge of the eastbound shipping and aggressively took on the 'wolfpacks'. Patrol bombers stretched their reach from the American coast, the Caribbean, Iceland, and Newfoundland, as well as from new escort ('jeep') carriers. U-boat losses began to climb. Amphibious landings in North Africa began in February and the Germans, paralyzed by the stunning cold of the Eastern Front, had to turn their attention to a new presence in the southern Mediterranean. In carefully secured settings, teams of American officers briefed their Allies on the tactics, techniques, and technologies used in the Battles of California and Hawaii and, for the first time, revealed the existence and effectiveness of the VT proximity fuze.

Jack Northrup and his and Glenn Martin's engineers worked feverishly on their XB-35. In view of his top-secret directions from Washington, every effort had to be made to ready the new B-35 for use not later than late 1944 or early 1945. His was the only long-range bomber design that could be ready by then and every possible resource was being devoted to help him.

His design team had been augmented by more engineers sent by the government, and together they decided to scrap the complex counter-rotating propellers in favor of more conventional paddle-bladed props, and some of the ambitious and complex remote-control defense gun positions were replaced by conventional manned turrets. The XB-35, a giant flying wing originally designed to have a wingspan of over 172 feet, was taking shape fast. Something to do with his bomber was also going on at Los Alamos, Northrup thought, but he couldn't find out what. He had been asked to increase the design payload from 16,000 pounds to over 26,000, and the design range from 8,150 nautical miles to 10,500. They had extended the wingspan to 207 feet and added two more engines, but he was puzzled about the size of the payload. He knew that some of the design payload would be the additional fuel needed to fly nonstop to Japan or Germany from the continental United States, but the rest of the increase was for a weapon or weapons. What kind of bomb weighed that much?

## The reality

In the final analysis, an American loss at Midway would have been a severe blow to US forces and to the morale of the country. However, it is certain that the basic and fundamental strength of the United States would not have been affected. Design and production on the West Coast would have been disrupted for a while, but there were more than enough other facilities to quickly take up the slack. The people of the United States could have sustained attacks and even an invasion, but they would never have agreed to an armistice with the Japanese. Of all of the mistaken analyses the Japanese leadership made regarding American reaction to the loss of Midway, and other defeats, that was their worst.

There would have been some very serious effects in Europe and the Soviet Union, but nothing final. Britain would have stood and fought, and held out to continue the struggle. The Soviet Union would probably have held Moscow and retaken Stalingrad, even with added forces and resources on the German side. The Soviets would have triumphed anyway, but it would have taken a bit longer, and many more Russians would have died.

Had Yamamoto decided to go along with the Army's plan to seize New Guinea and Australia, the same result would have come about; America would have prepared for its defense, accelerated carrier production and aircraft crew training, and built up its combat power for a counteroffensive. Arguably, if the Japanese had not concentrated on American targets, some of the ferocious desire for revenge would have been tempered, but not by much.

In the end, all that would have been lost was the additional blood and treasure of a six to eight month period. The Axis forces simply did not have the manpower and resources to hold the span of territory they had captured. They needed more luck, and a political system that accepted the cultures and peoples they conquered. Neither the Japanese nor the Germans had that kind of system, and instead they persecuted, terrorized, and inflamed their conquered peoples, causing a universal and unstoppable desire to resist them in any way possible. Further, the Imperial Japanese army and navy didn't have the logistic capability of sustaining a long-term transoceanic war. War needs fuel and ammunition in great quantities and fuel and ammunition are heavy and bulky and require a lot of shipping. Japan never had the logistic depth to support an all-out war in America's back yard.

Would America have invaded Guadalcanal even though it had lost three carriers? Probably. Both MacArthur and King knew the value of that airstrip to the Japanese and knew that they had to stop it being built in order to protect America's lines of communication to Australia. They also knew that if American aircraft could operate from Guadalcanal instead, the major Japanese base at Rabaul would be threatened. Once the Americans were on the island the Japanese would react quickly, and in this depiction of MacArthur's strategy the American invasion would have distracted Japanese attention from much more potentially damaging directions.

Even with a large defeat at Midway and the distraction of the United States, the war could even have been finished in mid-1945 anyway, but with a more difficult post-war recovery. The reverses at the beginning of the war and the brutal treatment of prisoners by the Japanese would have hardened American attitudes further and have given the war an even more desperate cast. The Manhattan Project would still have had the highest priority and once a bomber was available to deliver these new nuclear weapons there would have been no hesitation about using them. Jack Northup's elegant Flying Wings (with the unintended but welcome attribute of being nearly invisible to radar) could have delivered nuclear destruction to the very heart of enemy territory, and Tokyo and possibly Berlin would have been the first of several targets as the new fission weapons became available.

The enemy had sowed the wind, and they had reaped a whirlwind they could never have anticipated. Midway's loss would have only increased its force and ensured its inevitability.

The events presented in this chapter as following such a defeat turn on the decision of Lieutenant Commander McCluskey to turn towards Midway rather than northwest, which would have taken him towards the Japanese carriers. In reality he turned towards the Japanese, seeking the enemy rather than safety in the finest traditions of the U.S. Navy. He found the enemy carriers, and his strikes led to the sinking of all four of them. Midway was the critical, decisive defeat of the Imperial Japanese Navy that ultimately wrested initiative away from it.

## Bibliography

Baker, A.D., *Japanese Naval Vessels of World War II as seen by U.S. Intelligence* (U.S. Naval Institute Press, Annapolis, 1987).

Baldwin, Ralph B., *The Deadly Fuze: The Secret Weapon of World War II* (Presidio Press, San Raphael, 1980).

Boyne, Walter J., *Clash of Wings: Air Power in World War II* (Simon and Schuster, New York, 1994).

Francillon, R.J., *Japanese Aircraft of the Pacific War* (Funk & Wagnalls, New York, 1970).

Frank, Richard B., *Guadalcanal* (Penguin Books, New York, 1990).

Freeman, Roger A., *Mustang at War* (Doubleday, New York, 1974).

Gay, George, *Sole Survivor* (Midway Publishers, Naples, Florida, 1980).

Gunston, Bill, *Bombers* (Grosset & Dunlap, New York, 1978).

Hoyt, Edwin P., *Japan's War* (McGraw-Hill, New York, 1986).

McCullough, David, *The Path Between the Seas* (Simon and Schuster, New York, 1977).

Moore, John, Captain RN, *Jane's American Fighting Ships of the 20th Century* (Modern Publishing, New York, 1995).

Morison, Samuel Eliot, *The Two-Ocean War* (Little, Brown, Boston, 1963).

Prados, John, *Combined Fleet Decoded* (Random House, New York, 1995).

Smith, Peter C., *The Battle of Midway* (Spellmount, Staplehurst, 1976).

Wooldridge, E.T., *Winged Wonders* (Smithsonian Institute Press, Washington, D.C., 1985).

## Notes

1. For the purposes of this story, it is assumed that Lieutenant Commander Max Leslie of the *Yorktown* didn't find the Japanese carriers when Commander McCluskey turned towards Midway Island.

*2. For greater detail of this battle, see Minoru Genda, *Glorious Victory in the Pacific* (Asahi Shibun Press, Tokyo, 1944).

*3. *Ibid*.

4. John Prados' *Combined Fleet Decoded* (Random House, 1995) gives excellent detail of this remarkable area of the war.

5. This remarkable weapon was second in secrecy only to the atomic bomb during World War II. The U.S. government only reluctantly shared the technology with Britain in 1944.

*6. The Battle of Guadalcanal deserves much more attention than it has gotten. Coming so soon on the heels of an unbroken succession of Japanese victories it was the first true recovery of American initiative and the Allies' first step on the road back. Unfortunately, the success of the First Marine Division in the Solomons was eclipsed by the momentous events taking place in the East Pacific.

*7. Because of the uniqueness of San Diego's position as the only city in the continental United States to have suffered an attack by enemy forces in World War II, San Diego's War Memorial Museum at Balboa Park has been America's number one tourist attraction ever since.

*8. President MacArthur's Library Foundation was kind enough to allow the author access to the President's staff planning notes for this time period.

*9. Captain C. Gable's account of this battle in *Revenge! The ambush of Japan's Raid on Panama* (Silent Service Publishing, Norfolk, Virginia, 1976) gives additional insight into his deployment of his submarines into the path of the Japanese Special Attack Force.

# 6

# SAMURAI DOWN UNDER
# The Japanese Invasion of
# Australia

John H. Gill

Key British and American military leaders faced a bleak prospect in April 1942 when they gathered in London to discuss strategy. In Russia, the Red Army had succeeded in throwing the Wehrmacht back from the gates of Moscow, but had exhausted itself in the process. An operational pause had set in, but there was every expectation that the spring would bring a vast new German offensive. A similar pause had brought a temporary lull to the Western Desert after General Erwin Rommel's January attacks had carried his Afrika Korps deep into Libya, regaining much of the territory lost to the British the previous year. Much more threatening to Great Britain's immediate survival were the continued German successes in the Battle of the Atlantic, particularly Operation Drumbeat, the U-Boat campaign that was devastating shipping along the American east coast.

The picture was even worse in Asia, where the shock of Pearl Harbor and the sinking of the warships *Prince of Wales* and *Repulse* had been followed by an unbroken string of Japanese triumphs. In a seemingly irresistible tide of conquest, Japan's armed forces had forced the humiliating surrender of Singapore, crushed disjointed Allied resistance in the Netherlands East Indies, overrun the Philippines, evicted the British from Burma, threatened the last Allied link to China, bombed Australia, and seized bases on the northern shores of New Guinea. Even as General George C. Marshall, the head of the small U.S. delegation, was flying to England, Japanese carriers were rampaging through the eastern Indian Ocean, bombing facilities on Ceylon and adding to the Royal Navy's list of casualties, including the carrier *Hermes*. Nonetheless, from Marshall's perspective the London conference went well. America's military and industrial might was slowly unfolding and he believed he had won a British promise to launch an invasion of Western Europe in 1942. The British, having borne the brunt of Axis wrath thus far, were cautious and skeptical of an early cross-channel attack, but likewise looked for an opportunity to take the offensive some-

144

where in 1942. As they said their farewells, Churchill spoke of the two nations marching ahead 'in a noble brotherhood of arms', and Marshall headed home with hopes of a 'crescendo of activity' that very year.[1] What neither the British Prime Minister nor the American general yet knew was that the first notes of this particular crescendo would be sounded by their enemies on the other side of the world.

## Strategic points in the Australian area

While Allied leaders were planning in London, Japan's military strategists were debating next moves. Even before the first phase of conquests had been fully achieved, a General Liaison Conference between the Army and Navy General Staffs had decided, in early March 1942, that Japan, contrary to pre-war assumptions, would have to continue its offensive operations: 'In order to bring Britain to submission and to demoralize the United States, aggressive measures shall be taken by seizing opportunities to expand our acquired war gains'.

Although the policy adopted by the March Liaison Conference included 'measures such as the invasion of India and Australia', the exact actions to be taken remained under discussion for the next three weeks.[2] After rejecting the possibility of reconstituting and defending its existing gains, Japan had fundamentally three offensive strategic options in early 1942. First, it could advance into the Central Pacific and attempt to force the U.S. Pacific Fleet into a decisive naval battle by threatening a key American asset such as Midway or Hawaii. The second possibility was a drive into the Indian Ocean to destroy Britain's Eastern Fleet, weaken the British hold on India, and perhaps establish a link with Germany in the Middle East. Third was the 'Australia-first' option, with an adjunct push through the Solomons to Fiji and New Caledonia to isolate Australia from the United States.

As the heated interchanges accelerated through the month of March, Navy Captain Sadatoshi Tomioka argued passionately and persuasively in favor of the Australia option. Tomioka, assigned to the Plans Division in the Navy General Staff, was a vain but able officer, the top graduate in his class at the Naval War College. In his presentations, he highlighted several important advantages he expected Japan to gain by a direct attack on the Australian mainland. In the first place, a successful invasion would deny to the Allies the logical springboard for any counteroffensive against Japan's new holdings in the southwest Pacific. Moreover, as an arena where the Allies could exploit America's material superiority, Australia 'would be a weak spot in Japan's defensive armor unless it were either placed under Japanese control or effectively cut off from the United States'. Finally, Tomioka and his superiors saw an invasion of Australia as a key step in their campaign 'to break the fighting determination of the Allies', a crucial

consideration for a military culture that placed a high premium on the
psychological factor in war.[3]

At a conference in early April, while General Marshall was flying toward
London, the Japanese staffs quarreled and contemplated. Tomioka's principal adversary was Army Colonel Takushiro Hattori, who saw the Australia
option as a diversion of effort from the Army's traditional continental focus.
Meeting privately over tea one evening, Hattori was unable to shake his
Navy counterpart's conviction. Picking up his tea cup, Hattori said: 'The
tea in this cup represents our total strength.' He then spilled the tea on the
floor and added, 'You see it goes just so far. If your plan is approved I will
resign.'[4] Unfortunately for Hattori, Tomioka had by that time garnered the
support of the Combined Fleet, whose Chief of Staff wanted to ensure that
Imperial forces remained 'vigorously on the offensive' so that Japan would
not be put 'in a position of waiting for her enemies to attack without any
special advantages to herself'.[5] The Navy plan gained additional help from
Lieutenant General Tomoyuki Yamashita, the 'Tiger of Malaya', whose skill
and daring had brought about the surrender of Singapore several weeks
earlier. Overwhelmed, Hattori attempted to resign as promised, but was
reassigned to the staff of the 38th Division in China.

Tomioka had won the day, and the conference concluded on April 5,
1942, with a decision to move against 'strategic points in the Australian
area as speedily as operational conditions permit'.[6] The price for this victory,
however, was the Navy General Staff's acquiescence in Admiral Isoroku
Yamamoto's complex plan for the Combined Fleet's attack on Midway.
Though the Naval Staff 'pleaded vigorously, on occasion almost tearfully,
against the plan', Yamamoto would not be moved and Japan found herself
committed to conducting two simultaneous major offensives separated from
one another by thousands of miles of ocean.[7]

### Further pressure on Australia

The Japanese plan for the invasion of Australia envisaged two grand phases.
The first, scheduled for early May, would set the stage for later moves by
seizing Port Moresby on the southern coast of Papua (Operation MO) and
establishing a seaplane base on the tiny islet of Tulagi near Guadalcanal in
the Solomons. The second phase, Operation AU, would be the actual
invasion of northeastern Australia with the aim of seizing Allied air bases
that could threaten the Japanese stronghold at Rabaul and then driving
south so that land-based bombers could devastate the principal Australian
east coast ports and sever links to the United States. Japanese planners thus
calculated that there was no need to conquer or occupy all of Australia, a
prospect which Hattori and other Army staff officers predicted would
require ten or twelve divisions and impossible amounts of shipping. Instead,
Yamashita and the Navy developed a campaign plan that would leave

Japan in possession of bases in coastal enclaves as far south as Brisbane.[8] From these, Japanese aircraft could easily range Sydney, Canberra, and Melbourne, and possibly even strike as far as Adelaide, while patrol planes scoured the seas to the south and east.

Operation AU was slated to occur approximately one month after the capture of Port Moresby. It was thus timed to coincide with Yamamoto's offensive toward Midway in the hopes that the Combined Fleet would draw off the American Pacific Fleet, leaving the Australian invasion force unmolested by the U.S. carriers. Air bases and seaplane bases in the Solomons would provide flank protection to Operation AU and establish a foundation for a subsequent advance toward Fiji and New Caledonia. Other Japanese forces would loom menacingly in the Dutch East Indies, posing a constant threat to northwestern Australia and distracting Allied attention. As an addendum to the plan, Tomioka included the possibility of future amphibious attacks to seize Darwin and perhaps Perth 'to bring further pressure on Australia'.[9] Even without these acquisitions, however, the Japanese were confident that Operation AU would cut Australia off from any reasonable hope of succor and simultaneously deal a crippling blow to Allied morale.

The decision to invade Australia led to a rapid increase in Japanese military and naval might between New Britain and New Guinea. Headquartered at Rabaul was the newly established 8th Fleet, or Outer South Seas Force, under Vice Admiral Gunichi Mikawa, 'an intelligent, soft-spoken sailor of broad experience'.[10] Although the skilled Mikawa controlled the 8th Fleet's ships and a substantial contingent of naval guard and amphibious troops, Navy air was under Vice Admiral Nishizo Tsukahara's 11th Air Fleet. The Imperial Army, initially represented by Major General Tomitaro Horii's brigade-sized South Seas Detachment, was now supplemented by four infantry divisions (5th, 6th, 17th, 51st), two separate brigades (21st, 65th), and one of Japan's three recently-created tank divisions (2nd). General Yamashita, as the author of the outline plan, was designated to lead this large force as the commander of the new 17th Army.[11] Further, he was promised the use, at least temporarily, of two additional divisions should opportunities for easy conquest develop.

On April 23, 1942, Mikawa issued the directive for Operation MO, Outer South Seas Force Order No.13. Less than two weeks later, a large naval task force sailed from Rabaul under Mikawa's personal command, transporting Horii's South Seas Detachment, the 3rd Kure Special Naval Landing Force (SNLF), and other ground troops slated for the assault on and occupation of Port Moresby. Other elements of the 3rd Kure SNLF headed for Tulagi in the Solomons, while the fleet carriers *Shokaku* and *Zuikaku* of Vice Admiral Chuichi Hara's 5th Carrier Division steamed down from the Central Pacific to cover the invasion.[12] Mikawa exuded calm confidence and the troops 'were in high spirits as they embarked on their grand and ambitious scheme'.[13]

## Coral disaster

As the Japanese assembled their forces, the Allies struggled to find a way to gain the initiative. Marshall argued against any diversion from the build-up in Europe, but General Douglas MacArthur, in Australia after his escape from the Philippines, and Admiral Ernest J. King, Commander in Chief, U.S. Fleet, urged action in the Pacific. As commander of the new South-West Pacific Area (SWPA), MacArthur naturally stressed the importance of Australia, but King also recognized its significance as an Allied base for future operations, pointing out that the line of communications to the island continent was 'only barely less important' than the link between Hawaii and California. Owing to King's determination and good intelligence that 'an offensive in the South-west Pacific is shaping up', two American carriers, *Yorktown* and *Lexington*, were on hand to intercept Mikawa's task force as it sailed around the eastern end of Papua and into the Coral Sea.[14]

Unfortunately for the Allies, the Battle of the Coral Sea proved to be yet another in a long string of reversals, albeit not as disastrous as some of the earlier encounters. The battle began well enough for the Allies. American attack planes found part of Mikawa's force in the late morning of May 7 and sank the light carrier *Shoho*, jubilantly reporting 'Scratch one flat-top!' By excitedly concentrating on the hapless *Shoho*, however, they failed to damage any of the vulnerable transports and Mikawa quickly set about reassembling his scattered fleet behind the shelter of the Louisades. As *Shoho* was sinking, aircraft from 5th Carrier Division found and crippled the U.S. oiler *Neosho* while sending its lone escort, the destroyer *Sims*, to the bottom. That afternoon, Japanese Navy G3M Nell and G4M Betty bombers from Rabaul found Task Force 44, a small U.S./Australian surface force which was cruising south of the Jomard Passage with the mission to attack the Port Moresby invasion fleet. By skillful maneuvering and good luck, TF44 escaped this attack unscathed. The American and Australian sailors were less fortunate that night, when Mikawa led his cruisers and destroyers in an unexpected attack on the Allied ships. In a confused action, the Japanese Navy's superiority in night fighting resulted in TF44's lone light cruiser and two of its destroyers being sunk. Of the three remaining ships, both heavy cruisers (one American and one Australian) had suffered serious damage and were fortunate to evade detection as they slipped south to make their way back to Australia. Mikawa lost just one destroyer.

As the Allied ships were limping away from the Jomard and Mikawa was gathering up his flock of transports, the two principal carrier forces found one another. In a series of hard fought actions on May 8, American attack planes caused light damage to *Shokaku* before she and her sister ship disappeared in a heavy squall. The thick smoke from a fire aboard *Shokaku*, the poor visibility, and the lack of an overall attack commander led the U.S. Navy pilots to exaggerate their success. To their dismay, however, the American soon learned from signals intercepts that *Zuikaku* was unhurt and that *Shokaku*'s crew had quickly extinguished her fire and resumed operations. Meanwhile, the Japanese flyers struck a damaging blow against the U.S. carrier force. While the Americans were trying to find their targets in the rain, Japanese dive and torpedo bombers attacked under clear skies, pummeling *Lexington* and also managing a hit on *Yorktown*. Still capable of flight operations, *Yorktown* accepted most of the aircraft from both air wings while *Lexington*'s crew struggled to save their beloved ship. Despite extraordinary valor, *Lexington* was beyond rescue and had to be sunk that evening as *Yorktown* hurried away toward Pearl Harbor.

With the departure of the carriers and the destruction of TF44, the way to Port Moresby was open and Mikawa sailed back through the Jomard on May 9, only two days behind schedule. American bombers from Townsville attempted to hinder his progress, but achieved meager results for the loss of two B-17s to fighters from *Zuikaku*. Similarly, the few remaining Allied fighters and dive bombers at Port Moresby were overwhelmed by the Japanese after desperate fighting in the Papuan skies. With local air superiority, the veterans of the South Seas Detachment and the 3rd Kure SNLF landed at Port Moresby on May 12 and quickly broke the defenses of the demoralized and poorly-trained Australian 30th Brigade. Though some Australians managed to escape into the forbidding jungles, more than 3,000 went into captivity and, by mid-May, the first Japanese aircraft were operating from Port Moresby. The stage was set for Operation AU.

## Australia's darkest hour

The twin defeats at the Coral Sea and Port Moresby were devastating to Allied morale, compounded when it became clear that neither Japanese fleet carrier had suffered major damage. *Shoho* was a poor exchange for the loss of *Lexington* and the injuries inflicted upon *Yorktown*. As Australian Prime Minister John Curtin grimly told his countrymen, 'this is our darkest hour'.[15]

U.S.S. *Hornet* and *Enterprise* succeeded in diverting the two Japanese carriers from the Australian coast by feinting a raid toward Ocean and Nauru east of the Solomons in mid-May, but it was becoming increasingly clear to the Allies that Japan was preparing a major operation in the Central Pacific and both U.S. carriers were hastily recalled to Hawaiian waters. As *Hornet* and *Enterprise* steamed north, U.S. Pacific Fleet intelligence prepared an assessment that foresaw simultaneous Japanese thrusts toward the Aleutians, Australia, and the Hawaii/Midway area.[16] MacArthur's analysis was similar: 'The availability of large forces makes possible a strong enemy

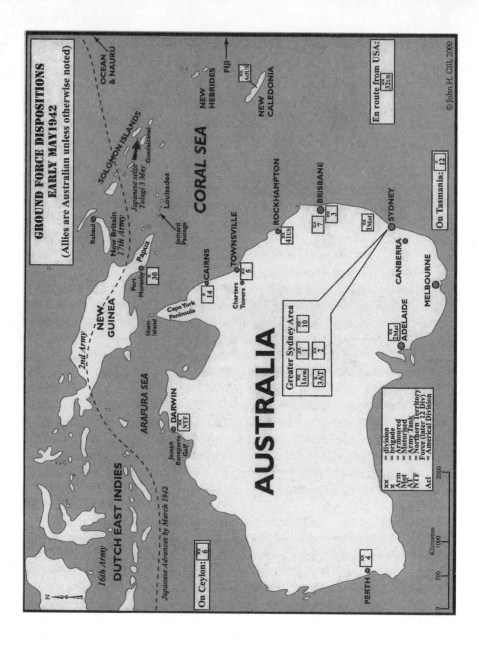

GROUND FORCE DISPOSITIONS
EARLY MAY 1942
(Allies are Australian unless otherwise noted)

OCEAN
& NAURU

SOLOMON ISLANDS

Japanese seize
Tulagi 3 May

Guadalcanal

Louisades

Jomard
Passage

Rabaul

New Britain
17th Army

Papua

Port
Moresby

NEW
GUINEA

2nd Army

CORAL SEA

NEW
HEBRIDES

Fiji

NEW
CALEDONIA

En route from USA:

xx
32US

xx
AdtUS

ROCKHAMPTON

BRISBANE

xx
3

xx
7

x
1Mot

SYDNEY

CANBERRA

On Tasmania:

x
12

ARAFURA SEA

DARWIN

xx
NTF

Joseph
Bonaparte
Gulf

CAIRNS

x
14

Charters
Towers

xx
5

TOWNSVILLE

xx
41US

Cape York
Peninsula

Horn
Island

Greater Sydney Area

xx
10

xx
2

xx
1

xx
1Arm

x
3AT

MELBOURNE

ADELAIDE

xx
2Mot

AUSTRALIA

DUTCH EAST INDIES

16th Army

Japanese Advances by March 1942

N

On Ceylon:

xx
6

PERTH

xx
4

xx    = division
x     = brigade
Arm   = Armoured
Mot   = Motorised
AT    = Army Tank
NTF   = Northern Territory
        Force (later 12 Div)
Acl   = American Division

Kilometres
0    500    1000    1500    2000

© John H. Gill, 2000

offensive effort of the most dangerous possibilities ... if Japan is not attacked elsewhere we can certainly look for an attack on Australia.'[17] With insufficient resources to respond to all three offensives, the Pacific Fleet had no choice but to concentrate on the Central Pacific threat, leaving MacArthur and the Australians to see to their own defense for the time being.

The Allied situation was not especially encouraging. Although Australia was in the process of forming a substantial army, in May 1942 less than half of the thirty-one brigades available in the country could be considered fit for combat operations and only four of these had any combat experience (five other brigades were still overseas and three, including the 30th, had been destroyed thus far). An Australian home guard of 50,000 men, the Volunteer Defense Corps, was providing invaluable assistance, but its members were generally too old for extended active service and there was hardly enough equipment for the regulars and militia, let alone these second-line troops. On the credit side of the ledger, the American 41st Infantry Division had reached Australia, the 32nd Division was en route, and American tanks were arriving to outfit the four Australian armored brigades. American Army and Marine units had also secured the island chains that guarded the line of communications back to the United States. With the exception of some elements of the 1st Marine Division, however, all of these units were newly formed and untested in battle.

The air picture was similarly worrisome and the naval situation absolutely gloomy. The fighting in the Dutch East Indies and over Port Moresby had depleted Allied air strength badly, so that many squadrons were operating with only half their intended number of aircraft. Pilots were also a problem. Many of the Australians were inexperienced while the Americans were an odd mixture of utterly green flyers newly arrived from the U.S. and tired, dispirited veterans of the repeated defeats in the Dutch East Indies. These problems were greatly exacerbated by the general inferiority of the Allied fighter aircraft (P-39s, P-400s, P-40s, and Australian Wirraways) when compared with the Japanese A6M Zeros and Ki-43 Oscars. In the wake of the catastrophes in the Java Sea and Coral Sea engagements, the U.S. and Australian naval forces had neither carriers, battleships, nor heavy cruisers to oppose a Japanese invasion. Until further American help arrived, the handful of remaining light cruisers and destroyers would be restricted to limited support missions well within the range of land-based aircraft. The best Allied naval leaders could hope for was some success on the part of their old S-model USN submarines.

## The fall of Townsville

While Admiral Yamamoto and the Combined Fleet were slicing through the waters of the Central Pacific toward their rendezvous with the U.S.

Pacific Fleet at Midway, Mikawa's armada steamed out of Rabaul and into the Coral Sea carrying Yamashita's invasion force to the Australian coastline.

Excellent intelligence work had alerted the Allies to the coming invasion, but the intended landing areas were still unknown as the Japanese transports approached the coast. Several problems contributed to this key intelligence gap. First, U.S. and Australian cryptanalysts had divined the general outlines of Operation AU, but, unlike the Midway invasion, the Allied intelligence officers did not have a near-complete operations order. Second, the Allies had only a limited ability to interpret Japanese Army codes. They thus had little success unearthing critical operational details of major Imperial Army activities. Finally, the limited number of U.S. analysts had been focused on Yamamoto as the more immediate danger and had not been able to devote as much time and energy to Operation AU. Though Australian intelligence also labored to penetrate the Japanese plans, there were neither enough specialists nor enough time to unravel the mystery before the Japanese struck.

Owing to these crucial holes in the intelligence picture, Allied strategists had to provide for the security of the entire east coast of Australia. Under plans prepared by Australian General T.A. Blamey, the Commander of Allied Land Forces, most ground troops were already concentrated in the strategically vital south-east from Brisbane to Melbourne, and these were bolstered by the arrival of the 2nd Division from Western Australia in late May. North of Brisbane, however, Allied leaders believed they could only attempt to hold Townsville and Rockhampton against a serious invasion; much of the intervening ground might have to be abandoned to the enemy in the short term. These two cities were therefore garrisoned with the 5th Australian and 41st U.S. Divisions respectively, the former also commanding the 14th Brigade recently sent to Cairns. The greater part of the operational aircraft were also concentrated around Townsville. Smaller garrisons were retained at other strategically important points: Northern Territory Force (soon to be 12th Division) at Darwin, 4th Division around Perth, and 12th Brigade on Tasmania.[18] The Australian government also improved its defensive posture by evacuating civilians, livestock, and potential war materiel from the area north of Townsville. Though resented at the time by many evacuees, this prudent and controversial move would deprive the Japanese invaders of equipment and supplies (especially fuel and motor transport) that they were relying on to sustain their offensive.

Tasked to defend Townsville, Major General E.J. Milford's 5th Division was the first to encounter the Japanese invaders. Yamashita's plan called for his own 5th Division to come ashore just north of Townsville while his 6th Division landed south of town to prevent reinforcements from pushing up along the coastal highway. Having served under Yamashita during the

Malaya campaign, the men of the 5th Division would have the honor of capturing the town itself while simultaneously pushing inland toward the cluster of Allied airfields at Charters Towers eighty miles to the southwest by road. At the same time, the 17th Division would assault the port of Cairns, evict the Australian garrison (mistakenly estimated to be a battalion), and begin to construct an airfield. As a final security measure, the 3rd Kure SNLF would capture two Allied airfields at the far northern tip of inhospitable Cape York Peninsula. In typical Japanese fashion, the plan was complex and daring to the point of recklessness, relying on the proven skill and ferocity of the Imperial armed forces to stun and overwhelm the defenders.

Timed to coincide with the assault on Midway, Yamashita's storm broke on the Australian coast on June 4, 1942. All three of his divisions quickly established footholds but losses were heavier than expected and the Australian militiamen, as some Japanese staff officers had predicted, were demonstrating unanticipated tenacity defending their homeland, even when badly outnumbered. Many of the first day's objectives were not achieved, much to Yamashita's annoyance, and there were problems unloading supplies under periodic Allied air strikes. The Imperial Navy was also experiencing difficulties. A destroyer and a transport were sunk, a cruiser damaged, and air superiority continued to elude the combination of land-based and carrier aircraft. Furthermore, disaster struck in the north when the ancient American submarine *S-38* put two torpedoes into one of the transports carrying the 3rd Kure SNLF. The resulting losses in men and equipment crippled the landing force and caused the temporary abandonment of the attacks on the Cape York airfields. Yamashita was also frustrated by supply and transportation problems. He had counted on seizing fuel, stores, vehicles, and coastal shipping to expedite the invasion, but Australian pre-planning and the exertions of the Volunteer Defense Corps had removed or destroyed most of these assets, leaving the Japanese largely reliant on what little they had brought with them. Despite these setbacks, the two Japanese carriers were safe and the 17th Army was well established ashore as night fell and commanders on both sides heard the first news of the Battle of Midway.

The catastrophe in the Central Pacific had almost immediate repercussions for Operation AU as *Shokaku* and *Zuikaku* were withdrawn to Rabaul out of effective range of Allied land-based bombers. Having made a commitment to the Australia operation, however, Imperial General Headquarters felt it had no option but to proceed. For the next several weeks, therefore, combat raged at both Cairns and Townsville, leaving the rusted wrack of battle that dots today's tourist beaches. The fighting in Townsville was especially vicious as the 5th Japanese Division had to pry the men of 11th Australian Brigade and Volunteer Defense Corps die-hards out of almost every building. By the end of the month the town was secure, but the leading Japanese infantry units were still more than fifty miles from Charters Towers and Allied aircraft hindered port unloading and airfield operations. At Cairns, the 17th Division had pushed back the Australian 14th Brigade with relative ease and two airfields were nearly complete despite routine visits from American bombers. Luckily, Lieutenant General Yasushi Sakai, the 17th's commander, contented himself with fulfilling his specific mission of seizing the port of Cairns and allowed the 14th Brigade to escape destruction. Progress was slow and hobbled by logistic difficulties which deprived him of mobility and supplies, particularly artillery ammunition. Nonetheless, Yamashita could take satisfaction in the occupation of the two Allied air bases on the Cape York Peninsula by the 5th Sasebo SNLF on June 19. Moreover, he was promised reinforcements. In addition to the 20th Division and the 2nd Tank Division, additional elements of the 6th Air Division were to deploy to Port Moresby and the new airfields in Australia. With these resources, he was confident that the Charters Towers runways would soon be in his hands.

The Allies responded to the invasion as quickly as scanty forces and Australia's limited transportation system would permit. As the enormous scale of the Japanese commitment became clear, MacArthur reasoned that another major amphibious landing was very likely beyond the Imperial Navy's capabilities, especially after Midway. He and Blamey thus stripped the southeast coast of Australian units and redirected the U.S. 32nd Division from Adelaide to Brisbane. The veteran Australian 7th Division was the first to arrive and almost immediately played a crucial role in smashing a Japanese offensive toward Charters Towers. Unfazed by headlong Japanese tank charges that had unnerved the weary 5th Division men, the 7th calmly shot up the enemy armored columns and ruthlessly cleaned up stray tanks that managed to slip behind their defenses. By halting the Japanese drive on Charters Towers, the 7th Division allowed Milford to strengthen his weak right flank where Yamashita had conducted small amphibious landings in an effort to break through along the coastal highway.

An operational pause followed the initial Japanese landings and attempted exploitation. However, while the two air forces battled for control of the skies and Yamashita waited for ammunition and reinforcements, Allied power steadily increased. By mid-July, the bulk of the 2nd Australian and 41st U.S. Divisions were in the battle zone and the first trains carrying the 1st Australian Armored Division were chugging north from Sydney. Supplying this growing force proved a major challenge, as the Japanese occupation of Townsville left the Allies dependent on a circuitous inland railroad link to Charters Towers. This arrangement was minimally satisfactory for the forces in the Townsville area, but the units near Cairns had to rely on a painfully lengthy road connection that was vulnerable to air interdiction.

Logistical obstacles notwithstanding, the new Allied units arrived just in time to blunt a renewed Japanese offensive. Yamashita, impatient with the lack of progress at Townsville, had decided to switch his reinforcements to Cairns to crush the 14th Brigade and, swinging wide inland, to sweep down on Charters Towers from the north, unhinging the Allied line in front of Townsville in the process. The assault opened at dawn on July 16, the newly disembarked 51st Division and 2nd Tank Division driving on Mount Garnet while the 17th Division attacked down the coastal road to establish a clean link to the forces at Townsville. The Japanese made rapid advances against the hopelessly outnumbered 14th Australian Brigade and its Volunteer Defense Corps auxiliaries at first, but resistance stiffened as elements of the 2nd Australian Division reached the front. Further slowed by concentrated air strikes, scarcity of fuel for his tanks, and the unanticipated appearance of the American 41st Division, Yamashita's offensive came to a halt just short of Mount Garnet in the first days of August. On the coast, however, the 17th Division's push, coordinated with an amphibious landing by the South Seas Detachment, cleared the road to Townsville against minimal opposition, but left the Japanese troops strung out over nearly 300 kilometers in a narrow corridor between the ocean and the inland mountains.

### 'I feel absolutely confident'

In the comfort of retrospect it seems clear that early August 1942 was the high water mark of the Japanese advance into the Southwest Pacific. At the time, however, there was no assurance of ultimate Allied success and Deputy Prime Minister F.M. Forde was by no means unjustified when he told MacArthur that his country was facing 'the greatest catastrophe that could have happened'. MacArthur's reply, on the other hand, has come to symbolize the resilience of the Allied troops and of the Alliance overall: 'Although the war clouds are black I feel absolutely confident.'[19] His sentiment was echoed by the men moving to the battlefront in Queensland. One Australian tanker of the 1st Armored Division recalled the pride and responsibility he and his squadron felt when people cheered them and their Grant tanks as they rolled through small stations on their way north. Others laughed and cheered themselves when a middle-aged woman on her way to a combat training session proclaimed 'I hope I never see one [a Japanese soldier], but if I do he will come off second best'.[20] The men would need all that determination and more in the months to come.

If the defensive victory against Yamashita's second offensive in Australia was the first Allied success of August 1942 in the Southwest Pacific, the invasion of Guadalcanal was the second. Frustrated by his inability to divert more forces to the Pacific even after the attack on Australia, and convinced that the Allies could and should take the offensive as soon as possible, Admiral King successfully promoted a plan to seize Guadalcanal and the Japanese seaplane base on nearby Tulagi. Though nine months of incredibly hard fighting lay ahead, the landing of the 1st Marine Division on August 7 was the first step on a path that would isolate the Japanese invaders in Australia and ultimately set the stage for the explosion of Allied power through New Guinea to the Philippines and beyond.

While the U.S. Marines and the Japanese 18th Army were locked in the bitter struggle for Guadalcanal, the Australian and American armies were being reorganized to take the offensive in Australia. This process led to considerable friction between the two Allies. MacArthur had wanted to keep American troops under U.S. commanders, but the exigencies of the dire situation precluded a tidy arrangement along national lines. To the egocentric MacArthur's intense irritation, there was no alternative to an intermingling of units that would lessen his direct operational role. U.S. I Corps under American Lieutenant General Robert L. Eichelberger was thus duly constituted with one American and two Australian divisions at Mount Garnet, while Australian Lieutenant General S.F. Rowell moved the headquarters of I Australian Corps to Charters Towers to assume command of the troops facing Townsville. Both corps ostensibly came under Blamey as Commander of Allied Land Forces, but MacArthur often intervened directly, causing no end of frustration to the already harried commanders and staffs. Despite the frequent collisions between the senior Australian and American generals, all were agreed upon the common goal. As Blamey noted later: 'From the outset it was decided between General MacArthur and myself that as soon as possible we would move to the offensive against Japan as far north as we could proceed.'[21]

With the command structure somewhat in order, I U.S. Corps in the Cairns area attempted a limited attack toward Ravenshoe on August 20, while I Australian Corps distracted the Japanese at Townsville. Led by the American 41st Division, the attack made some initial gains, but quickly ground to a halt in the face of stubborn resistance compounded by the inexperience of the green U.S. troops. The Australian militia battalions in the 2nd and newly-organized 11th Divisions did little better, but the two weeks of fighting taught the Allies important tactical lessons and shook a lot of dead wood out of the leadership positions. Despite fairly heavy losses, the American and Australian units emerged from the August fighting tougher, wiser, and more formidable.

The Japanese, however, also gained a success in August when a large convoy was able to evade ineffectual Allied bombing efforts to bring the 20th Division, and even more important, a significant resupply of fuel and

ammunition, to Cairns. With these resources, Yamashita planned what
came to be his last major offensive.

## A final desperate phase

Yamashita's September attack surprised the Allies, who were busy planning
their own offensive operation. While the 7th Australian Division decimated
an ill-conceived diversionary advance by Horii's South Seas Detachment
southwest of Townsville, the Japanese 17th Division found the weakly-held
right flank of U.S. I Corps near Koombooloomba and achieved a deep
penetration. Worse, the 20th Division and the 2nd Tank Division were able
to punch through the center of U.S. I Corps, isolating some units, over-
running others, and spreading fear in their wakes. For Yamashita, it began
to seem like a repetition of the triumph in Malaya.

Yamashita's satisfaction proved very brief indeed. While badgering
Washington for more troops and equipment, MacArthur had gathered a
reserve of two divisions (II Australian Corps), albeit untried ones, to launch
a massive Allied assault on the Cairns front. This large force was still
training and stocking munitions when the Japanese attacked, and the Allied
commander waited for the initial fury of the enemy assault to expend itself
before he unleashed his counterstroke. Preceded by a short but intense
artillery bombardment and an all-out air assault on the Japanese air bases,
the 1st Australian Armored Division crashed into the 20th Division's lines
north of the Ravenshoe–Mount Garnet road on September 13. With utterly
inadequate anti-tank weapons, the 20th had no hope of stopping the well-
trained Australian tankers despite the self-sacrificing bravery of the Japanese foot-soldiers. By nightfall, the Australian armored spearheads were
deep behind Japanese lines, leaving numerous pockets of isolated, but
desperate and determined, defenders for the American 41st Division to
eradicate. The 20th's commander, Lieutenant General Kane Yoshihara, was
almost killed when his forward headquarters was overrun, but he escaped to
the 79th Infantry Regiment's command post and radioed for help. His pleas
brought an uncoordinated counterattack by the 2nd Tank Division's 3rd
Tank Brigade on the morning of September 14. Ill-prepared for tank-
versus-tank engagements, the Japanese armor suffered seventy percent
casualties as they tried to close with the Australian Grants and Stuarts.
Lacking adequate infantry support, the victorious Australians reluctantly
withdrew some ten kilometers during the night, but their dramatic success
had so disordered the Japanese that Yamashita had to pull back or risk
watching his command be taken apart piece by piece.

The action on September 13–14 gave the Japanese a healthy respect for
Allied tanks, but the Australian tankers and American G.I.s could not
achieve a breakthrough. As elsewhere in the Pacific, the tactical skill and
ferocious tenacity of the Japanese infantry made every mile's progress slow

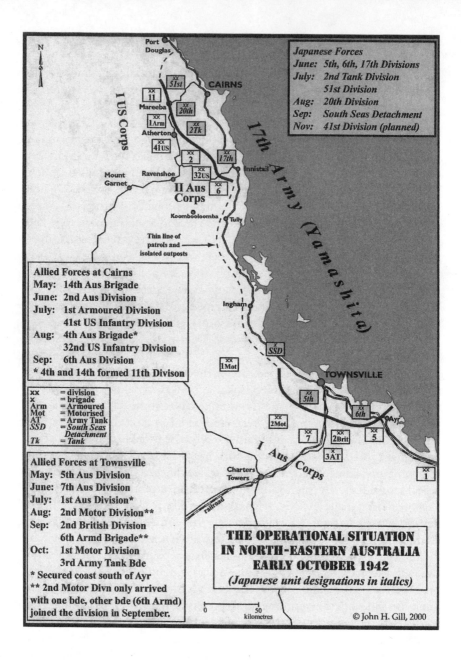

N

Port Douglas

CAIRNS

Mareeba

Atherton

Mount Garnet

Ravenshoe

I US Corps

XX 51st

XX 11

XX 20th

XX 1 Arm

XX 2 Tk

XX 41 US

XX 2

XX 32 US

XX 6

II Aus Corps

XX 17th

Innisfail

Koombooloomba

Tully

Thin line of patrols and isolated outposts

17th Army (Yamashita)

Ingham

X SSD

XX 1 Mot

TOWNSVILLE

XX 5th

XX 2 Mot

XX 6th

Ayr

XX 7

X 2 Brit

XX 5

X 3 AT

XX 1

Charters Towers

I Aus Corps

railroad

**Japanese Forces**
June:  5th, 6th, 17th Divisions
July:  2nd Tank Division
        51st Division
Aug:   20th Division
Sep:   South Seas Detachment
Nov:   41st Division (planned)

**Allied Forces at Cairns**
May:   14th Aus Brigade
June:  2nd Aus Division
July:  1st Armoured Division
        41st US Infantry Division
Aug:   4th Aus Brigade*
        32nd US Infantry Division
Sep:   6th Aus Division
* 4th and 14th formed 11th Divison

| | |
|---|---|
| xx | = division |
| x | = brigade |
| Arm | = Armoured |
| Mot | = Motorised |
| AT | = Army Tank |
| SSD | = South Seas Detachment |
| Tk | = Tank |

**Allied Forces at Townsville**
May:   5th Aus Division
June:  7th Aus Division
July:  1st Aus Division*
Aug:   2nd Motor Division**
Sep:   2nd British Division
        6th Armd Brigade**
Oct:   1st Motor Division
        3rd Army Tank Bde
* Secured coast south of Ayr
** 2nd Motor Divn only arrived
with one bde, other bde (6th Armd)
joined the division in September.

**THE OPERATIONAL SITUATION
IN NORTH-EASTERN AUSTRALIA
EARLY OCTOBER 1942**
*(Japanese unit designations in italics)*

0        50
kilometres

© John H. Gill, 2000

and costly. Nonetheless, when MacArthur called a halt to the offensive on September 30 his troops had retaken Ravenshoe and inflicted disproportionate losses on Yamashita's command. The contrast in losses was greatest in armored vehicles. A second tank battle had erupted on September 20 when the Japanese 2nd Tank Division attempted to overcome technical inferiority by resorting to a night attack. One Japanese column was detected and destroyed when the lead vehicle opened fire too soon, but a second column threw parts of the 1st Armored Division and 41st Division into temporary confusion. Japanese command and control quickly collapsed, however, and most of the Allied defenders held firm, leaving the isolated and disjointed elements of the 2nd Tank Division to succumb to unremitting Allied fire the following day. As a result of fights like this, by the end of the battle the 2nd Tank Division was a wreck. Though less successful and more costly to the Allies, the timely intervention of the American 32nd Division over the same period had sufficed to check the Japanese 17th Division and restore the situation on the U.S. I Corps right flank.

September not only brought the first successful Allied counterattack, it also provided the first tentative glimmer of hope that the balance in the entire theater was beginning to shift in favor of the Allies. In the first place, significant reinforcements were arriving in Australia. Although the naval situation remained precarious and the fighting around Guadalcanal absorbed most of the available Allied ships, MacArthur's and Curtin's consistent pleas for help resulted in the appearance of increasing numbers of replacement aircraft and crews. The 'Germany-first' strategy and the strategic crisis in North Africa also limited the number of new ground troops available, but Churchill agreed to divert the British 2nd Division en route to India in exchange for retaining the already legendary 9th Australian Division in Egypt. Even more important in Australian eyes was the return of the veteran 6th Division and a growing inventory of modern equipment, especially artillery, to outfit and replenish the existing Australian formations.

Beyond these material gains, the Allied troops were learning, albeit painfully, that the conquerors of Malaya, Java, Burma, and Papua were not invincible. This was a critical psychological victory, as important in its own way as the physical success achieved in crippling the 2nd Tank Division or inflicting punishing losses on the Japanese bomber fleet. The Allied armies and air forces were also slowly gaining in battlefield competence while the Japanese, renowned for their combat prowess, were already beginning to turn to the tactics of desperation: mass infantry attacks with inadequate support. Yamashita's 17th Army was by no means a spent force, but its combat advantage over the Americans and Australians was slipping away.

Yamashita, perceiving the slow shift in the tide of the campaign, urgently requested reinforcements. Competing demands for shipping to support

Guadalcanal delayed the departure of his designated reserve division, the 41st, until November, so he launched Sakai's 17th Division in a spoiling attack against the vulnerable right flank of I U.S. Corps in early October. This time, however, the Allies held, and the Japanese 53rd Regiment, which had broken through a weak point in the line, was surrounded and annihilated over the course of the next three days. The attack and severe logistical problems did, however, cause the postponement of MacArthur's next offensive and granted the Japanese 8th Area Army time to dispatch the 41st Division from Rabaul.

Unfortunately for Yamashita, the 41st would never reach Australia's shores. The Allied air forces, though still inadequately supplied with men and machines, had grown in experience, skill, and numbers since the first Japanese raid on Darwin in February. Now under the extraordinarily competent leadership of American Major General George C. Kenney, they were increasingly taking the fight to the enemy and had made Japanese air operations from Cairns and Townsville nearly impossible. They had also received numbers of new B-25s and, when signals intelligence indicated that the Japanese were organizing a large convoy to reinforce the 17th Army, Kenney made detailed preparations to destroy it. The result was a disaster for Yamashita. While three Royal Air Force Spitfire squadrons kept Japanese fighters at bay, Kenney's American and Australian flyers caught the 41st Division's convoy with little air cover and wrecked it. In addition to the loss of most of its heavy equipment, an estimated 4,000 men of the division were killed, drowned, or wounded during the two-day battle. The disaster not only left the 41st a hollow shell, it also seriously depleted Japanese shipping at a time when the simultaneous struggles on Guadalcanal and Australia were placing an impossible logistics burden on slender Imperial resources. Though Yamashita continued to hope for reinforcements and adequate resupply, this Second Battle of the Coral Sea proved to be the last attempt to send substantial assistance to the 17th Army.

As the scattered remnants of the Japanese 41st Division assembled at Port Moresby, the tide had truly turned in the Battle of Australia. In the first place, by late 1942 Allied military power in the Australian theater was quickly growing to unassailable proportions, despite Marshall's continued insistence on priority being given to Europe. Though naval strength remained problematic, ground force strength and tactical competence were steadily improving. Furthermore, an increasingly effective Australian resistance movement was tying down Yamashita's troops and disrupting his supply efforts. Most important, however, was the change in the air balance. While Japan relied on inexperienced pilots flying obsolescent Nells, Bettys, Sallys, Oscars and other types, Kenney's air forces were increasing in overall numbers and in pilot quality. Kenney's squadrons were also receiving greatly superior aircraft, such as the B-25 bombers used to good effect in the destruction of the 41st Division's transports, RAF Spitfires, and P-38 Lightnings, which began to arrive in November. These Allied advantages compounded the woes of Yamashita's army. Casualties were a problem, but much more serious was the general deterioration of his logistic situation. Grave shortages of ammunition, fuel, and food, left his large force physically weakened, largely immobile, and unable to apply large caliber firepower except in the most dire circumstances.

In addition to these tactical and technical considerations in the immediate theater of operations, the broader strategic situation was also developing to the Allies' advantage. By January 1943 it was clear to Imperial General Headquarters that Guadalcanal could not be held without an enormous Japanese effort, an effort that was not certain to succeed. Even if Japanese power sufficed to transport massive reinforcements to the island, it was obvious that those forces, like Yamashita's, could not be sustained at anywhere near the level required for offensive operations. The Allied conquest of Guadalcanal in February 1943 and their subsequent advance up the Solomons effectively outflanked the Japanese foothold in Australia and granted Allied aircraft even greater access to Yamashita's lines of communications through Papua and across the Coral Sea. The arrival of the Japanese 35th and 36th Divisions in New Britain and the Solomons during early 1943 temporarily stemmed, but could not halt, the mounting Allied pressure.

On the other side of the Coral Sea, the Allies were also advancing. When the American 32nd Division and the Australian 2nd reached the coast near Innisfail on December 14, 1942, the two division commanders celebrated by sending General MacArthur a canteen full of seawater with an American flag painted on one side and an Australian flag on the other.[22] Their waggish gift symbolized the separation of Yamashita's 17th Army into two isolated enclaves and foretold the end of the bold Japanese enterprise in Australia. Many dreary months of fighting remained as the Allies slowly contracted the circle of fire around Yamashita's dwindling force, but at Christmas MacArthur was able to direct his staff to begin planning the invasion of Papua and New Guinea. Though he had hoped to 'fight the Battle of Australia in New Guinea', the Japanese attack on Australia actually made the coming Allied operations at Port Moresby and elsewhere easier. By consuming enormous amounts of materiel and more than 100,000 men, Operation AU left Japan's forces gravely weakened. In March 1943 the Imperial General Staff thus adopted a defensive strategy designed to cripple the Allies with heavy casualties and to create the conditions for a counterstroke. Faced with simultaneous Allied thrusts in New Guinea, the Solomons, and the Central Pacific, however, the Japanese strategy gradually collapsed and MacArthur could justifiably, if grandiloquently, claim that 'the sacrifices of our united forces in the defense of the

Australian homeland have paved the way for the ultimate destruction of the Japanese Empire'. From his broader perspective, Marshall could be equally pleased. As he surveyed the Allied strategic situation in May 1943, he could happily record that he was 'very gratified to see Tunisia become the Nazi Townsville'.[23]

## The reality

Speculative scenarios provide a useful laboratory for historical analysis, allowing us to gain a better understanding of what actually happened by exploring what might have happened. In general, our fictitious forays diverge from reality along two paths. On the one hand, we can examine the changes that might have resulted from specific incidents – cases, for example, where a shift in luck, skill, or perseverance might have altered the outcome of a battle. These experiments with history require little alteration of actual events but might yield significant results. Consider the potential catastrophe for the Allied cause had the Japanese carrier aircraft attacked *Yorktown* and *Lexington* on May 7, 1942, instead of blasting the unfortunate *Sims* and *Neosho*. On the other hand, our speculative examinations can reveal areas where larger, farther-reaching changes would have been needed to alter events. This line of investigation brings us to strategic, institutional, and attitudinal aspects of the historical situation. The Japanese pre-war policies on air crew recruitment and training provide one example of this avenue of research; the Allied decision to pursue the Germany-first strategy is another.

The present chapter detours from reality in both ways. At the lower, incidental level, it posits a new outcome to the Battle of the Coral Sea, one in which the Japanese are more determined and suffer fewer losses than they actually did, and are thus allowed to continue with the assault on Port Moresby. The battle becomes thereby both a tactical and strategic success for Japan. In reality, of course, the Imperial Navy achieved a tactical victory by sinking the fleet carrier *Lexington* for the loss of the light carrier *Shoho*, but the Allies simultaneously gained strategically by thwarting the seaborne attack on Port Moresby and reducing the potential danger to Australia. Perhaps even more important were the heavy losses inflicted on the Japanese carrier air wings involved in the battle and the damage done to *Shokaku*. As a result of Coral Sea, both units of the 5th Carrier Division were absent at Midway, where their participation would have given the Imperial Navy six fleet carriers against three American and might have tipped the balance in Yamamoto's favor.

At the strategic level, two important shifts were introduced to make this scenario possible. First, the Imperial Army makes a strategic commitment to the Southwest Pacific which did not exist in reality. The Japanese Army, institutionally focused on China and the Soviet Union, had almost no interest in expanding operations in New Guinea and the Solomon Islands, let alone Australia, which military planners believed would require ten or twelve divisions and an impossible level of logistical support. Hoping that the expected German successes in the summer of 1942 would create an opportunity for a Japanese attack against the USSR, Army planners therefore kept troop allocations to the Southwest Pacific to a bare minimum (General Horii's South Seas Detachment, which was little more than a reinforced regiment). Given the Army's predominance in Tokyo, the Japanese Navy's urge to extend its Pacific conquests was quashed.[24] Senior American and British decision-makers were thus correct in assessing a Japanese invasion of the Australian mainland as a very unlikely prospect. Indeed, Japan's only real hope for a successful invasion of eastern Australia would have been to exploit the momentum of their early victories by attacking in February or March 1942.

The second 'strategic' change is within the Japanese Navy. This chapter assumes that the Navy General Staff's interest in the Southwest Pacific would have resulted in the provision of two fleet carriers and other shipping for the invasion of Australia. While such an operation would have stretched and perhaps exceeded Japanese maritime capabilities, the principal obstacle was Admiral Yamamoto and the Combined Fleet. Obsessed with orchestrating the 'decisive battle' with the U.S. Pacific Fleet, Yamamoto would have brooked no diversion of precious carrier assets to Australia. His iron determination and vast prestige doomed the Navy General Staff's plans for the southwest area. At a crucial planning conference in April 1942, he threatened to resign if his plan for the Central Pacific was not adopted. The Navy General Staff capitulated and the Imperial Japanese Navy set its course irrevocably toward Midway.[25]

## Bibliography

Frank, Richard B., *Guadalcanal* (Penguin, New York, 1992).

Fuchida, Mitsuo, and Okumiya, Masatake, *Midway: The Battle that Doomed Japan* (U.S. Naval Institute Press, Annapolis, 1992).

Hay, David, *Nothing Over Us: The Story of the 2/6 Australian Infantry Battalion* (Australian War Memorial, Canberra, 1984).

Hayashi, Saburo, *Kogun: The Japanese Army in the Pacific War* (Greenwood Press, Westport, 1978).

Hopkins, Major General R.N.L., *Australian Armour* (Australian War Memorial and the Australian Government Printing Service, Canberra, 1978).

Horner, David, *Crisis of Command* (Australian National University Press, Canberra, 1978)

Horner, David, *High Command* (Allen & Unwin, Sydney, 1992).

Horner, David (ed.) *The Commanders* (Allen & Unwin, Sydney, 1984).

Horner, David (ed.), *The Battles that Shaped Australia* (Allen & Unwin, St Leonards, 1994).

Lundstrom, John B., *The First South Pacific Campaign: Pacific Fleet Strategy December 1941–June 1942* (U.S. Naval Institute Press, Annapolis, 1976).

Madej, W. Victor (ed.), *Japanese Armed Forces Order of Battle* (Game Marketing Company, Allentown, 1981).

McKernan, M., and Browne, M. (eds.), *Australia: Two Centuries of War and Peace* (Australian War Memorial, Canberra, 1988).

Milner, Samuel, *United States Army in World War II, The War in the Pacific, Victory in Papua* (Department of the Army, Washington, D.C., 1957).

Morton, Louis, *United States Army in World War II, The War in the Pacific, Strategy and Command: The First Two Years* (Department of the Army, Washington, D.C., 1962).

Pogue, Forrest C., *George C. Marshall: Ordeal and Hope* (Viking Press, New York, 1966).

Robertson, John, *Australia Goes to War* (Doubleday, Sydney, 1984).

Toland, John, *The Rising Sun* (Random House, New York, 1970).

Trigellis-Smith, Syd, *All the King's Enemies: A History of the 2/5 Australian Infantry Battalion* (Headquarters Training Command, Australian Army, George's Heights, 1994).

United States, Department of the Army, Office of the Chief of Military History. Japanese Monographs series: Monographs 22, 37, 71, 96, 105, 116.

Willmott, H.P., *Empires in the Balance* (U.S. Naval Institute Press, Annapolis, 1982).

Willmott, H.P., *The Barrier and the Javelin: Japanese and Allied Pacific Strategies February to June 1942* (U.S. Naval Institute Press, Annapolis, 1983).

## Notes

1. Churchill, quoted in Forrest C. Pogue, *George C. Marshall: Ordeal and Hope* (Viking Press, New York, 1966), pp.318–19.
2. Both preceding quotes are taken from 'General Outline of Policy of Future War Guidance', adopted by Liaison Conference on March 7, 1942, as published in Louis Morton, *United States Army in World War II, The War in the Pacific, Strategy and Command: The First Two Years* (Department of the Army, Washington, D.C., 1962), pp.611–13.
3. Mitsuo Fuchida and Masatake Okumiya, *Midway: The Battle that Doomed Japan* (U.S. Naval Institute Press, Annapolis, 1992), pp.73–82.
4. Quoted in John Toland, *The Rising Sun* (Random House, New York, 1970), vol.I, p.378.
5. Combined Ugaki quote from Morton, *op.cit.* pp.215–16, and Fuchida and Okumiya, *op.cit.* p.75.
6. Quoted with slight rearrangement from Combined Fleet Operations Order No.1, November 5, 1941, in Morton, *op.cit.* p.204.
7. Fuchida and Okumiya, *op.cit.* p.82.
8. For Yamashita's plan, see John Robertson, *Australia Goes to War* (Doubleday, Sydney, 1984), p.104.
9. Japanese Army and Navy agreement of February 16, 1942, quoted in Samuel Milner, *United States Army in World War II, The War in the Pacific, Victory in Papua* (Department of the Army, Washington, D.C., 1957), p.10.
10. Quote from Richard B. Frank, *Guadalcanal* (Penguin, New York, 1992), p.44. The 8th Fleet was actually not established until July 1942.
11. Japanese deployments have been advanced by several months. All of these units actually arrived in the general New Guinea area in late 1942 and early 1943.

17th Army was organized on May 2, 1942. The tank divisions were organized in August 1942.

12. The Carrier Striking Force under Vice Admiral Takeo Takagi included two cruisers, six destroyers, and an oiler, as well as Hara's two carriers.

13. Japanese account quoted in John B. Lundstrom, *The First South Pacific Campaign* (U.S. Naval Institute Press, Annapolis, 1976), p.98.

14. Two preceding quotes are from U.S. Pacific Fleet estimates from April 1942 in Lundstrom, *op.cit.* pp.79–81.

15. Speech of December 8, 1941, quoted in David Horner (ed.), *The Battles that Shaped Australia* (Allen & Unwin, St Leonards, 1994), p.34.

16. Nimitz to King, May 15, 1942, in Lundstrom, *op.cit.* p.160.

17. MacArthur statements from April 28 and May 6, 1942, in David Horner, *High Command* (Allen & Unwin, Sydney, 1992), pp.192–3.

18. With the exception of 14th Brigade (at Port Moresby with 30th Brigade), these were the actual Allied dispositions in May–July 1942. David Horner, *Crisis of Command* (Australian National University Press, Canberra, 1978).

19. Quoted in Horner, *High Command*, p.186.

20. Mrs. M. Bryson, quoted in Horner (ed.), *The Battles that Shaped Australia*, p.120.

21. Blamey's memoirs, quoted in M. McKernan and M. Browne (eds.), *Australia: Two Centuries of War and Peace* (Australian War Memorial, Sydney, 1988), p.263.

22. Inspired by the action of U.S. Marines on Iwo Jima.

*23. Both quotes are invented.

24. Saburo Hayashi, *Kogun: The Japanese Army in the Pacific War* (Greenwood Press, Westport, 1959), pp.41–8; and Fuchida and Okumiya, *op.cit.* pp.77–82.

25. H.P. Willmott, *The Barrier and the Javelin* (U.S. Naval Institute Press, Annapolis, 1983), pp.67–8.

# 7

# THE JAPANESE RAJ
## The Conquest of India

David C. Isby

The Japanese conquest of the British Indian Empire was one of the most dramatic successes of World War II. It was not a goal of Japan's opening offensive against the Allies in 1941–2, but it followed, domino-fashion, from the military success that this offensive achieved. The Empire's fall was the direct result of decades of unrest preceding the outbreak of war, which had undercut the legitimacy of British rule in many eyes, not only in the sub-continent but also in Britain. It was also made possible by Japan's willingness to use intelligence of this weakness to commit much of their strategic reserve – in ships, divisions, and fuel oil – that had been intended to maintain the defensive perimeter, to an offensive against India instead.

Throughout history, empire has succeeded empire. The British Indian Empire would surely have lasted but a scant few years more had it not been itself defeated and replaced by a Japanese successor as part of the tide of conquest that swept all Asia in 1942. Yet the same forces that had doomed the British Raj turned out also to make sure that the Japanese Indian Empire, and its impact on India and the sub-continent, would be even briefer than its predecessor.

### Overstretch that succeeded

The British Indian Empire had been generally peripheral in pre-war Japanese strategic thinking, including the issue of how its independence movement could best be used to Japanese advantage.[1] However, as the Japanese strategy moved towards one of confrontation with Western imperialism and economic presence in Asia, India took on additional importance.

The Japanese pre-war strategic reassessment of India initially saw it as the base of support of hostile forces in the Nan-yo, the resource-rich areas of Southeast Asia that were the Japanese strategic focus. They did not apply much of their limited planning resources to how this base function could be attacked, interdicted, or disrupted, or even what Japan's overall policy

166

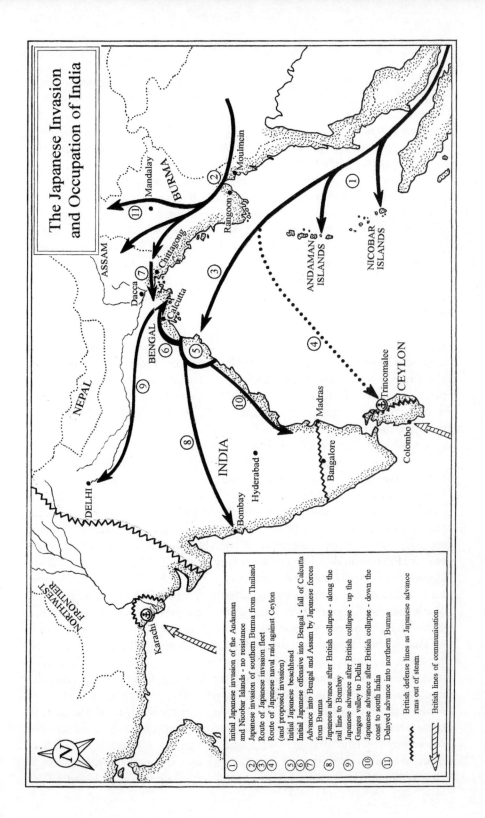

The Japanese Invasion
and Occupation of India

① Initial Japanese invasion of the Andaman
and Nicobar Islands - no resistance
② Japanese invasion of southern Burma from Thailand
③ Route of Japanese invasion fleet
④ Route of Japanese naval raid against Ceylon
(and proposed invasion)
⑤ Initial Japanese beachhead
⑥ Initial Japanese offensive into Bengal - fall of Calcutta
⑦ Advance into Bengal and Assam by Japanese forces
from Burma
⑧ Japanese advance after British collapse - along the
rail line to Bombay
⑨ Japanese advance after British collapse - up the
Ganges valley to Delhi
⑩ Japanese advance after British collapse - down the
coast to south India
⑪ Delayed advance into northern Burma

〰〰〰 British defense lines as Japanese advance
runs out of steam

⇗⇗⇗ British lines of communication

should be towards Indian nationalism and anti-imperialism. Yet the absence of planning and long-range thinking was easier to reconcile in the case of Japan than in the other combatants' strategy. This was because of the increasing tendency, as strategic options became narrower, to focus on a largely post-rational optimism that, if enough spirit imbued the leadership, enough guts, enough love of Japan, the way would become clear. Thus, rather than a specific plan, or even commitment to a planning purpose, the Japanese approach to India would be guided by an ability to respond to opportunities. More rationally, the Japanese stressed the achievement of what today would be called a 'rapid reaction' capability, stressing the principle of activeness. Realizing they were unlikely to prevail in a major battle of attrition, the Japanese made a point of being able to decide, plan, and act quickly to take advantage of transitory advantages. This was a goal of Japanese military thinking at the tactical, operational, and strategic levels alike.

This meant it was not a great stretch or a violation of precepts when, in the opening stages of the war, Japan came to realize that India would become a key member of the Greater East Asia Co-Prosperity Sphere, even though pre-war strategy had looked to Burma to provide its western perimeter.[2] Even Burma was a late addition, and Japanese operations there were originally intended only to cut off the Burma Road to China rather than opening a major front against the Allies.

The Liaison Conferences held in Tokyo in November 1941 had stressed the use of political and indirect penetration against India rather than direct military conquest.[3] This reflected Japanese caution at the potential for an open-ended ground war in Asia, as in China. Yet, within a few months, a number of changes would force the Japanese to re-assess their strategic perceptions of India. One factor that drew the Japanese towards a greater strategic focus on the sub-continent was the prospect of inter-allied cooperation. Even though Japan and Germany were not to be partners in a drive against the Soviet Union, the German successes in North Africa, the Middle East (including the abortive revolt in Iraq) and the possibility of a drive into south Asia from the southern flank of the Soviet Union, all suggested that German-Japanese cooperation could emerge into a valid strategic concept.

That it did not was not the fault of Ambassador Hiroshi Oshima, the Japanese ambassador in Berlin. He may never have understood the weakness in much of German strategy and their disinclination to look beyond the immediate operational situation.[4] But he and his German counterparts could both see that the British were having to divert additional resources to the western approaches to India, and that this could have the advantage of weakening the British ability to respond to a Japanese attack from the east. They also raised – but did not resolve – the issue of whether the objective of a move against India would be the disruption of Britain's world-wide lines of communication or whether it would be a continuation of Japan's expansion into Burma from Southeast Asia. The Germans were, naturally enough, most interested in an attack on Ceylon and subsequent attacks into the Indian Ocean. This would have a more direct potential impact on the Allied position in North Africa and the Middle East than it would on the battles that would shape Japan's future. In response, in Berlin in December 1941 Ambassador Oshima proposed a synchronized German-Japanese march on India. 'After the capture of Singapore, Japan must turn towards India. When Japan attacks India from the East, it would be most advantageous if German troops threaten India from the west'.[5]

Yet, even though German troops were never to get within striking range of India, the Japanese were encouraged to look in that direction by what proved to be an illusion of cooperation. This made sure India would be included in the objectives that expanded after the victories of 1941–2, even though it appeared remote from more immediate Japanese objectives.

However, as Japanese pre-war planning was swept away after the fall of Singapore, by what came to be called the 'victory disease', the 'Greater East Asia Co-Prosperity Sphere' was redefined to include India.[6] How this was implemented was not a foregone conclusion, for Japanese strategy and planning remained largely service-specific. The Japanese Navy reacted to the victories of 1942 by planning larger advances, focussing on Hawaii but also including India.[7] In the words of Admiral Matome Ugaki, chief of staff to the Combined Fleet, 'Our strategy aimed at an invasion of Hawaii, Fiji, Samoa and New Caledonia as well as dominating over India and the destruction of the British [Indian Ocean] squadron'.[8] However, the plans for the invasion of Australia were being finalized at this point, and the Japanese recognized a simultaneous attack on India as posing insurmountable problems.[9] Therefore, if both India and Australia were part of Japan's newly expanded strategic objectives, they would have to be prioritized.

## The plan is nothing, planning is everything

In early 1942, Prime Minister Tojo was the main supporter of operations against India.[10] He was opposed in this by Generals Count Hisaichi Terauchi (commander in chief of the Southern Army, with headquarters at Saigon) and Hajime Sugiyama (chief of the Army General Staff), and the various intelligence agencies. In addition to concern about Japan's strategic direction, they remained concerned about the dangers of success, which would leave Japan in occupation. They saw the Indians as incapable of establishing an orderly state after the British were driven out. These leaders had little time for non-Japanese allies and even distrusted their own collaborators of the Indian National Army (organized on Tojo's orders), much as they had originally distrusted the Burmese collaborators who they were now trying to organize to support Japanese control.[11]

Yet the Army found India a possible option, in part, as an alternative to ambitious naval plans for an expansion of the defensive perimeter throughout the Pacific.[12] It at least would not result in the piecemeal commitment of forces that the Navy's strategy would entail. If a decision was made for a move against India, planning would have to begin in January–February, at the end of the Malaya campaign. Any move against India before the May monsoon might mean delaying the campaign to occupy upper Burma, including the vital airfields at Mandalay and Lashio, controlling access to China. This would mean the forces now committed to Burma would have to deal with the remaining British and Chinese forces in upper Burma through the monsoon, with few resources available.

In early 1942 the Japanese saw the same two basic strategic options as the Germans (and British) did for offensive operations. A move against India could either strike at Ceylon, which then gave them the option of threatening Britain's Indian Ocean lifelines around the Cape of Good Hope; or strike directly at India, with a cross-border attack being launched from Burma as soon as the campaign there concluded. The mechanisms of attack were also undecided. Naval raids – the Navy's preferred option – and invasion were both considered.[13] The two invasion options were planned as 'Operation Number 11' and 'Operation Number 21', against Ceylon and India respectively.[14]

Japan's attacks against British forces seemed irresistible in the spring of 1942. The triumph of Singapore was followed by the relentless advance in Burma, despite Chinese intervention and the difficult terrain that, together with Japanese shoestring logistics, slowed their advance more than did the British. The question that had to be resolved was where the next target would be. Obviously, the conclusions of November 1941 were now overtaken by events.

The need to improvise follow-on strategic planning – where there was neither the time nor inclination for an extensive analysis of alternatives – started when Japan diverged from pre-war planning after the initial objectives of 1941–2 were met.[15] The legacy of pre-war planning meant that the Japanese realized that an improvised direct assault against India represented a gambler's throw of resources. It could lead to immediate or long-term disaster. However, the reality of the overall strategic situation meant that the Japanese recognized that if they did not win a battlefield victory over the Allies in the first six months, they were unlikely to win in the end. India was obviously the base from which the Allies' industrial superiority would allow the eventual build-up of forces and re-occupation of Burma and, beyond that, Southeast Asia. The Japanese were also under no illusions that the political turmoil in India might prevent this.

Implementing this high-risk strategy would be difficult. It would mean sending to India the exhausted troops from the Malaya and Java campaigns.

They would comprise the follow-up echelons. The divisions that would be responsible for the initial assault would have to be brought down from the central reserve in Japan and Manchuria. This was itself a risk. The divisions that had gone into Malaya had greatly benefited from intensive training in French Indochina, but there would be no time for that if the follow-on operations were to have the benefits of strategic momentum from Japan's victories.

Whether the target was to be Ceylon or India itself, an option including an invasion would require pulling together convoys of Japan's relatively few – and now increasingly vital – fast merchant ships. This meant disrupting scheduled convoy sailings and ensured that strategic stockpiles of petroleum, steel, and other strategic materials would be reduced to a level far below what was considered acceptable.

In addition to requiring new strategic re-planning, the Japanese advances also brought them into contact with new Asian populations. The Japanese came increasingly to see themselves as their propaganda presented them, as the deliverer of Asia from white control. The brutality of their own decades-long rule in Korea and their war against China never crossed the perceptual filter this view gave Japanese decision-makers. The contradictions that were increasingly pushing the British Indian Empire towards its end – how an Empire that legitimated its mobilization for war on the grounds of democracy and self-rule could deny this to an Indian Empire led by an Anglicized elite – did not exist in the Japanese context. Thus, the Japanese were surprised by the increasing tension between ruler and ruled in their new empire, and that this was not limited to the ethnic Chinese that were the first targets of their repression.

## The defense of India

The British were hastily improvising a defense of India. They had not previously considered a threat to India from the east.[16] With the threat coming so soon after the defeat at Singapore, there was little that could be done. Many of the available reserves – a division of British infantry, a wing of Hurricane fighters – had been lost in that debacle and the subsequent one in Java. On March 31, the British Joint Planning Staff assessed that if the Japanese decided on a bold offensive strategy against India, there was a danger of British defeat.[17]

The British were in a poor position to defend against any of the Japanese options. Churchill explained to a secret session of the House of Commons: 'Alternatively [to an invasion of Australia] the Japanese may invade India. There is no doubt of their ability, if they choose to concentrate their efforts, to invade and overrun a large part of India, to take Calcutta and Madras, and certainly to make very cruel air raids upon defenseless Indian cities'.[18] The Commander in Chief in India, Field Marshal Wavell – with only one

British and six poorly trained and equipped Indian divisions available outside the Northwest Frontier – saw the main threat as coming overland from Burma, but he was overruled by the Chiefs of Staff in London, who redeployed his British division to Ceylon.[19]

The Bengal Administration, adjacent to Burma, was in no shape to be in the front line of a major conflict. It was unable to cope with the influx of refugees and military reinforcements, at the same time matched by a resurgence in nationalist unrest. Districts such as Contai, Midnapore, and Dacca were in open revolt much of the time.[20] The limited number of British troops available rendered the internal security situation paramount. There was the threat of widespread insurrection, which increased as it increasingly appeared to much of the Indian population that the Japanese advance was unstoppable and that British rule in India was doomed.[21]

The Indian nationalist leadership divided on the Japanese threat that had appeared on their doorstep. The Congress Party, mainstream of Hindu nationalism, had opposed participation in the war, which had been entered into by the Viceroy without asking Indian approval. However, Congress was not united. Leaders such as Jawaharlal Nehru offered stronger Indian participation in the war effort in return for immediate independence or at least its guarantee. Radical members of the Congress party that had already diverged from the leadership pre-war, such as Subhash Bose, saw the Japanese as a positive force and sought their assistance.

The Muslim League, recently diverged with a claim for their own country as part of the former Empire, were more open to cooperation with the British, but were concerned about the threat of Hindu domination. Marxists such as M.N. Roy advocated strong allegiance to the cause of the United Nations that included the Soviet Union. Mahatma Gandhi promoted a policy of passive non-cooperation to the Japanese as the only moral policy. In short, there was little unity that could be 'operationalized', either to rally a patriotic defense against the Japanese invasion or to rise in support of it to gain independence.

An attempt to deal with the nationalist unrest that was undercutting the defense of India led to the British dispatch of the Cripps mission in March, 1942. This brought Sir Stafford Cripps, the British politician who had been most sympathetic to at least the Congress Party's approach to Indian nationalism in pre-war years, to make a deal. Between the nationalists' desire to use the moment of greatest peril for maximum political leverage and Churchill's and the Viceroy's unwillingness to make concessions at such a time, there was little common ground. Psychologically and politically, May 1942 found the British Indian Empire at the weakest point in its history. The Indian population had been impressed by Japanese power. The seemingly unstoppable advance had an impact on civilian and soldier alike similar to that which was seen in France in 1940 and in North Africa at the peak of Rommel's advance. As a result of this overall assessment that no resistance could be made to Japanese landings in the Calcutta area until at least June, the Admiralty believed emphasis should be on 'denial measures' such as preparation for demolitions.[22] The discussions of a wide-scale 'scorched earth' policy further reduced morale. No word had yet leaked out to India of Japanese atrocities in Southeast Asia, or that non-Chinese were not to be spared the full weight of Japanese rule.

## Japan invades India

The key decision was made by the Japanese to make a rapid thrust outside of what had been seen as their strategic sphere of influence and defensive perimeter only a few months before. The strike at India would have to be approved by the highest levels of both services and the government. The Japanese strategic goal was now to block access to China not by controlling airfields, but by defeating the British Indian Empire. Implementing the Clausewitzian concept of center of gravity with a vengeance, it aimed to deprive the Allies of bases from which they could both resupply China and mount an offensive to retake Southeast Asia.

The eventual plan was a variation of Operation Number 21 proposed by General Shojhiro Iida, 15th Army commander. He favored an offensive into the plain of the Ganges.[23] The final compromise was marrying the go-now approach with the amphibious component of Operation Number 11. It subsumed the plan, already advanced, for an Indian Ocean raid by Japan's carrier striking force supported by fast battleships and oilers. This force would remain committed to the action, but after their attack on Ceylon and the installations there, they would pursue any surviving British forces before covering the arrival of two slower follow-on forces, one a large invasion convoy, the other of battleships and their escorts to provide shore bombardment and to prevail against any surviving British battleships that tried to challenge the invasion force.

What was key in motivating this Japanese change of strategy, the decision that the strategic reserve would have the greatest value if committed against India rather than elsewhere, was improved intelligence. The Japanese had been weak on intelligence regarding their British opponents pre-war, until the capture of French Indochina had given them a base.[24] Then, aerial reconnaissance over Malaya had shown them how weak the British position was. The Japanese thus came late to grasp that for a numerically weaker attacker, intelligence is key, with its ability to locate the transitory advantages that an opportunistic planning process and a rapid deployment capability might exploit.

Before the war the Japanese had not achieved good intelligence coverage of the sub-continent. They greatly over-estimated the size of the forces in India well into 1942, believing there were a half-million men in thirty

(seven British, twenty-three Indian) divisions.[25] However, they may have
had a general idea that the newer, high-numbered Indian Army divisions
were raw and insufficiently trained, with the cadre of pre-war officers and
NCOs stretched very thin indeed. The Indian Army had never planned for
massive expansion, and its recruiting, training, and induction was still very
much dependent on 'hand crafting' in the hands of regimental officers and
NCOs. Nor was there an effective program in place to bring training lessons
from other fronts home to those units still forming in India.

But there were other intelligence sources that were able to convince the
Japanese that a strike directly at India would work as required. This was an
area where the Germans helped. German-Japanese cooperation had indeed
remained largely illusory, but intelligence was one area where the potential
pay-off was the highest, when disruption to British secure cable communications through the Middle East forced a greater reliance on longer routes
or, more frequently, radio messages. The Germans proved to be able to
intercept and decode long-haul communications between India and Britain,
which were then passed to the Japanese in a degree of inter-Axis cooperation
that had not been previously achieved.

From these reports the Japanese extrapolated the weakness of the forces
defending India – key information, to be sure – and, more importantly, the
sense of confusion and defeatism amongst the British, the idea that a
Japanese offensive move would be hindered more by their own limitations
than the resistance of the British Indian Empire. The Japanese were able to
realize for themselves that here was an area where the enemy really was
weakest in spirit – that neither Englishmen in London or Delhi, nor the
majority of Indians, were willing to make sacrifice to defeat the Japanese
because of the decline in the perceived legitimacy of British imperial rule –
and that this undercut any material advantages they might have.

To take advantage of this transitory crisis – before Churchill was able to
provide top-down leadership or the Indian Army was able to start
addressing the problem of the defense of India in an effective way – meant
striking before the monsoon set in mid-May.

The first stage of the operation was opened in mid-March, with the
invasion of the Andaman Islands (evacuated by their limited British garrison) as the Japanese Navy entered the Indian Ocean in earnest. In the first
two weeks, Vice Admiral Chuichi Nagumo's First Air Fleet operations failed
to sink the British battlefleet, which retired out of range, but sank the
carrier *Hermes*, the cruisers *Dorsetshire* and *Cornwall*, and large numbers of
smaller warships and merchant ships throughout the Indian Ocean. Once
the British air and naval threat had been reduced, the Japanese inflicted
heavy damage to the port at Trincomalee, including the tank farm and the
dockyard. The carriers then ranged northwards and repeated the same
treatment against Bengal, striking airfields and military installations around

Calcutta and Chittagong. This time, however, the port installations were not hit.

So far, this was consistent with the original plan for an Indian Ocean raid, although a few weeks in advance. But among the effects of concentrating Japan's carrier strength was preventing long-range reconnaissance aircraft from shadowing the troop convoy and the battle squadron as they entered the Indian Ocean under radio silence. The British, however, through U.S. supplied decrypts and other intelligence sources, were soon able to realize that this was not simply a carrier raid. However, whether Ceylon or India would be the target remained uncertain. Ceylon nevertheless received most of the reinforcements.

Thus it came as a surprise when, in early April, the Japanese seaborne invasion of India commenced with the main thrust, utilizing two divisions, coming ashore southwest of Calcutta at Balasore in Orissa state. Other, smaller forces came ashore between Chittagong and the right flank of the beachhead. By the standards of invasions, it was a small one, and the logistics were improvised and run on a shoestring even by Japanese standards. It was weeks before the first follow-on divisions were able to come ashore.

But while the Japanese were at risk from an immediate counterattack, they were strong enough to secure their beachhead from the immediate local counterattacks the British were able to launch. In early 1942 the British lacked a central reserve in India, their ability to move reserve formations down from the Northwest Frontier and the interior being limited by civil unrest which affected movement on the railroads and created problems with the infrastructure. These actions were not widespread, and the increasing civil unrest did not amount to a general rising, but the cutting of rail lines and destruction of telegraph lines at key moments prevented the British from shifting reserves against the Japanese beachhead.[26] The British responded by arresting the Congress party leadership, Gandhi, and many other leading Indian nationalists.

As a result the British were unable to launch a large-scale counterattack that could have pushed back the overstretched Japanese invasion. While to the British this appeared the proverbial 'stab in the back', it was rather the lack of reserves and British planning itself that prevented such an operation. The counterattacks launched were those envisioned by GHQ India in their initial defense plan, not a single hammer blow but rather multiple blows by uncoordinated, reduced-strength brigade forces.[27] In a series of battles in the initial weeks of the campaign, both before and after the Japanese capture of Calcutta, the British launched a number of counterattacks, which, because of the problems experienced by British commanders, ended up operating independently.

These counterattacks over the crucial weeks of the campaign were often marked by great heroism by British and Indian troops alike, and were often tactically proficient or clever but, in the end, were operationally futile. In this way, they resembled the offensive operations of the combined arms 'jock columns' in the Desert at the same time.

The initial Japanese carrier air attacks had defeated the limited British airpower in Ceylon and Bengal – the latter a numerically inferior force of Hawker Hurricanes and Curtiss Mohawks – and ensured there would be little air opposition to the invasion. Japanese bomber aircraft had been able to move forward to the airfields at Mandalay and Rangoon soon after they were taken, and these now launched a series of countervalue attacks on the cities of Bengal, especially Calcutta. As in Burma, the shock of the air attacks was much greater than the damage inflicted and led to the British decision not to try and defend Calcutta.

What happened after the Japanese flag was raised in Calcutta was exactly what was envisioned by the India Command's Joint Planning Staff in their assessment of March 14, 1942.[28] This included '(a) a big refugee problem, (b) a serious internal security problem, (c) the probability of fifth column activities in Bengal, (d) large scale desertion of labor from threatened areas paralyzing all industrial and transport activities, (e) breakdown in civil administration, (f) large scale looting, and (g) general loss of morale throughout the population of India which could not escape having an effect on the Indian forces.'

The arrival of the monsoon in mid-May was accompanied by the end of the British retreat from Burma, adding an overland threat to Bengal in addition to that from the expanding Japanese beachhead. The British thought the monsoon would bring a halt to military operations. What it actually did was impede the logistically light Japanese a great deal less than the British. As in Malaya and the Philippines, the Japanese demonstrated in India that they were able to function at the end of a supply line that was limited and frayed. The Japanese operated on appropriated food – causing starvation in the areas through which they advanced – and impressed transport.

By May, the Japanese threat to India was achieving the proportions that the British Joint Planning Staff had estimated two months earlier: eleven divisions by sea and two more advancing over the border from Burma.[29] Once Calcutta had been captured, the Japanese were faced with their next decision, of a main advance. The ultimate decision was for a drive westward, with Bombay as the ultimate objective.

The prospect of an advance across the sub-continent, with open flanks and a torturous supply line leading back to Japan, was a daunting one. Ceylon-based submarines had already started to exact losses from Japanese troop and supply convoys. But there was not the strong resistance that could have crumpled the over-stretched Japanese advance. Key to this was the British view – in Delhi, though not in London – that the situation was hopeless.[30] As with the French in 1940, this gave the potential for even limited operational and tactical defeats to have strategic results and to prevent available depth and resources from being effectively utilized. The fall of the Indian Empire resembled in many ways the fall of France. It was unable to recover from tactical and operational defeats because the national will and ability to resist was low. Many of the Indian divisions proved as unable to resist as equally untrained and under-equipped French reservists did in 1940.

There was no mass rising of Indians to meet the Japanese, though the unrest did greatly hinder British military efforts. It did not matter that only a minority of the educated classes in the Indian Empire would say 'better the Japanese than the British' or, in the case of many Muslims, 'Better the Japanese than the Hindu-dominated Congress Party', just as only a minority of Frenchmen actually did say 'Better Hitler than Leon Blum' in the years before their defeat in 1940. These attitudes rather showed that they did not have the will that could be mobilized for a war effort involving all of society and its economy the way Stalin was able to mobilize the Soviet Union in 1941 and – without the use of secret police – Churchill mobilized Britain in 1940.

The Indian Empire was also suffering from a crisis of legitimacy in 1942. In some ways it was not the educated Indians who wanted independence that were important. The British had devised the military elements of the Indian Empire so that they did not matter, the manpower being provided by those groups that had traditionally been associated with the British Army. Resources for the war effort were, as required, to be provided by a top-down command economy. But increasingly, not the Indians, but the British leadership (and the Anglicized Indians who were also part of the leadership classes of British India) did not believe in the Empire. They were unwilling to fight and die for the maintenance of British rule in India, to endure any struggle, as Britain had been in 1940.

This led to the collapse of resistance throughout the sub-continent. The Japanese largely advanced into a vacuum. The advance was slowed by no more than the summer heat and the general anarchy as British rule collapsed. The British held on in Ceylon, in the south – the Japanese did not think it worthwhile advancing there – and in the Punjab and Sind, with the port of Karachi providing a haven for reinforcements. Additional British divisions arrived in May and June,[31] and U.S. aircraft arrived to provide air cover. This reflected the decision to go with Operation 21 rather than Operation 11 as the model for the invasion, which limited the Japanese ability to move against British lines of communication running to those areas they still held. While Ceylon would become increasingly isolated as the Japanese expanded southwards, they were unable to pull together the additional resources that would have been required for an invasion.

## Attempting an occupation

The most immediate result of the fall of Delhi and the flight of the viceregal government to Karachi was its benefits for the Japanese position in China. Without the logistics and communications support that came from bases in India, Allied airpower in China largely eroded away. The Japanese ability to make advances in China was limited only by the increasing shortage of their own resources which, in turn, was compounded by the invasion of India.

As the Japanese occupation of the vast majority of the sub-continent began, the first reaction of the Indian populace was curiosity.[32] They had been totally unarmed as a result of British policy, intended to prevent active resistance as well as to create feelings of powerlessness, so could not have offered active resistance even had they been so motivated. The Indian population was also faced with more immediate problems of a non-functional economy. There was widespread destruction of infrastructure and industry, as there had been in Burma and the Andaman Islands.[33] This meant that the potential for widespread food shortages soon became very real.

In the aftermath of their occupation of major objectives in India, the Japanese repeated their practice, as in Hong Kong, Singapore, and Rangoon, of having British prisoners sweep streets, perceiving this to be a ritualized act of public humiliation. However, as in the previous incidents, this had the effect of increasing respect for the British military among the population, seeing them maintaining discipline under difficult conditions. This, along with the immediate economic disruption, led to the now-departed British rule quickly being recalled with nostalgia by many Indians.

Ill-prepared to control much of India at the same time as it was trying to do the same in China, the Japanese took over the British system of administration, including its non-European personnel, wherever feasible. As a result, it appeared to be a continuation of the Raj under a new, more brutal and less effective, leadership. Effectively, the administration was rooted in the hands of a relatively few Japanese military officers, with the Army proving to be considerably more brutal and repressive than the Navy in practice.

Indian nationalists, while happy to be relieved of British rule, did not find the Japanese sympathetic to their demands for self-determination. To the Japanese, the Congress Party leadership was not seen as fit material for collaboration. The Japanese may have used the rhetoric of removing a dying imperialism from Asia and reviving Asia for the Asians, but when they were presented with the reality of the leadership that the British had jailed earlier in 1942, they decided to leave them in jail. The Japanese decided that these were basically no more than brown Englishmen, and if they had resisted the rule of a distant British emperor, they were even more likely to resist the rule of a Japanese one.

Gandhi, despite his worldwide stature, was subject to continued confinement. When his followers in Orissa State tried to meet Japanese extraction of in-kind food taxes with non-violent resistance, they were met with heavy firepower and Gandhi himself was threatened with summary beheading. Fortunately for the Japanese, calmer heads in Tokyo prevented this, but it was a clear demonstration of the rapidly developing tensions between the occupiers and occupied. Throughout India, the general attitude towards the Japanese followed that of the Andaman islanders who first experienced their occupation: impressed by their energy, efficiency, and discipline but horrified by their atrocities and the brutality inherent in their system.

The Japanese had soon brought into India their own army of Indians recruited from prisoners of war and ethnic Indians in Southeast Asia after their victories in Singapore and Hong Kong.[34] These units had seen little fighting in the Japanese conquest of India, being mainly used for logistics and second-line duties, including occupation. They were important in allowing the Japanese to try and legitimize their authority by borrowing the cause of Indian nationalism. However, the disintegration of the 'voluntary' Indian National Army in December, 1942, showed how ineffective the Japanese were at dealing with the realities of India in anything other than the direct top-down attempt to work through the control of local intermediaries that had characterized their actions from Korea through China into Southeast Asia.[35]

The Bengal famine of 1943 led to the first major crisis of Japanese rule. It took several million lives and reflected the poor harvests in much of India and the loss of rice imports from Burma. The Japanese had commandeered much of the remaining transportation assets to support their continuing military campaigns against the British in the south and west, so there was little ability to shift food. Despite repeated air attacks on Ceylon, which suppressed much of its offensive capability, Japan continued to collect taxes in rice at the height of the famine, as it had in similar circumstances in Java.

The Japanese did try to alleviate hardship in the areas of India they occupied. They tried to increase rice yields. They tried to introduce sweet potatoes and other alternative crops. Conscript labor was rounded up whenever it could be identified – which in India often meant in urban areas – under military direction and was sent to the field for what amounted to slave labor either in agriculture or on infrastructure repair. Fugitives from this conscription were soon on the move throughout Japanese-occupied India.

But, in the final analysis, the Japanese Indian Empire was faced with widespread famine conditions because of its inability to cope with the lack of petrol, the disastrous collapse of internal communications, and the continued destruction of war, including the loss of coastal shipping. In response, the Japanese attempted to build and repair infrastructure. Their efforts at building airbases and railroads were more intense than those that the British had tried to put in place before they were defeated. The Japanese made massive use of prisoner and conscript labor, as in Southeast Asia.

Despite the declaration of the nominal independence of India in these efforts, the Japanese did not invest heavily in building Indian institutions or forces that they could use. They showed no real interest in respecting either the traditional cultures of the sub-continent or in the modernized and educated classes and their capabilities. The Indian National Army was rebuilt after its December, 1942, collapse, but while its manpower strength was considerable, it had little real effectiveness. Like the puppet forces in Japanese-occupied China and Manchuria, it was used primarily for internal security.

This approach to occupation led to the Japanese becoming increasingly familiar with the indigenous tradition of revolt in the sub-continent. This had been focused against foreign rule since long before the British appeared and was now reflected in increasing, if disorganized, opposition to Japanese rule. This was combined with the view of educated Indians that the Japanese offered all of the oppressive features of British rule without any of its enlightenment. Throughout Indian society, there was a hatred of the Japanese military police. This was compounded by widespread Japanese use of mass executions and torture, especially where espionage or sabotage was suspected. Gratuitous executions became a mark of Japanese rule.

### Japan loses the Empire

The fate of Japan's Indian empire was not determined by events in the sub-continent itself, but rather by the decisive battles fought against the United States in the Pacific. The Japanese also found that they could no more complete the military occupation of the sub-continent than they could that of China. They could hold most of what was militarily and economically valuable, but occupying the frontiers of British India or even, beyond that, the passes of the Hindu Kush that provide a natural forward defense, was far beyond Japan's capability.

In the long term, the sub-continent was peripheral to both Britain and Japan. The British, short on resources, were so absorbed by the struggle for Europe and the Mediterranean that the preservation of an Indian Empire that would almost inevitably end or be transformed soon after the conflict was a distant third priority.

The British defeat in India accelerated the inevitable process of the British move to junior partner in the Anglo-American alliance. This forced the

British to adjust policies to U.S. requirements if they wanted to receive the necessary resources to continue the conflict. This was among the motivating reasons behind the British grant of independence, in the form of 'dominion status', to the remaining four British-occupied provinces of western India – Punjab, Sind, Baluchistan, and the Northwest Frontier – in 1943. There was considerable unrest at this. The Sikhs of the Punjab were particularly reluctant to become part of the new state, so were given autonomy and had to be given the chance to opt out post-war.

With most of India occupied by the Japanese, the British had to give greater weight to the Muslim population of the west, with the new dominion being a Muslim-majority area. But the British realized that the Muslim League, under Ali Jinnah, had already been diverging on a course towards partition. This had been opposed by the Congress Party and the Hindu majority but, as they were now under Japanese occupation, they had to be content with promises of their own dominion on liberation.

In the new dominion, named 'Pakistan', the British also established a government-in-exile of an independent India. The need to have at least a nominally Indian government involved also forced the British to transfer back almost all of the seven Indian Army divisions that were overseas at the time of the Japanese invasion. These would, along with newly formed Pakistani Divisions (equipped by the U.S., though still trained by the British) and U.S. and British divisions, be the forces that would have to eject the Japanese from India.

This new Indian government was not built around Indian nationalist leaders – since these were already in Japanese custody – but was drawn from major landowners in the Punjab and refugees, including a number of the native rulers of pre-war 'non-British' India. Whenever possible, the British made sure that leaders linked with the Indian Army and the 'martial races' of India received the political power.

This series of changes reflected U.S. political pressure. Since U.S. air-power and extensive ground troops had been deployed into Karachi and up into the Punjab, American domestic political concerns insisted that this had to be seen as a battle for liberation, not to re-establish the British Indian Empire. There was little even the most stalwart empire loyalists in London could do about the situation.

The period between late 1942 and 1944, the two years prior to the Anglo-American move back into India, included limited grand offensives towards Bombay and Delhi and moves to secure control of the air and sea around Japanese-controlled India. This involved the build-up of strategic bombers in and around Karachi. These hit targets throughout South Asia. Ceylon, which previously had been reinforced only by means of hard-fought Malta-style convoy battles, was now turned into a jumping off point for air and naval operations that severed the Japanese logistic lifeline except for a trickle flowing in overland from Thailand.

The Japanese were unable to put in place a system of indirect rule that might have secured their Indian Empire, for as the Allies advanced the Indians looked to them increasingly as liberators. The Allied offensive was a slow and deliberate one compared to Japan's lightning victory, but in the end it was inevitable that Japan was unable to hold its Indian Empire. The Japanese flag was hauled down – in Delhi, Calcutta, and throughout India – and replaced with the flag of an independent Dominion of India that had been created expressly to defeat it.

It is readily apparent that Japanese occupation transformed the Indian movement towards independence. While pre-war Indian nationalists such as Nehru had shown sympathy for a policy of non-alignment with pre-war great power competition, the effects of the Japanese occupation were to burn the necessity for collective security into the post-war Indian consciousness as effectively as it did that of the French in Europe. Post-war Indian policy was shaped by the need to reconcile this requirement with the nationalist impetus of many of their policies. This prevented the move towards international isolation that the Japanese occupation had on Burma.

Post-war, India took a different course than it would have if the pre-war nationalists had led the movement to independence. As it was, independence came with liberation. Those few of the pre-war leaders who survived Japanese captivity – Gandhi had starved himself to death in a fruitless hunger strike – were seen as irrelevant. The leaders of the Dominion of India were landowners, native princes, and men thrust forward from the Indian Army, conservative pragmatists. While strong nationalists, they realized India's future would lie primarily with the United States and secondarily with Britain, much as the leaders of Australia and New Zealand did. This included membership in U.S.-led regional defense organizations.

The Dominion of India's pragmatic focus extended to the Dominion of Pakistan. While regretting partition, they saw this as reflecting necessity and removing the potential irritant of the Northwest Frontier. Relations between the two countries, within the Commonwealth, were cordial. The Dominion of Pakistan also joined post-war U.S.-organized regional security organizations. Ceylon's wartime British occupation was reflected in it remaining a colony for many years thereafter.

The Japanese occupation of India, even where brief, has left lasting resentment. On the positive side, there was only a brief spate of building. Japanese had a passion for building and public works where the Western colonial powers had tended to leave well enough alone where it had not benefited the imperatives of control or benefited the extractive economy. In the Andaman Islands the Japanese built roads and airfields and port facilities where the British had been content to have the minimal amount that the islands' plantation-and-prison economy required.

The ephemeral Japanese Raj had, however, been for the Empire a strategic success. Despite defeats in the Pacific and eventual defeat in India, the Japanese had blocked the resupply routes to China long enough for the rotten Nationalist Government to finally fall apart in late 1944. Much of the Japanese Army in China was transferred to Indochina, where its mass was able to slow Allied advance to a crawl along the Mekong River. The badly wounded Soviet Union, whose forces had met the American General Patton in Eastern Poland, decided to honor its treaty of neutrality with Japan, freeing more divisions from the Kwangtung Army in Manchuria. Exhausted in Europe, Britain's Atlee Government had no more taste for war, especially after Singapore was recovered. Even the remorseless Americans were brought around with the quiet Japanese offer to evacuate the Philippines. The Treaty of Lima in 1946 left Japan with most of Indochina and China and a few small problems named Ho Chi Minh and Mao Tse-Tung.

## The reality

The changing Japanese options and plans regarding India are those that were actually considered. As it was, the Japanese settled for 'The Indian Ocean Adventure' of spring, 1942, to support their invasion of Burma. It was 1944 before the Japanese tried an overland invasion of India, which was defeated.

The British plans for the defense of India are the actual ones. The events once the Japanese invade are taken from British appreciation of the 'worst possible case' of a Japanese invasion, which Japan could have used an intelligence advantage to achieve.

The British failure in the invasion is assumed. Initial British defensive plans collapsed in both the 1941 invasion of Malaya and the 1944 invasion of India. In the latter case, there were enough resources, space, and time available to compensate for the initial Japanese success. That was unlikely to be the case in spring, 1942.

The Indian unrest and the arrest of nationalist leaders are those that actually took place in August, 1942, brought forward by a few months. Today's India was shaped by the emergence of the Japanese threat in 1942, transforming the independence movement.

The conduct of the Japanese occupation is taken from that in China and in Southeast Asia, with India-specific information taken from their occupation of the Andaman Islands. Unlike the Germans in the Channel Islands, the Japanese did not set out to make the Andamans a model occupation. The eventual Japanese defeat in India is what they experienced in Burma writ large.

# Bibliography

Boyd, Carl, *Hitler's Japanese Confidant: General Oshima Hiroshi and MAGIC Intelligence, 1941–1945* (University Press of Kansas, Lawrence, 1993).

Broomfield, J.M., *Elite Conflict in a Plural Society* (University of California Press, Berkeley, 1968).

Chatterjee, A.C., *India's Struggle For Freedom* (Chuckerbutly & Chatterjee, Calcutta, 1947).

Drea, Edward J., *In the Service of the Emperor* (University of Nebraska Press, Lincoln, 1999).

Ellsbree, W., *Japan's Role in Southeast Asian National Movements 1940–45* (Harvard University Press, Cambridge, 1953).

Fay, Peter Ward, *The Forgotten Army: India's Armed Struggle for Independence, 1942–45* (University of Michigan Press, Ann Arbor, 1993).

Goldstein, Donald M., and Dillon, Katherine V. (eds.), *Fading Victory: The Diary of Admiral Matome Ugaki, 1941–45* (University of Pittsburgh Press, Pittsburgh, 1991).

Hayashi, Saburo, and Coox, Alvin D., *Kogun: The Japanese Army in the Pacific War* (Marine Corps Association, Quantico, 1959).

James, Robert Rhode (ed.), *Winston S. Churchill: His Complete Speeches, vol.6* (Cassell, London, 1974).

Lebra, Joyce (ed.), *Japan's Great East Asia Co-Prosperity Sphere* (Oxford University Press, Kuala Lumpur, 1975).

Ohmae, Toshikazu, 'Japanese Operations in the Indian Ocean', in David C. Evans (ed.), *The Japanese Navy in World War II in the Words of Former Japanese Naval Officers* (U.S. Naval Institute Press, Annapolis, 1986).

Prasad, Bisheshwar, *Defense of India: Policy and Plans* (Orient Longmans, Delhi, 1963).

Sudata, Deb Chaudbury, *Japanese Imperialism and the Indian National Movement: A Study of the Political and Psychological Impact of Possible Invasion and Actual Occupation* (University of Illinois at Champagne-Urbana, Ph.D. dissertation [UMI 9236439], 1992).

Takushiro, Hattori, *The Complete History of the Greater East Asia War, vol.2* (500th Military Intelligence Service Group, Tokyo, 1953).

Toland, John, *The Rising Sun* (Random House, New York, 1970).

Voigt, Johannes H., *India in the Second World War* (Arnold-Heinemann, Delhi, 1987).

## NOTES

1. See generally W. Ellsbree, *Japan's Role in Southeast Asian National Movements 1940–45* (Harvard University Press, Cambridge, 1953), and Joyce Lebra (ed.), *Japan's Great East Asia Co-Prosperity Sphere* (Oxford University Press, Kuala Lumpur, 1975).
2. Lebra, *op.cit.* p.x.
3. Johannes H. Voigt, *India in the Second World War* (Arnold-Heinemann, Delhi, 1987), p.86.
4. Carl Boyd, *Hitler's Japanese Confidant* (University Press of Kansas, Lawrence, 1993), p.38.
5. John Toland, *The Rising Sun* (Random House, New York, 1970), p.245.
6. *Ibid.*
7. Saburo Hayashi and Alvin D. Coox, *Kogun: The Japanese Army in the Pacific War* (The Marine Corps Association, Quantico, 1959), pp.42–3.
8. Donald M. Goldstein and Katherine V. Dillon (eds.), *Fading Victory: The Diary of*

*Admiral Matome Ugaki, 1941–45* (University of Pittsburgh Press, Pittsburgh, 1991), p.128.

 9. Japanese Ministry of Foreign Affairs, Document No.4076, *Translated Records* (University Publications of America).

10. A.C. Chatterjee, *India's Struggle For Freedom* (Chuckerbutly & Chatterjee, Calcutta, 1947).

11. *Ibid.*

12. Edward J. Drea, *In the Service of the Emperor* (University of Nebraska Press, Lincoln, 1999), p.34–6.

13. *Ibid* p.36.

14. Hattori Takushiro, *The Complete History of the Greater East Asia War, vol.2* (500th Military Intelligence Service Group, Tokyo, 1953), p.156.

15. On naval planning for the Indian Ocean, see Toshikazu Ohmae, 'Japanese Operations in the Indian Ocean', in David C. Evans (ed.), *The Japanese Navy in World War II in the Words of Former Japanese Naval Officers* (Naval Institute Press, Annapolis, 1986), pp.106–10.

16. Bisheshwar Prasad, *Defense of India: Policy and Plans* (Orient Longmans, Delhi, 1963), pp.136–9.

17. *Ibid* p.139.

18. On April 23, 1942. Robert Rhode James (ed.), *Winston S. Churchill: His Complete Speeches, vol.6* (Cassell, London, 1974), p.6618.

19. Voigt, *op.cit.* p.106.

20. J.M. Broomfield, *Elite Conflict in a Plural Society* (University of California Press, Berkeley, 1968), p.305.

21. Voigt, *op.cit.* p.107.

22. *Ibid* p.107.

23. *Ibid* p.183.

24. See generally Hayashi and Coox, *op.cit.* pp.31–6.

25. *Ibid* p.44.

26. This is what actually happened in August, 1942, when historically India was in danger from a post-monsoon Japanese advance.

27. Prasad, *op.cit.* pp.170–83.

28. *Ibid* pp.153–5.

29. *Ibid* p.160.

30. Voigt, *op.cit.* p.144.

31. *Ibid* p.168.

32. Deb Chaudbury Sudata, *Japanese Imperialism and the Indian National Movement: A Study of the Political and Psychological Impact of Possible Invasion and Actual Occupation* (University of Illinois at Champagne-Urbana, Ph.D. dissertation [UMI 9236439], 1992), p.228.

33. *Ibid* pp.229–32.

34. See generally Peter Ward Fay, *The Forgotten Army: India's Armed Struggle for Independence, 1942–45* (University of Michigan Press, Ann Arbor, 1993).

35. *Ibid* p.201.

# 8
# GUADALCANAL
# The Broken Shoestring

John D. Burtt

There was anger in the man's eyes, anger as he watched his men — unbeaten in battle, unbowed by lack of supply or sleep, undaunted by debilitating terrain or fanatical enemy — load landing craft to leave the island they had defended for two months. Everything in his personality and training told him to stay and keep the island and its valuable airfield out of the hands of his enemy. But his superior feared disaster and ordered him to evacuate. So Major General Alexander Vandegrift watched in anger as his First Marine Division withdrew from Guadalcanal.

## The situation

After the setbacks at Coral Sea and Midway, Japanese plans changed a little, but they continued to pursue the strategic initiative. The Imperial Japanese Navy postponed, then cancelled its push south to take New Caledonia, the Fijis, and Samoa. Instead it formed the Eighth Fleet, stationed at Rabaul, to guard its southern conquests and approaches. Vice Admiral Gunichi Mikawa, a soft-spoken warrior, commanded the Eighth Fleet, a collection of cruisers and destroyers. Foiled at Coral Sea, the Army chose to continue its advance against Port Moresby, New Guinea, with an overland assault across the Owen Stanley Mountains, landing at Buna on the island's north coast on July 21, 1942.

Almost overlooked were Japanese moves in the southern Solomons. On May 3, they landed on Tulagi Island and began establishing a seaplane base, primarily for reconnaissance. Two weeks later a recommendation to build an advanced airbase on the nearby island of Guadalcanal was made to the Imperial Navy General Staff. Such an airbase would strengthen the outer perimeter of Japan's advance and put pressure on the supply line between the United States and Australia. The Staff approved the airbase on June 13. On July 6, 2,600 men of the 11th and 13th Naval Construction Units arrived to begin work.

Meanwhile, United States Army and Navy leaders were locked in

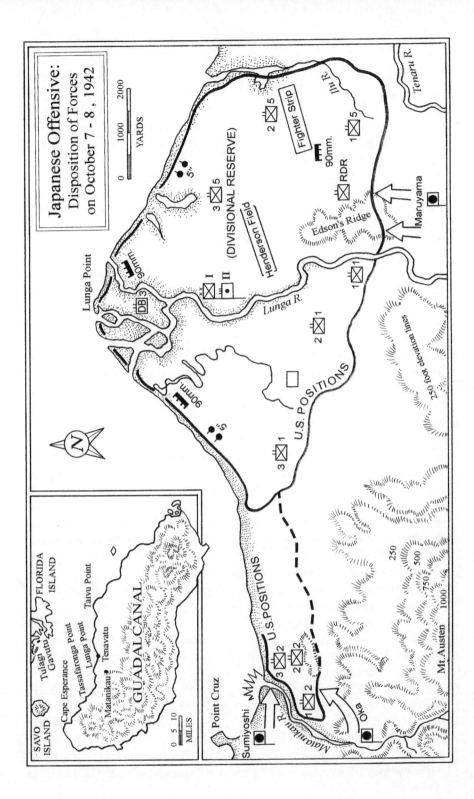

contentious discussions on how to take advantage of the victory at Midway. General Douglas MacArthur wanted all assets assigned to support his plan to move up through New Guinea, but the U.S. Navy was reluctant to commit its limited carrier forces to the narrow waters there. On July 2 a compromise between Army and Navy plans was reached, and the three-task Operation Pestilence was born. The Navy would seize the Santa Cruz Islands and Tulagi in the Solomon Islands as Task One. MacArthur would occupy the rest of the Solomons, Lae, Salamaua, and the northwest coast of New Guinea in Task Two. The final task was the seizure of the Japanese base at Rabaul. Word of the arrival of construction units on Guadalcanal forced a modification of Task One to include the capture of the new airfield before it became operational. Operation Watchtower was born.

Overall command of the U.S. Navy in the South Pacific was entrusted to Rear Admiral Robert L. Ghormley. Until his assignment to the Pacific he was the Special Naval Observer in London. Under Ghormley was Rear Admiral Richard K. Turner, assigned as the Amphibious Force Commander. The aircraft carriers *Enterprise*, *Wasp*, and *Saratoga* under Vice Admiral Jack Fletcher would provide support. The First Marine Division, commanded by Major General Alexander A. Vandegrift, would make the actual landing.[1]

Vandegrift's Marines went into Watchtower as a cobbled together organization. He had only two of his three regiments, the First and Fifth Marines. The Seventh Marines were stationed on Samoa protecting that vital island. To replace the Seventh, the Second Marine Regiment of the Second Marine Division on the Atlantic coast was hastily built up and sent west. In addition to these three infantry regiments, Vandegrift would have the Eleventh Marine Artillery Regiment, First Raider Battalion, First Parachute Battalion, and the Third Defense Battalion. The last, armed with 90 mm anti-aircraft guns and 5-inch coastal batteries, would be crucial to the defense of the island. In total some 19,000 troops would be committed to this first offensive.

There was very little hard information on the targets and less time to get it. The Marines headed for Guadalcanal knowing little about the terrain, landing beaches, climate or, even worse, enemy dispositions. Fortunately, plans were made assuming an enemy garrison of some 7,500 troops — double what was actually on the target islands. Loading of the transports with supplies and men was chaotic, leading to the operation's unofficial nickname: Shoestring.

After a week of sailing, eighty-two ships of the Navy's Task Force 61 entered the waters near their objective and opened fire on August 7, 1942.

## The first phase

The landings on Guadalcanal met virtually no resistance. The First and Fifth Marines landed east of the airfield and moved inland. The field was captured the next day, with the Japanese construction units retreating into the jungle. Across the channel, more difficulty was experienced in securing Tulagi, Florida, and the smaller islands of Gavutu and Tanambogo. The First Parachute Battalion suffered almost sixty percent casualties on Gavutu, forcing Vandegrift to release the divisional reserve, the Second Marines, to finish the job. At the end of August 8, however, resistance had effectively been eliminated, and the uncompleted airfield on Guadalcanal captured.

The invasion caught the Japanese completely off guard. They assumed they had the initiative and had done little to prepare for what should have been an obvious Allied step following Midway. In part, the lack of foresight and preparation was due to the poor communication between Army and Navy leaders – the Army still did not know about the Midway disaster. The first Japanese reaction to the invasion was an air attack by Rabaul-based bombers, originally intended for a bombing run on Port Moresby and still armed for that mission. Eighteen Mitsubishi G4M Betty bombers arrived in early afternoon and were rudely met by the covering force of U.S. carrier fighters. Six Japanese aircraft were shot down without inflicting a single hit. An attack later in the day by nine Aichi D3A Val dive-bombers (operating beyond their capability of returning to Rabaul) did manage one hit on the destroyer *Mugford*, but none of the nine attacking aircraft survived. Attacks the next day managed to hit the transport *George Elliot*, but cost seventeen of the twenty-three aircraft involved. In two days of attacks, the bomber force at Rabaul was nearly wiped out.

Swift naval reaction came from Admiral Mikawa. He initially hesitated because his fleet had never trained together, but he knew that the enemy had to be attacked. He sortied with his full force, heading south. His Eighth Fleet was a tough, confident group of five heavy cruisers (*Chokai*, *Aoba*, *Kako*, *Kinusaga*, and *Furataka*), two light cruisers (*Tenryu* and *Yubari*) and one destroyer (*Yunagi*). With little hard information, Mikawa simply planned to attack the enemy at night. Japanese doctrine of nocturnal torpedo attacks had proved effective in all their modern wars and was augmented by excellent optics, flashless powder, and extremely powerful, long-ranged 'Long Lance' torpedoes, carried by all Japanese cruisers and destroyers.

Mikawa's force was sighted several times in its passage, but the sightings were delayed in a clumsy chain of communications. The Americans had meanwhile lost a good portion of their covering force. Fletcher informed Turner he was pulling his carriers south earlier than planned due to the increasing number of torpedo aircraft being thrown at them. He sailed at midday on August 9, leaving protection of the beachhead to the force of Allied cruisers and destroyers commanded by Rear Admiral V.A.C. Crutchley, Royal Navy. Crutchley had been the commander of the

Australian Squadron prior to his appointment as Turner's deputy for Operation Watchtower in deference to the Allied nature of the naval forces involved. Crutchley positioned his forces in two groups, on either side of Savo Island, some fifteen miles from the beachhead. The southern group consisted of the heavy cruisers H.M.A.S. *Canberra* and U.S.S. *Chicago*, with the destroyers *Patterson* and *Bagley*. The northern group had the American heavy cruisers *Vincennes*, *Quincy*, and *Astoria*, and the destroyers *Wilson* and *Helm.*[2] Further out, the destroyers *Blue* and *Ralph Talbot* picketed the approaches to the anchorage.

Mikawa managed to evade the picket destroyers and enter the area south of Savo Island at 0143 on August 9. By the time *Patterson* radioed a warning the Japanese had launched torpedoes and opened fire. *Canberra* took the brunt of fire and was quickly put out of action. *Chicago* lost her bow to a torpedo and limped off to the west and out of the fight before she could respond with anything more than a few shots from her 5-inch secondary batteries.

The brief battle with the southern force split the Japanese column, four of the heavy cruisers in one, the rest of the ships in the other. The two columns swept north and within minutes encountered the Allied northern group, still unaware that the Japanese were upon them. The three U.S. cruisers were not ready for the storm of fire that struck them from both sides and were only able to respond feebly before being inundated with shells and torpedoes. All three were effectively destroyed in fifteen minutes of firing.

Mikawa assessed his situation. His ships had expended half their ammunition and torpedoes, and were scattered by the brief fight. His flagship *Chokai* had suffered the only real damage during the exchange when a salvo from *Quincy* killed some thirty crewmen around the cruiser's chartroom. His staff estimated two hours to reassemble in order to push on to the transport anchorage. Unaware that the American carriers had departed, he felt justifiably concerned for his ships should they linger too long off the island and be caught by aircraft in daylight. He chose caution and sailed north. Ironically, on his way home the American submarine *S-44* torpedoed and sank the cruiser *Kako*.

He left chaos behind: four cruisers sunk or sinking, over 1,700 men killed or wounded. The success of the landings had been reversed in forty minutes of battle at sea. Feeling incapable of defending the remaining ships, especially without air cover, Turner chose to withdraw. The withdrawal carried away 1,800 Marines of the Second Marines and most of the construction equipment needed to complete the airfield. Vandegrift's Marines were left with enough ammunition for four days of fighting and about one month's worth of rations, including food the Japanese had left behind.

When reconnaissance noted that the American ships were gone, the Japanese assumed that only a small force had been left on the island. They had previously estimated the Americans to be in divisional strength, but the lack of naval support let them downgrade their estimate. The 17th Army was given the assignment of taking the airfield back. It designated the 35th Infantry Brigade under Major General Kiyotaki Kawaguchi, augmented by troops from the 4th and 28th Infantry Regiments, to carry out the recapture. The 28th under Colonel Kiyoano Ichiki was immediately available on Guam. It had been originally tasked with occupying Midway, but lost that job after the naval disaster. It now began its move while the 17th Army prepared detailed orders. By August 15 Ichiki's first 900 men were ready to deploy to Guadalcanal. His specific orders were to recapture the airfield if possible, and if not, to await reinforcements, expected in ten days. To support the move, the Imperial Japanese Navy began to transfer its carriers south toward the island.

On Guadalcanal, the Marines kept busy. In the absence of their own construction equipment they made use of that left behind by the Japanese – trucks, explosives, steam rollers, and two narrow gauge locomotives. On August 12 they named the emerging airstrip Henderson Field, after Major Lofton Henderson, a Marine flight leader killed at Midway. The next day an amphibious Catalina made the first landing there.

Elsewhere the Marines were learning the hard way about their two enemies: the terrain and the Japanese. A small patrol, investigating a report of Japanese wishing to surrender, was virtually wiped out, with the survivor spreading tales of flashing swords used on his comrades. A tentative push westward across the Matanikau River achieved little success but proved how difficult operations in the jungle would be.

Then the plans of both sides came together in a week of frantic activity. On August 19, Colonel Ichiki and the first half of his regiment were landed at Taivu Point, some twenty miles east of the Marine perimeter. He moved swiftly toward his objective. The reinforcements from 35th Brigade were preparing to follow up this landing, with support from Japan's carrier force.

The 20th of August was a momentous day for the Marines – nineteen Grumman F4F Wildcat fighters and twelve SBD Dauntless dive-bombers landed at Henderson. The Wildcats were slower than the Japanese Zeros, but they could dive faster and were better armored. In addition, their six .50-caliber machine-guns were very effective against the lightly armored Zeros and Bettys. The SBDs could carry a 1,000-pound bomb, which was more than the Bettys could, and could deliver it accurately – as the Japanese carriers at Midway had found out. With these planes on Guadalcanal, the stakes became markedly greater for both sides. The Marines now had land-based teeth.

That night, at around 0300 hours, Ichiki attacked the Marine line on Alligator Creek, erroneously noted on the Marines' maps as the Tenaru River. Ichiki sent three of his four rifle companies straight ahead without reconnaissance or other probes. The Japanese waded through withering fire from the 2nd Battalion of the First Marines and 37 mm anti-tank cannons firing canister. Although the line was breached momentarily, the Japanese attack failed. At dawn the 1st Battalion, First Marines, swept in on the southern flank of the Japanese and, with the aid of four light tanks, virtually annihilated the entire force. For a cost of forty-four Marines, some 800 Japanese soldiers were killed. Ichiki radioed his failure, then committed suicide.

The defeat sent shock waves through the Japanese chain of command, but bigger things were already happening. On August 24 the carriers went at it again, for the first time since Midway. The Japanese had two of their best on hand, *Shokaku* and *Zuikaku*, with 140 aircraft tasked with finding and destroying the U.S. carriers as payback for the Midway debacle. The light carrier *Ryujo* and her thirty-three aircraft were detached with a small escort to attack Guadalcanal and suppress the now active airfield there. A third approaching force was the reinforcement convoy carrying Ichiki's second echelon and the 5th Yokosuka Special Naval Landing Force. Opposing them were Fletcher's carrier groups. Originally there were three such groups, but in a controversial decision Fletcher sent the *Wasp* south to refuel, taking a third of the U.S. aircraft out of the coming fight, leaving *Saratoga* and *Enterprise*, with 150 aircraft, to engage in what would be called the Battle of the Eastern Solomons.

The Americans struck first in the early afternoon, finding and over-whelming the *Ryujo*; but as the main U.S. strike was engaged against this small carrier, the big Japanese carriers were also found. The Japanese had already spotted the U.S. flattops and *Enterprise* came under heavy attack by a force of twenty-seven Val dive-bombers and ten Zeros. Over half the attacking planes were destroyed, but they succeeded in hitting the *Enterprise* with three bombs. Damage control parties got the fires under control, but a half hour after the last bomb hit her she lost steering control and began circling, almost hitting one of her escorts. Her speed was reduced while the problem was being fixed, but the damage crews never got the chance. A second Japanese strike force attacked. Ironically, the thirty-plus planes of this attack group almost missed the *Enterprise* completely, but were drawn toward her when patrolling U.S. aircraft attacked them. Another ten planes were shot down, but the Wildcats, low on ammunition and fuel, couldn't stop the onslaught against the crippled carrier. Three more bombs hit her, creating uncontrollable fires. With the Japanese surface force of cruisers and battleships bearing down, the big carrier was abandoned, then scuttled with a spread of U.S. torpedoes.

The death of the *Big E* marked the end of the carrier duel. Both sides retired. The Japanese had traded a small carrier for *Enterprise*, but had suffered severe losses in aircraft. *Saratoga* withdrew to rejoin *Wasp*. The next day, planes from Henderson found the reinforcement convoy still pushing for Guadalcanal and severely damaged it. They sank a destroyer and one transport, and inflicted severe damage on the convoy's flagship, the light cruiser *Jintzu*. Guadalcanal's teeth were sharp.

The convoy's repulse ended the first phase of the campaign. The results were a mixed bag for both sides. Guadalcanal's airfield had been captured and put into service by the United States, making the surrounding seas dangerously interdicted for Japanese ships, especially during the daylight hours. But the beachhead was suffering from lack of supply and the U.S. logistics chain moved slowly. With no port facilities on the island, supply ships had to use their own landing craft to beach supplies, a time-consuming process limited to two to three ships at a time. Worse, the night belonged to the Imperial Japanese Navy, which added a major time constraint to the whole process. The U.S. supply ships had to arrive early in the morning, unload, and depart prior to darkness. The Japanese had severely hurt the U.S. Navy by sinking *Enterprise* but lost too many aircraft and trained crews doing it. Their Navy had wrested control of the night waters off the island from the Allies with their stunning victory off Savo Island, but didn't follow that victory up with an effective blockade. The Army's initial counterthrust by Colonel Ichiki was a complete disaster.

## The second phase

The failure of Ichiki's infantry attack and the repulse of the reinforcement convoy caused a storm of acrimonious argument at all levels of the Japanese military. The Army was angry at the Navy for limiting the troops sent to the island; the Navy was equally angry for the Army's handling of the attack. One point was incontestable. The United States Marines and their airfield at Guadalcanal constituted a serious breach in the Empire's outer perimeter – Japanese ships were suddenly at risk within 200 miles of the airfield. The breach called for a more serious effort against the beachhead. Kawaguchi's brigade, assembling at Rabaul, might not be enough.

The airfield was the most restrictive problem. It had to be retaken or suppressed. Suppression could take several forms. Bombing could keep the airfield unusable if the attacks were strong enough. The distance from Rabaul to Guadalcanal was 565 miles. This was well within the range of the Betty bombers, but only long range Zeros could accompany them and, at that, they would be at the edge of their operational range. Worse, the bombers usually attacked at altitudes between 20,000 and 25,000 feet, where the Zeros were not at their best. Suppression could also come from the sea through bombardment by the Imperial Japanese Navy. Knowing full well the power of aircraft against ships, the Navy would have to operate in a risky environment and make full use of their nighttime capabilities. This was an attractive option since the enemy's capital ships had left the area, driven away by Mikawa's success. The final option was to retake the airfield by ground assault or at least interdict it by artillery fire. This would require transporting men and equipment to the island. Along with the risk posed by Allied aircraft, the Japanese had no port facilities and little capability for beachhead supply. But this was the ultimate answer to the problem. Surprisingly, given their concerns about supplying their own troops, they appear to have not considered the tenuous supply situation of the Marines and an attack on the Guadalcanal problem from that angle. They chose the more direct approach.

Plans for an all-out aerial assault were made, their only short-term option. Recognizing the problems of maintenance and pilot fatigue inherent in such a long flight, the Imperial General Staff ordered an advanced airbase begun at Buin, New Georgia. In the meantime, Kawaguchi would transport his forces to the anchorage at Faisi on Shortland Island, closer to their final destination, while the Army and Navy worked out a plan of operation.

For the next week, weather permitting, Japanese planes made a concerted effort to suppress Henderson field with little success. The Marine aircraft, reinforced by Army P-400 fighters (the inferior export version of the P-39 Aircobra), as well as orphan Wildcats and SBDs from the *Enterprise*, were well warned of the approaching attackers through the coastwatcher system in the Solomons and their own radar. They took a heavy toll of the bombers and their escorts. On August 30 the Japanese tried a fighter sweep, sending eighteen of their best carrier fighter pilots alone. The Zeros were very effective against the low flying Army P-400s, shooting down four of the seven, but the F4F Wildcats shot down half the Zeros while losing two of their own. A bombing attack later in the day diverted to attack the destroyer-transport *Calhoun* in the Sound, sinking her. The day ended with more aircraft arriving at Henderson to reinforce the Marine and Army planes, now dubbed the Cactus Air Force.

The following day, *Saratoga* was torpedoed while protecting the supply line to Guadalcanal. Damage to its propulsion system was serious and the ship was sent to the West Coast, out of the fight. Along with her went Admiral Jack Fletcher. With *Saratoga* homeward bound, the U.S. carrier force in the South Pacific was reduced to *Wasp* until *Hornet* could arrive.

General Kawaguchi assembled five full battalions, nearly 6,500 fighting troops, at Faisi; this comprised all three battalions of the 124th Infantry Regiment, the 2nd Battalion of the 4th Infantry, and the Kumo Battalion. The remaining two battalions of the 4th Infantry were on the way. The 17th Army had also redirected the 2nd (Sendai) Infantry Division to be the primary attack force. Kawaguchi was ordered to transport his infantry and land them west of the Marine perimeter, near Tassafaronga, then proceed to establish artillery positions on the Matanikau River.

The problem of how to get the troops to the island with Henderson still operational was partially solved by the institution of what became known as the Tokyo Express. Japanese destroyers, loaded with some 150 soldiers and forty tons of supplies, were fast enough to run to the island, drop their passengers, deliver a brief bombardment of the airfield, and race north to get out of the danger zone. Its most serious drawback was the inability to transport heavy equipment, such as artillery and tanks. The Navy designated two seaplane carriers, *Nisshin* and *Chitose*, to provide that capability.

Kawaguchi's move began auspiciously on September 4. Led by the light cruiser *Sendai*, eleven destroyers landed Kawaguchi and nearly 1,000 troops at Tassafaronga before proceeding east to bombard the airfield. Instead, the Japanese found the destroyer-transports *Little* and *Gregory* running a patrol line northwest of Lunga Point. Armed with only 4-inch guns, the two U.S. ships were overwhelmed by the Japanese and sunk. The following day, the Cactus Air Force gained a small measure of revenge when they sighted, attacked, and scattered a large barge convoy carrying troops to the island. But over the next seven days, Kawaguchi's force was landed safely with only two destroyers damaged on the return trips.

On the American side, Vandegrift established his defensive perimeter in a semicircle around Lunga Point, using the First Marines to the east and the Fifth Marines to the west, each with a battalion in reserve. To the south, facing dense jungle, he set a series of strongpoints manned by Raiders, Paratroopers, engineers, and pioneers. The Third Defense Battalion had its coastal guns trained out to sea. In reserve, Vandegrift had the Second Marines; its third battalion was transported to the Lunga Point perimeter on September 10, but the other two battalions stayed on Tulagi. A second grass airstrip, called Fighter One, was established a mile to the east of Henderson, allowing better disbursement of planes and supplies, but the strip was difficult to keep unflooded. His defensive situation, however, was more serious than just limited manpower and limited supply. The daily bombardments and bombing, as well as the unhealthy environment, were debilitating his troops. Over 900 men were down with malaria, with more falling sick every day.

At higher levels, doubt was settling in, especially with Ghormley. All available intelligence indicated a massive Japanese buildup of ships, planes, and troops moving toward Guadalcanal. To counter the threat, Ghormley had a single Marine division at the end of a tenuous supply line, two carriers to support and protect the beachhead, and no other resources available. The Army pushed to have the island evacuated and the resources transferred to the Southwest Pacific effort, as demanded by General MacArthur, but the Navy held firm. Despite the pessimism, Ghormley and his superiors were well aware of the propaganda issue involved with the island battle: Guadalcanal had become a symbol of the Allied turnaround in the Pacific War. Success would be an enormous benefit to the war effort; conversely, failure would be disastrous, especially if the Marines were lost.

On September 7, however, Ghormley did take an overdue step. He created Task Force 64, a collection of cruisers and destroyers under Rear Admiral Norman Scott, to help protect and counter the nightly Japanese naval activity off the island. In addition, more aircraft, this time from the damaged *Saratoga*, reinforced the Marines' airpower. On September 11 he sent Turner to visit Vandegrift to get the Marines' first hand assessment of the situation. Vandegrift was adamant about his ability to hold the island and its airfields, even in the face of Ghormley's stated inability to support him fully. He told Turner, however, that without better supply and more troops, all he could do was hold on to what he had; he could not advance any further. He wanted his missing regiment, the Seventh Marines. Turner agreed to try to get them.

Natives had been reporting Japanese to the west of the perimeter, some 200–300 of them. Vandegrift decided he needed more information and assigned Colonel Merritt 'Red Mike' Edson, of the First Raider Battalion, to make a landing near Tassafaronga to reconnoiter. Edson combined the depleted First Parachute Battalion with his Raiders to build up to 850 troops. On September 12, they boarded the destroyer-transports *McKean* and *Manley*, plus two smaller boats. Just as they were embarking, natives appeared with a new assessment of Japanese strength, placing it at 2–3,000. Edson discounted the new reports as native exaggeration.

His landing was initially unopposed, and the Marines found ample evidence of recent landings, including stacks of food and other stores, plus two anti-tank guns. Probing further inland, the Raiders ran into a battalion of Japanese from the 4th Infantry who had landed the night before. A sharp firefight ensued with the Japanese being reinforced by troops from a second battalion, also landed the previous night. Edson's men lost their radio and went into a defensive position near the coast. Using T-shirts, they spelled out HELP on the beach, which was soon spotted by a roving SBD. Supported by air attack and bombardment from destroyers, the Raiders were successfully evacuated but suffered some fifty casualties.

Both sides felt good about the raid – Edson returned with valuable information from the documents he captured. Vandegrift now knew approximately how many Japanese he faced – well over 6,000 troops of the 35th Brigade. In addition, U.S. bombardment of the area destroyed a substantial amount of Japanese supplies. Kawaguchi felt pleased because the Marines had been repulsed.

With the new information, Vandegrift brought the Second Marines' 2nd Battalion over from Tulagi, and renewed his request for the Seventh Marines. He sent the two battalions of the Second Marines westward, to take up positions on the Matanikau River. Holding this line, he believed, would keep Japanese artillery, except for their largest guns, out of range of Henderson Field.

On Espiritu Santo, Turner loaded up the newly arrived Seventh Marines and, with *Wasp* and *Hornet* in support, sailed for Guadalcanal. On September 15, however, the reinforcement convoy ran into a Japanese submarine. Commander Takaichi Kinashi's *I-19* maneuvered to within 1,000 yards of *Wasp* and fired six torpedoes. Three hit the carrier and detonated the gasoline storage tanks and the forward bomb magazine. The destroyer *O'Brien* and the battleship *North Carolina* were also hit in Kinashi's incredible salvo. Thirty minutes later, fires still raging, *Wasp* was abandoned and sunk with American torpedoes. With his air support cut in half and his sole battleship requiring major repairs, Turner turned back, not willing to risk further damage to his depleted escort forces.

Over the next few days, patrols from Kawaguchi's Brigade and the Second Marines clashed west of the Matanikau. The firefights, aided substantially by close support from the Marine aircraft, were inconclusive, except to show Vandegrift that the Matanikau was currently as far west as he could push with the limited troop strength he had. He called for another attempt to get the Seventh to the island.

Kawaguchi, stung by the air attacks, called for an increased effort to put Henderson out of commission. Naval personnel at Rabaul put together a reinforcement convoy, built around *Nisshin* and *Chitose*, to carry 150 mm guns to Kawaguchi – these would be able to reach Henderson Field from the area the Japanese held. The six escorting destroyers also carried the first troops from the Sendai Division. The Imperial Navy General Staff also upgraded their bombardment plans. Offshore bombardment by destroyers was having very limited effect; bigger guns were needed. The first suggestion was heavy cruisers, but other staff members argued for battleships and their 14-inch guns. Both plans were approved. A total of five bombardment vessels – three heavy cruisers and two battleships – were sent south, along with the reinforcements.

Ghormley reluctantly approved the second attempt to land the Seventh Marines. He had a single carrier group for support, but intelligence indicated the Japanese carriers were not in the immediate area. Turner sent Scott's Task Force 64 ahead of the reinforcement convoy to sweep the Slot free of Japanese ships and interdict additional Japanese reinforcements. Scott's TF64 consisted of the heavy cruisers *San Francisco* and *Salt Lake City*, the light cruisers *Helena* and *Boise*, and the destroyers *Farenholt*, *Duncan*, *Laffey*, *Buchanan*, and *McCalla*. He prowled south of Guadalcanal by day for several days, awaiting word of Japanese intruders. Meanwhile, at Espiritu Santo, the Seventh Marines embarked again. On September 21 a B-17 spotted the Japanese reinforcement convoy heading south. Unfortunately, none of the U.S. scouting aircraft spotted the Japanese cruisers or battleships, which had lagged behind the smaller ships due to a problem with a battleship's engineering plant.

Near midnight, Scott had his ships in line off Cape Esperance. The destroyers *Farenholt*, *Laffey*, and *Duncan* led the cruisers, followed by the two remaining destroyers. *Helena* had the latest and most modern radar set, but much of the information provided by radar was lost in the undisciplined radio communications between the ships. In hindsight, Scott should have had his flag on the ship with the best intelligence capability, rather than on *San Francisco*.

At approximately 2330 hours, *Helena*'s radar picked up five ships, coming straight toward them. This was the cruiser bombardment force, commanded by Rear Admiral Aritomo Goto, consisting of the heavy cruisers *Aoba*, *Furataka*, and *Kinugasa*, flanked by the destroyers *Fubuki* and *Hatsuyuki*. A column shift of 180° was ordered and mishandled by TF64, leaving the lead destroyers out of the column. While he sorted out his ships, the enemy sailed closer, apparently unaware of the U.S. ships directly in front of them. Finally, at 2346 hours, crossing the Japanese line with all ships, the U.S. line opened fire.

The deluge of 8-inch and 6-inch shells shocked the Japanese – there had been no U.S. naval opposition to the Japanese Navy since Mikawa's victory.[3] The unexpected fire pounded Goto's flagship *Aoba*, killing the admiral. The Japanese didn't respond for a few minutes, which should have been fatal to the entire force; but Scott, unsure of the situation and aware his destroyers were in the line of fire, ordered a short cease-fire to make certain the targets weren't American. *Aoba* careened out of the Japanese line in full retreat, on fire with all turrets out of action, but *Furataka* and *Kinugasa* protected her well, concentrating their fire on *San Francisco*. Several hits killed Scott and most of his staff, and started major fires on the U.S. flagship. The Japanese traded blows with the Americans and launched torpedoes to their withdrawal. The U.S. cruisers turned away when the torpedoes were spotted, but the light cruiser *Boise* was hit by the salvo, severely damaging it. In a side action the U.S. destroyers inundated the *Fubuki* with shells and left her sinking. The initial stages of the battle were a complete American success – the Japanese were driven off with severe damage, leaving the United States in control of the night time waters off Guadalcanal for the first time since August 9.

Command of TF64 now fell to Captain Ernest Small of *Salt Lake City*. With two cruisers damaged, he chose not to chase the fleeing Japanese but to collect his ships and assess the damage. *San Francisco*'s crew fought hard to save their ship and had started to succeed when *Helena*'s radar contacted a new group of ships, including two 'large' ships, heading toward them. Small moved to intercept the new group with *Farenholt* and *Duncan* leading *Salt Lake City* and *Helena*, trailed by *Laffey*. The destroyer *McCalla*, slightly damaged in the shootout with *Fubuki*, stayed with the wounded U.S. cruisers as they made their way slowly back to the Lunga Point anchorage.

The second Japanese group was the battleship bombardment force, commanded by Vice Admiral Takeo Kurita. He had trailed far enough behind to miss the fireworks that had pounded Goto. His ships were in three lines, with his two battleships, *Kongo* and *Haruna*, flanked by three destroyers on either side. His first inkling of trouble came from the retiring *Furataka*, which reported U.S. warships in the Slot. The unexpected news stunned the admiral as much as the opening salvos must have Goto, and for a few minutes his force continued its approach. As Kurita made up his mind to retire and reassess the new situation, his flanking destroyers spotted the U.S. column across their path. The Japanese turned to retire but the battle was upon them.

Kurita's force was being tracked on *Helena*'s radar, and at about 4,000 yards Small decided to open the dance. *Laffey* fired starshells just as the two battleships illuminated the lead destroyers with searchlights. The shock of confronting battleships was hammered home as both ships fired their broadsides at *Farenholt* and *Duncan*. One 14-inch shell detonated the *Duncan*'s forward magazine and the resulting explosion broke the destroyer in half. *Farenholt* was luckier, but only marginally: the 1,500-pound shells shattered the smaller ship and left her on fire and sinking. The sacrifice of his destroyers gave Small a chance to strike back. Both cruisers fired on *Haruna*, exploding one 5-inch secondary position, but the big battleship's heavy armor shrugged off most of the other hits.

The return fire was deadly. Small died when *Salt Lake City*'s bridge was hit. Both forward turrets were destroyed and only a quick flooding of the forward magazine saved the ship from a massive explosion. *Helena* was hit harder, losing all power. Kurita, however, didn't follow up his devastating fire, continuing his course to retire. His flanking destroyers sent a salvo of torpedoes toward the American ships to cover the retirement; two disemboweled the drifting *Helena* and she sank quickly.

The following morning, planes from Henderson found the damaged *Aoba* and an escorting destroyer and sank both, exacting a measure of revenge for the previous night's slaughter. *Salt Lake City* was able to limp back to the anchorage but no farther, as her battle damage finally overcame the crew's ability to keep her afloat. The Battle of Cape Esperance had started with a significant victory for the United States, the first time the Navy had gone toe to toe with the Japanese and come out ahead. The brush with Kurita, however, had turned the victory into a hard defeat. Scott had gone into battle with nine ships; now only the destroyer *Laffey* was battle ready. *San Francisco* and *Boise* would have to head home for major repairs. Over 700 U.S. sailors had died.

The impact of the battle was immediate. At Espiritu Santo, Ghormley, confidence again shaken by the loss of Scott and TF64, ordered Turner to abort the reinforcement run. Once again, the Seventh Marines would not be joining their division. Worse, the battle started up the question of Guadalcanal's future once again. The loss of eight ships stretched current resources almost to breaking point. No one in the South Pacific or Washington doubted that the United States would soon be able to 'out-material' their Japanese opponents; but the future wasn't going to arm or feed the Marines on Guadalcanal at that moment.

While the Americans began rearguing their commitment to Guadal-canal, the Japanese were also rethinking their position. The clash off Cape Esperance had cost them *Aoba* and two valuable destroyers, along with the cruiser *Furataka* damaged enough to be sent home for major repairs. Damage to *Haruna* was minimal, but the repercussions of the surprise and Kurita's precipitous withdrawal created an atmosphere of contention that stymied progress for a full day. The 10,000 troops of the Sendai Division were ready for transport to the island, which was now more complicated with active U.S. interference at night. More naval forces were allocated reluctantly. Transport plans were made and set in motion.

Critical to the success of the transportation was a convoy of six fast transport vessels, each with its own landing craft and effective anti-aircraft protection. The vessels would carry over 4,500 of the Sendai troops along with 100 mm and 150 mm guns and ammunition, the First Independent Tank Company (with ten Model 97 light tanks), and provisions. The remaining troops, equipment, and supplies would be delivered by normal Tokyo Express destroyer runs over a ten-day period. To protect the convoys and to suppress U.S. air activity, another bombardment force was put together, this time with the battleships *Hiei* and *Kirishima*. This attack would be followed with more bombardments as necessary.

On Guadalcanal, Vandegrift was dealing with the loss of the Seventh Marines. He pulled the last of the Second Marines out of Tulagi, and sent them to join their sister battalions on the Matanikau defensive line. He reiterated to his superiors his determination to hold the island as long as he had Marines to fight and aircraft to fly.

On the night of September 24, the Japanese battleships – missed once again by U.S. scouts – opened fire on Henderson Field from over 29,000 yards. Guided by observation aircraft launched for that purpose, the bat-tleships pounded the area with nearly 1,000 heavy shells over the next ninety minutes. The effect was devastating. Henderson Field was rendered unusable, over eighty percent of the SBDs damaged or destroyed, and all aviation gas wiped out. The lone bright spot for the Americans was the survival of Fighter One and over half of its fighter aircraft. Although they were able to get fighters in the air to meet the afternoon bombing attack, the first group of transport destroyers made their run without interference.

The move had been spotted, but there was nothing the United States could do about it that day. The lack of resistance led the Japanese to start the high speed convoy toward the island.

U.S. air operations began sporadically the following day, with emergency supplies and planes being flown in. Refueling was still the critical item but was aided by the discovery of small 'emergency' stashes. But resistance to the approaching convoy was minimal. At midnight, September 26, the six transports, along with a large Tokyo Express run of destroyers, made their anchorage at Tassafaronga and commenced landing their troops. There was no reaction until daylight. The Japanese, confident in Henderson Field's suppression, found themselves under attack early on the 27th. Three of the transports were destroyed during the day-long battle, but almost all of the troops and most of the supplies survived the onslaught. That night the Japanese retaliated with another bombardment by the heavy cruisers *Chokai* and *Kinugasa*. A more ominous development for the Americans was the initial artillery fire from newly arrived 150 mm guns, with enough range to reach Henderson Field from west of the Matanikau. Fortunately for the Marines, ammunition for these guns was still in short supply.

Vandegrift sent a warning to his superiors that an estimated 10,000 enemy troops had landed. The news arrived at the same time as word that a fuel convoy of four ships had been attacked by Japanese carrier aircraft and stopped, with the loss of U.S.S. *Meridith*. The stranglehold on the island seemed to be tightening.

As Vandegrift dug his troops in waiting for the Japanese attack he knew was coming, the fate of the island was being discussed at the highest levels in Washington. Ghormley's assessment that he could not support the Marines logistically was fed by his natural pessimism. It overshadowed Vandegrift's insistence that he could hold the island. The loss of TF64 left the South Pacific with one carrier, two battleships, three heavy cruisers and four light cruisers, against the Combined Fleet under Yamamoto that contained four heavy carriers, two light carriers, four battleships, and eight heavy cruisers in the immediate area. Holding out the necessary escort for the surviving carrier *Hornet*, the ratio of forces was clearly against the Americans at this point. Twice he had tried to reinforce the beachhead and had failed both times. Supply was becoming more difficult to deliver. He saw little hope in the situation.

Ghormley's gloomy assessment sparked a renewed debate in Washington between Army Chief of Staff General Marshall and his naval counterpart Admiral King. With MacArthur in Australia pushing his Southwest Pacific plans, the Marshall–King debate finally went all the way to the White House. On October 3, President Roosevelt made it clear that most of the nation's efforts had to focus on Europe, and that the Pacific's time would come. More importantly, he told King point blank to supply the Marines as best he could, but if he couldn't, to withdraw the troops. American public opinion, the President told his commanders, would not accept the loss of the First Marine Division. King left the meeting and sent the President's orders to Ghormley.

On Guadalcanal, the Japanese were ready to move. With his troops landed, the Sendai Division's commanding general, Lieutenant General Masao Maruyama, prepared a detailed plan of attack. He would lead most of his troops southward to attack the American perimeter from its inland side. He split this force into three columns. The left column, commanded by Major General Nasu, consisted of the three battalions of the 29th Infantry Regiment. The right column, under Major General Kawaguchi, contained two battalions of the 230th Infantry, plus the 3rd Battalion, 124th Infantry. The center column was the divisional reserve under Maruyama's direct control and consisted of the 16th Infantry's three battalions. Artillery and mortar units broke down their weapons and were to join the march. Coordinated with this landward assault, Maruyama ordered a supporting attack at the Matanikau. The Sendai's artillery commander, Major General Tadashi Sumiyoshi, would command on this front with two groups. The first, under Colonel Oka, would be the two battalions from the 124th Infantry, plus a battalion from the 4th Infantry. This force would march inland and attack the Marine line from the south up the east bank of the river. The second group consisted of the First Independent Tank Company plus the remaining two battalions from the 4th Infantry, which would attack straight across the river. Maruyama's plan thus set over 15,000 troops into motion against the Marines.

On October 1, Nasu's column stepped off into the jungle. Maruyama planned to attack five days after starting his march and set the attack date for October 6. Heavy air raids would commence to prepare the way on October 5, with the Navy adding another bombardment that night. But what looked like a simple march proved anything but that in reality. Steep terrain, deep gorges, and dense jungle hampered the marching troops. Navigating solely by compass, obstacles had to be overcome rather than avoided, and the pace was very slow and exhausting, especially for the artillerymen carrying their guns. Four days after starting, Maruyama's headquarters reached a small valley he estimated was only four miles from the U.S. lines. But the scouts he sent out either got completely lost or returned to report nothing but jungle. He radioed Sumiyoshi that the attack date would have to be postponed until October 7.

His Matanikau diversion commander got the order but failed to send it on in time to stop the pre-attack air raid. The Zeros and Bettys appeared as they always did over Henderson Field, but this time most of the bombs hit the West bank of the Matanikau and a ridge south of the airfields. Vandegrift rightly assumed the Japanese would attack those positions. The ridge in question was 1,000 yards long, with two knolls rising 80 and 120 feet above sea level. It commanded the southern approach to Henderson Field, located less than a mile behind it. The Marines began beefing up the defenses in those areas. Edson's Raiders had that particular responsibility, flanked by battalions of the First and Fifth Marines. The troops began digging in and stringing barbed wire. The batteries of the Eleventh Marines registered around the ridge. Dense jungle precluded any semblance of a continuous line: Edson's men set up mutually supportive platoon-sized strongpoints 100 yards apart.

Maruyama's plan continued to unravel. Pushing forward during the daylight hours of October 7, he expected to be in position to attack soon after nightfall. But by nightfall, he had barely begun to reach the outskirts of the Marine lines. Brief firefights erupted along the Marine line as Japanese scouts probed. But the left and center columns had less than a battalion near contact; the rest of the column stretched back into the jungle. In addition, Kawaguchi's column on the right, having strayed off on a course parallel with the Marine lines, reported jungle in all directions. Once again Maruyama sent the word to postpone the attack a full day.

While his 17th Army superiors in Rabaul received word of the postponement, Sumiyoshi's diversionary force on the Matanikau did not. Pursuant to orders he did not know were changed, Sumiyoshi attacked at 2330 on October 7. But even his own attack had coordination problems. Colonel Oka, with the main force approaching from the south, had been delayed by the same jungle conditions that had hampered Maruyama, and at the appointed hour he wasn't in position to attack. Consequently the First Independent Tank Company, with a battalion of the 4th Infantry in support, attacked alone. The Japanese artillery, seventeen 75 mm and 100 mm guns, struck the positions of the 3rd Battalion, Second Marines, near the mouth of the river. The first wave of five tanks made it through the barbed wire and over the first machinegun positions before being destroyed by massed anti-tank fire and the heroic actions of individual Marines.[4] The second wave was destroyed quicker. Massed artillery fire from the Eleventh Marines' forty guns stopped the infantry cold. One side of Sumiyoshi's attack was stymied.

Three hours later, Oka's three battalions stormed out of the jungle, striking, by sheer good luck, the seam between the two Second Marine battalions. Oka's troops forced their way onto the ridge, but the massed Marine guns began to take their toll on the exhausted attackers. Counterattacks caught the Japanese in a vise and pushed them back off the hill. Sumiyoshi again sent his two remaining battalions against the river lines, trying to support Oka's attack, but they achieved little. By morning the Japanese had withdrawn, leaving almost 700 dead on the field, including over half the tank crews that had attacked.

The Marines spent the daylight hours working on their defenses on what was now being called Edson's Ridge. The Raider commander pulled his troops back some 200 yards from the positions that had been probed earlier. The Eleventh Marine guns registered their weapons carefully in front of the new lines. On the Matanikau front, the Second Marines hunted down the small detachments of Japanese that had infiltrated during Oka's attack.

Shortly after dark on October 8, Maruyama attacked, using his very limited artillery and mortar support. One battalion from the left and center columns each charged the lines and were disrupted by accurate and massed artillery fire. Maruyama reinforced the assault with two more battalions an hour later and put severe pressure on the Raiders. Japanese soldiers began pushing through the gaps between strongpoints, threatening to flank and breach the thin line. Edson ordered his troops to pull back to his last line built near the large knoll on the ridge. With the aid of 37 mm cannons firing canister, the Raiders repulsed two more assaults. Vandegrift stripped companies from the First and Fifth Marines to bolster the thinning line, but the Fifth Marines ran into Japanese from a battalion of the 16th Infantry that had broken through and was heading for the airfields. A savage fight broke out, and ended with the arrival of Marine tanks. The Japanese remnants withdrew to positions near the Fighter One airstrip, where engineers and other rear area troops destroyed them.

Exhaustion and artillery fire finally stopped Maruyama's attack, and he pulled back into the jungle leaving over 2,000 of his troops dead on the field. He was unaware of the 16th Infantry's breakthrough or their position inside the Marine perimeter. It had been a very close battle – the fact that the three battalions of Kawaguchi's column failed to engage was decisive.[5] Devoid of supply, the Sendai Division began a torturous trek back to their Matanikau lines.

## The final phase

Vandegrift's Marines had fought ably and well, but even he knew how close it had been. As his troops tended their dead and wounded, they also dug in deeper and hunted down Japanese infiltrators. He sent his report to Ghormley: we held and are holding, but we need more troops.

Ghormley's nerve failed on receiving word of the big Japanese attack. Fearing another such attack would wipe out the Marines, he told Vandegrift that troops were available but unable to get safely to the island, and ordered him to prepare for evacuation. Ten transports would arrive to get the troops out, and all equipment was to be destroyed prior to leaving. Vandegrift was livid, arguing that if empty ships could make it to the island, full ones could as well. But Ghormley would not sway.

The evacuation convoy got underway that same day. The cruisers *Portland*, *Atlanta*, and *San Juan*, along with fifteen destroyers, under Rear

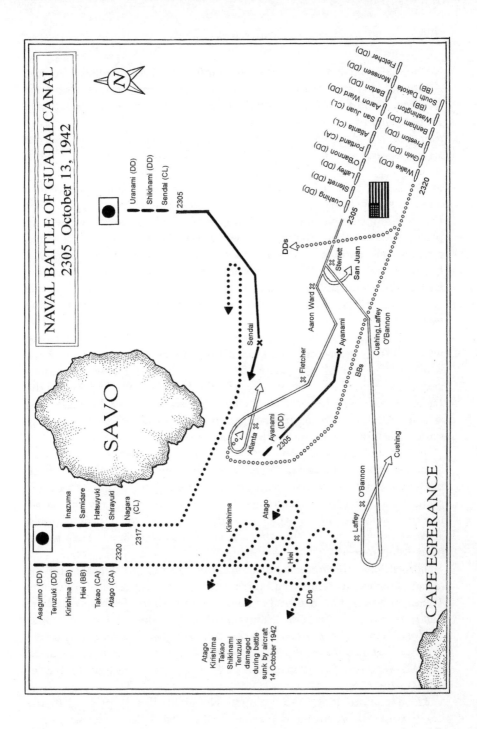

NAVAL BATTLE OF GUADALCANAL
2305 October 13, 1942

SAVO

CAPE ESPERANCE

● Uranami (DD)
Shikinami (DD)
Sendai (CL)
2305

● Asagumo (DD)
Teruzuki (DD)
Kirishima (BB)
Hiei (BB)
Takao (CA)
Atago (CA)
2320

Inazuma
Samidare
Hatsuyuki
Shirayuki
Nagara (CL)
2317

Sendai ✕

Fletcher ✕✕

Ayanami (DD)
2305

Atlanta ✕✕

Aaron Ward ✕✕

Sterrett
San Juan

DDs

BBs

Ayanami ✕

Cushing,Laffey
O'Bannon

Kirishima
Atago

Hiei

DDs

Kirishima
Atago
Takao
Shikinami
Teruzuki
damaged
during battle
sunk by aircraft
14 October 1942

Laffey ✕ O'Bannon

Cushing

Cushing (DD)
Laffey (DD)
Sterrett (DD)
O'Bannon (DD)
Portland (CA)
Atlanta (CL)
San Juan (CL)
Aaron Ward (DD)
Barton (DD)
Monssen (DD)
Fletcher (DD)
Wake (DD)
Gwin (DD)
Preston (DD)
Benham (DD)
Washington (BB)
South Dakota (BB)
2305
2320

Admiral Mahlon Tizdale, escorted the transports. Also providing cover was the newly recreated Task Force 64, now consisting of the battleships *Washington* and *South Dakota* and the destroyers *Walker*, *Gwin*, *Preston*, and *Benham*, under Rear Admiral Willis Lee. The carrier *Hornet*, with its escort of four cruisers and six destroyers, provided very careful air cover, as well as the stepping stone for those Guadalcanal aircraft capable of using her flight deck.

The U.S. convoy was spotted soon after its departure from Espiritu Santo and the Japanese took its significance the wrong way. They assumed that the convoy meant significant reinforcements. Much discussion was taking place in Rabaul after Maruyama's defeat. His report of severe losses and continued close attack by Marine aircraft pointed again to the importance of closing Henderson Field down. Coordination problems had stymied the effects. The Japanese Navy again prepared to roll out its big guns while the Army sent orders for the 38th Division to prepare for transport to the island. Word of the big U.S. convoy added incentive for the Japanese.

On October 12, Lee and his ships arrived off Lunga Point. As they waited, TF64's destroyers began evacuating Tulagi of the troops left there, while the battleships, guided by aircraft, bombarded Japanese positions west of the Matanikau. The pounding by the 16-inch shells demoralized the Japanese, although Lee intended solely to disrupt further Japanese land assaults. A B-17, however, reported a large group of Japanese ships heading south – including what looked like battleships.

Turner and the transports arrived the following day and began the laborious process of loading. Vandegrift's staff had prepared a pull-back plan that kept the front lines covered as much as possible. Engineers grouped equipment for demolition. As the work continued, air scouts reported Japanese ship movements. Turner realized the Japanese would arrive that night, well before the evacuation was completed. They would have to be stopped.

Turner gave the immediate interception mission to Tizdale and his cruiser-destroyer force, leaving his battleships to be the last line of defense. Tizdale established his line west of Lunga Point with the destroyers *Cushing*, *Laffey*, *Sterret*, and *O'Bannon* leading Tixdale's flagship, the heavy cruiser *Portland*. The light cruisers *Atlanta* and *San Juan* followed with the destroyers *Aaron Ward*, *Barton*, *Monssen*, and *Fletcher*. Behind them, if needed, was Lee's Task Force, with its four destroyers leading the battle-ships.

The Japanese, under Vice Admiral Nobutake Kondo, flagged in the heavy cruiser *Atago*, advanced in three divisions. The light cruiser *Sendai* and three destroyers (*Ayanami*, *Shikinami*, and *Uranami*) would sweep through the Slot, scouting for the bigger ships. The light cruiser *Nagara* and four destroyers would escort the main column, consisting of the heavy cruisers

*Atago* and *Takao*, and the battleships *Hiei* and *Kirishima*, with two more destroyers. Kondo's plan was simply to destroy any U.S. ships he found and bombard Henderson Field in a repeat of his September 24 success.

At 2305, October 13, *Portland*'s radar picked up three ships east of Savo, and Tizdale moved his line to intercept. *Sendai*'s keen lookouts spotted the U.S. column and reported the finding to Kondo. *Sendai*, *Shikanami*, and *Uranami* opened fire on the approaching U.S. ships and maneuvered for a torpedo attack. The U.S. line replied, but got the worst of the shooting. A Japanese shell punctured destroyer *Sterret*'s forward magazine and a massive explosion left the ship sinking. *Cushing* led other lead destroyers off against a lone Japanese destroyer spotted in front of them.

*Portland* opened fire with her radar controlled 8-inch guns and scored heavily on the Japanese light cruiser, but too late to stop the torpedo attack. The U.S. line found itself in a swarm of Long Lance torpedoes and the cruiser *San Juan* was hit. Even as the light cruiser lurched out of the line, another torpedo tore the destroyer *Aaron Ward* in half. The *Cushing* and her two companions caught the *Ayanami* trying to maneuver for a lone torpedo attack and sank her, while *Sendai* succumbed to massed fire from *Atlanta* and *Portland*.

As the U.S. ships were finishing off the *Sendai*, the two other Japanese columns came into contact from west of Savo Island. *Nagara* and her four destroyers sent more torpedoes toward the U.S. line, sinking the *Fletcher*; but Tizdale's attention was drawn to the capital ships that opened up at his column from 8,000 yards. *Portland* and *Atlanta* opened fire on the battleships while the destroyers engaged the *Nagara* and her escorts. *Hiei* and *Kirishima*'s shells hammered the cruisers, but the U.S. return fire seemed to do little.

Then Fate changed sides. Up to that point, the Japanese were winning the battle. Three U.S. destroyers had been sunk and a cruiser damaged, with two more U.S. cruisers under fire by a superior force. Each battleship's 14-inch broadsides could deliver almost 12,000 pounds of destruction, while the *Portland* could answer with only 2,400 pounds per broadside. But one of the *Portland*'s 8-inch shells hit *Hiei*'s bridge, destroying her main fire control and killing everyone there. The battleship careened out of control, disrupting the entire Japanese line. In addition, while the Japanese were concentrating their fire on the U.S. cruisers, the destroyers *Cushing*, *Laffey*, and *O'Bannon* closed unnoticed and opened fire with guns and torpedoes on the Japanese flagship. The attack set fires all along the cruiser's length, while one torpedo destroyed a boiler room. The sudden and unexpected barrage also killed Kondo on *Atago*'s bridge.

The loss of their commander coupled with the out of control *Hiei* created chaos within the Japanese ranks. *Takao* and *Atago's* destroyers turned their full fury on the daring U.S. destroyers, sinking *Laffey* and *O'Bannon* and leaving *Cushing* a twisted wreck. The *Kirishima* circled and continued to battle with the U.S. cruisers trying to protect her wounded consort. Her accurate fire pounded *Atlanta* into a sinking hulk.

Further to the east, *Nagara* and her destroyers spotted and tangled with Lee's approaching column, but *Washington*'s 16-inch shells convinced the Japanese to turn back. As they passed just south of Savo, the Japanese fired another round of torpedoes. They missed their intended targets— *Portland* and her two remaining destroyers – but the long-ranged weapons continued on and one of them hit *Takao*, nearly disemboweling the heavy cruiser.[6]

Lee came within range and, while his destroyers carried on a long range duel with the *Nagara* group, the two battleships opened fire on the bigger targets. Sadly, *South Dakota*'s first broadside went against the wrong target, scoring a damaging hit on U.S.S. *Barton*, but her fire was soon directed against the Japanese, hitting the wounded *Takao* hard. *Washington* and *Kirishima* traded blows at 7,000 yards' range. The U.S. battleship's armor withstood the 14-inch shells well, but one hit jammed one of her forward turrets. In return she hit the *Kirishima* many times with 5-inch and 16-inch shells, seriously damaging her armament and propulsion.

*Hiei* regained control after ten minutes and led the Japanese withdrawal. Lee, noting them retiring, wanted to follow, but Turner ordered him back to the anchorage. With Lee's destroyers detached and serious damage to *Washington*'s firepower, Turner felt further pursuit was dangerous. Lee's mission had been accomplished. The evacuation anchorage had been protected. The following day, as the U.S. continued their evacuation loading, aircraft from *Hornet* and Henderson Field found several of the Japanese ships limping for safety and sank them: *Kirishima*, *Atago*, *Takao*, and two destroyers all went under.

The Naval Battle of Guadalcanal had cost the United States dearly. *Atlanta* and five destroyers were sunk, *Washington*, *Portland*, and *San Juan* were damaged, and over 800 sailors had died. These losses further convinced Ghormley that his decision to evacuate was the correct one. For the Japanese, the irreplaceable loss of *Hiei*, two heavy cruisers, and a light cruiser, plus 1,100 sailors, represented a devastating loss. But the American victory off the island was a hollow one. Fought defensively, it had no strategic impact; the island was still being evacuated.

The Japanese sent their usual array of bombers and Zeros the following day, but did not seriously interfere with the U.S. operations. Japanese observers in the hills overlooking the Marine perimeter began to realize what was taking place and sent word to Sendai Division headquarters, but Maruyama's men were not in position or shape to take advantage. They were in the midst of retracing their steps back to Japanese lines sans food and equipment. A single probe across the Matanikau elicited a spirited response by Marine artillery.

By the evening of October 13 loading was complete, and the engineers began setting off their demolitions. The resulting explosions and fires destroyed construction equipment, ammunition dumps, artillery pieces, and tanks, a fireworks display most Marines remembered sadly as they sailed away from their island. The following day, Henderson and Fighter One were destroyed by heavy bombardment from B-17s.

Three days later, Japanese troops entered the abandoned beachhead in strength and sent word of their 'victory' to their superiors in Tokyo. The world was once again treated to pictures of the Japanese soldiers standing over their conquest, arms raised in celebration.

## Summary

Operation Shoestring had been launched before the United States was materially ready for a major offensive campaign waged on land, sea, and air. Regardless of logistics, the Americans won on virtually all fronts. Despite that record, the campaign was lost in the one area that counted the most – in its commander's head. Ghormley took counsel of his fears and lost the drive to see the battle through. A commander with a bolder, more aggressive attitude would have seen past the problems and kept the Marines on the island, making the Japanese beat them.

Ironically, the Japanese showed great boldness in pushing through the needed troops and supplies despite the interdiction capabilities of Henderson Field. Their boldness had its drawbacks as they tried to attack a strong defensive perimeter with little support other than their manpower. The battles cost them irreplaceable soldiers, sailors, and airman, and the materiel losses, particularly in the air and at sea, were devastating. But their resolve didn't waver, and that turned defeat into victory.

## The reality

In the real battle there were two key differences from the story just related. First, the Americans did not take the counsel of their fears. Turner, for example, pushed the Seventh Marines through to the island in spite of losing *Wasp*. When Ghormley's confidence faltered in early October, Admiral 'Bull' Halsey, an aggressive and confident fighter, replaced him. The Americans hung on and dared the Japanese to push them off.

The second difference lay with the Japanese, who continually underestimated the Americans. When Ichiki's attack failed, General Kawaguchi's Brigade was sent to try. When his September attack failed, the Japanese sent the Sendai Division. The Japanese high command failed to take the threat seriously and apply their resources in a bold concentrated manner. This mistake allowed the Marines to hold on despite the shoestring nature of the operation.

## Bibliography

Bergerud, Eric, *Fire in the Sky: The Air War in the South Pacific* (Westview Press, Boulder, 2000).

Dull, Paul S., *A Battle History of the Imperial Japanese Navy (1941–1945)* (U.S. Naval Institute Press, Annapolis, 1978).

Dupuy, Trevor N., *The Harper Encyclopedia of Military Biography* (Harper Collins, New York, 1992).

Frank, Richard B., *Guadalcanal* (Random House, New York, 1990).

Loxton, Bruce, *The Shame of Savo: Anatomy of a Naval Disaster* (U.S. Naval Institute Press, Annapolis, 1994).

Morison, Samuel Eliot, *History of United States Naval Operations in World War II, vol.V: The Struggle for Guadalcanal, August 1942–February 1943* (Little, Brown, Boston, 1975).

## Notes

1. Alexander Archer Vandegrift was born in Charlotteville, Virginia, on March 13, 1887. He attended the University of Virginia before enlisting in the U.S. Marine Corps in 1908. He served in Mexico, Haiti and Nicaragua before undertaking a series of staff positions during which he helped draw up amphibious landing manuals. He took command of the First Marine Division two months before leading it into the South Pacific. After the war he served as Commandant of the Marine Corps and vigorously argued against any mention of a 'defeat' on Guadalcanal for the rest of his life. See Trevor N. Dupuy, *The Harper Encyclopedia of Military Biography* (Harper Collins, New York, 1992).

2. The destroyer U.S.S. *Jarvis* has been listed by some historians as part of the northern group. In fact, she was damaged by the air attack the day before the Savo Island battle. One account has her sailing past the southern group and the oncoming Japanese and sinking in some unidentified place after the battle: Samuel Eliot Morison, *History of the United States Naval Operations in World War II, vol.V: The Struggle for Guadalcanal, August 1942–February 1943* (Little, Brown, Boston, 1975), p.36.

3. One of the popular but unsubstantiated myths surrounding this initial stage of the battle was that Goto believed he was being attacked by Japanese ships, never considering that the U.S. would risk the night waters off Guadalcanal. According to the myth, the last thing he said was *'Bakayaro'* ('stupid bastards').

4. One such hero was U.S. Marine Private Joseph Champagne, who reached out as a Japanese tank churned up his foxhole and put a grenade in the tracks. The tank, with ruptured tracks, slewed away into the surf, where it was destroyed by a 75mm gun: Richard B. Frank, *Guadalcanal* (Random House, New York, 1990), p.350.

*5. Kawaguchi's failure to bring his troops into the battle created a major personal feud between him and Maruyama, who accused the general of deliberately withholding his troops. The controversy grew, involving staff officers throughout Japan, and ended only when Kawaguchi was killed in a plane crash on Saipan three years later: Masao Maruyama, *Triumph of the Will: Defeat into Victory on Guadalcanal* (U.S. Naval Institute Press, Annapolis, 1955), p.236.

6. This was not the first time during the Guadalcanal battle that a ship torpedoed a friendly vessel. Post-war analysis into the loss of the H.M.A.S. *Canberra* during the Savo Island battle indicated that the U.S.S. *Bagley* probably fired the torpedoes that doomed the Australian vessel: Loxton, *The Shame of Savo: Anatomy of a Naval Disaster* (U.S. Naval Institute Press, Annapolis, 1994), chapter 18.

# 9
# THERE ARE SUCH THINGS AS MIRACLES
## Halsey and Kurita at Leyte Gulf

Christopher J. Anderson

By the autumn of 1944 even the most dedicated Japanese naval officer could recognize that things were not going well in his country's war with the United States and its allies. Beginning with their seizure of the Marshall Islands in February, the third year of the war had been marked by a string of Allied victories. Everywhere, it seemed, the Americans were inexorably advancing in a vast and overwhelming tide that was seizing all of the territory gained during the heady days of 1941 and 1942.

In the summer of 1944 the situation had taken a further turn for the worse when, in response to efforts to defeat American forces fighting to secure the Marianas Islands (including the critical island of Saipan), Admiral Jisaburo Ozawa's First Mobile fleet had been decisively defeated at the Battle of the Philippine Sea on June 19–20, 1944. Known derisively by the Americans as the 'Great Marianas Turkey Shoot', the disaster had cost Ozawa all but forty-seven of his 473 operational aircraft, as well as two of the emperor's precious aircraft carriers. With the Marianas Islands in American hands, Japanese planners knew that the enemy was now within range of the home islands. Soon, waves of American B-29 bombers would be exacting revenge for the December 7, 1941, attack on Pearl Harbor by mercilessly bombing Japanese cities. In the wake of Ozawa's defeat, Prime Minister Hideki Tojo, who had done so much to propel his nation into conflict with the United States, was forced to resign. After the fall of Saipan one prescient Japanese observer was overheard to remark that, 'Hell is on us.'

### 'Act faithfully and well'

To forestall this, Japanese planners met in July 1944 to try and determine what to expect next from the enemy and to prepare a course of action that could be followed in response to whatever direction the Americans struck. The resulting *Sho* (victory) plan, which required that all available resources

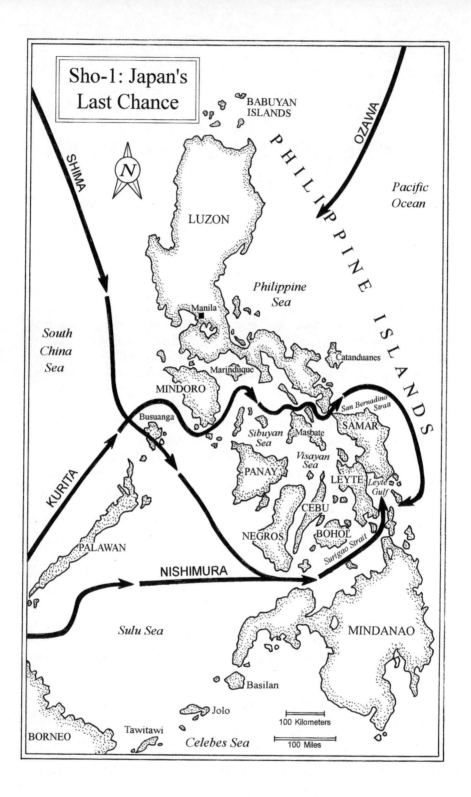

Sho-1: Japan's Last Chance

be carefully husbanded until needed, provided four alternative defensive operations that could be activated as soon as the Americans made their next move. *Sho*-1 would be activated in response to an attack on the Philippines, *Sho*-2 for the Kuriles and Ryukyus, *Sho*-3 for southern Japan, and *Sho*-4 for northern Japan. Each of these plans was considered to be an all or nothing operation intended to provide one last opportunity to secure a decisive victory over the Allies and forestall Japan's total collapse. For any of these plans to be successful, however, the Japanese would need to achieve a level of cooperation among their forces that had heretofore been lacking. They would also need time to train pilots who could replace those lost in the Marianas Islands.

Time ran out in October 1944. In preparation for the upcoming American naval offensive, Rear Admiral William F. Halsey began a series of air attacks starting as far to the north as Okinawa and working southward to the Philippines. Intended to confuse the enemy as to the time and place of the next attack and to further weaken their defenses, the Japanese responded by sending out what available aircraft they had to drive off the American planes.

Admiral Soemu Toyoda, the commander in chief of the Combined Fleet, was in Formosa on October 12 when Halsey's aircraft struck that island. Believing the attack heralded the start of the invasion of Formosa, Toyoda ordered a partial activation of *Sho*-2 and sent every available aircraft to attack the Americans. Unfortunately, the air battles in the first weeks of October were merely a repeat of what had happened four months previously. Vice Admiral Shigeru Fukodome commented after the American raid that 'our fighters were nothing but so many eggs thrown at the stone wall of the indomitable enemy formation.'[1]

Although the Japanese achieved limited successes – sinking two Allied cruisers – the air battles of September and October were a serious setback to the possible success of the *Sho* plan. The poorly trained Japanese pilots were simply no match for the Americans; slightly more than half of the thousand aircraft that the Japanese had gathered since June fell to Halsey's planes. The battle over Formosa seriously diminished what little airpower the Japanese now had available to implement whichever of the *Sho* plans finally became necessary.

Meanwhile, as Halsey's aircraft were clearing the skies of Japanese planes, the massive American fleet began to assemble at Hollandia and elsewhere along the coast of New Guinea to begin its journey north. Although there had been a good deal of wrangling between General Douglas MacArthur, who favored an American landing to liberate the Philippines, and Admiral Chester Nimitz, who favored bypassing the Philippines altogether in favor of an attack on Formosa, by September MacArthur's appeals had their desired effect and President Franklin Roosevelt had made the decision to launch the next Allied attack on the Philippines. Scheduled to begin with an invasion of Leyte on December 20, 1944, the date of the invasion was advanced to October after Halsey excitedly reported that the island was poorly defended and could be taken with little effort.

Believing that the moment had arrived to return to the Philippines, the Americans prepared to launch a massive combined operation against Leyte. As was to be expected, MacArthur would be in overall command of the operation. Lieutenant General Walter Krueger's Sixth Army would land on the island while Vice Admiral Thomas Kincaid's massive 700-ship Seventh Fleet supported the operation from Leyte Gulf. Meanwhile, in the unlikely event that the Japanese fleet was able to sail south toward the invasion fleet, Halsey, operating under orders not from MacArthur but Nimitz, was commanded to use his Third Fleet to 'cover and support forces of Southwest Pacific in order to assist the seizure and occupation of objectives in the Central Philippines ... and destroy enemy naval and air forces in or threatening the Philippines Area... In case opportunity for destruction of major portion of enemy fleet offers or can be created, such destruction becomes the primary task.'[2]

Although the two principal American fleets were operating under different commanders – Kinkaid under MacArthur and Halsey under Nimitz – it was believed that operations had been going so smoothly up to this point that a split command would not pose any major difficulties to the success of the operation.

Despite the assembly against them of the most powerful naval force ever known, the Japanese remained unaware of exactly where the Americans would strike next – and therefore unable to activate the appropriate *Sho* plan – until the morning of October 17, when Japanese observers on the tiny Philippine island of Suluan reported that they spotted American ships. The men of the Sixth Ranger Battalion came ashore on Suluan, Dinagat, and Homophon to secure these islands in preparation for the arrival of Kinkaid's Seventh fleet. Reports of the American advance on the Philippines were received by Admiral Toyoda, who realized that the time had come to initiate *Sho*-1 and finally check the American advance.[3] After further discussion among senior Japanese naval officers, at 1110 on the morning of October 18, 1944, Admiral Toyoda gave the order to execute *Sho*-1.

Although Toyoda was unhappy with the prospect of launching his fleet in the face of an enemy overwhelmingly superior in air and naval power, later commenting that making the decision to activate *Sho*-1 was 'as difficult as swallowing molten iron',[4] he knew that the loss of the Philippines would sever the home islands from their valuable oil supplies in the East Indies, which would have a catastrophic effect on the Japanese war effort. If Japan were to have any hope of survival, therefore, the Philippines must be retained.

*Sho*-1 called for the Japanese to order what remained of their widely scattered forces to converge at Brunei, where Admiral Takeo Kurita would lead them to attack the American fleet at Leyte Gulf. If he arrived quickly enough, it was hoped that Kurita could destroy Kinkaid's Seventh Fleet before the Americans became strong enough to secure total control of the archipelago. To prevent Halsey's Third Fleet from coming to the aid of Kinkaid, the Japanese planned to use an additional force to entice the Americans northward.

Toyoda knew that in order to lure Halsey away from the landing area he would have to provide a target that was sufficiently tempting to ensure the Americans' pursuit. Since the air battles at the Philippine Sea and Formosa had destroyed what little remained of Japanese naval airpower, the decision was made to offer up the empire's remaining aircraft carriers as bait. This sacrificial force was commanded by Ozawa and consisted of four carriers, two battleships that had been converted to aircraft carriers by the addition of improvised flight decks, and eleven cruisers.[5] As carriers had come to dominate naval operations by this point in the war, it was reasoned that the site of what remained of Japan's carrier force would be too lucrative a target for the aggressive Admiral Halsey to pass up.

After arriving in Brunei on the 20th, Kurita and his staff briefed the assembled officers aboard his flagship, the cruiser *Atago*. The plan called for Kurita to split his force into two wings that would travel to Leyte on two separate routes. To the north, the First Strike Force under the overall command of Kurita consisted of five battleships, including *Yamato* and *Musashi*, the largest and most powerful battleships ever built, seven cruisers, and fifteen destroyers. This force would travel across the Philippine archipelago via the Sibuyan Sea. After passing through the San Bernadino Strait, Kurita would travel around Samar and descend on Kinkaid from the north. Meanwhile, a smaller but still potent force of two battleships, one cruiser, and four destroyers, led by Vice Admiral Shoji Nishimura, would strike Leyte from the south after crossing the Sulu Sea, traveling past Mindanao through the Surigao Strait. As the two forces traversed the narrow passages toward Leyte, what little ground-based aircraft that remained to the Japanese would take to the sky and provide air cover. If everything went well, the two pincers would arrive almost simultaneously at Leyte on the 25th.

Every one of the officers present for Kurita's briefing knew that this was a desperate gamble that was likely to result in the sinking of many of the emperor's finest ships. They also knew that they had no other option but to proceed. If they succeeded they could save their embattled country. If they failed, they would at least ensure that the imperial fleet met an honorable end. Before the briefing finished Kurita addressed his officers:

I know that many of you are strongly opposed to this assignment. But the war situation is far more critical than any of you can possibly know. Would it not be a shame to have the fleet remain intact while our nation perishes? I believe that Imperial General Headquarters is giving us a glorious opportunity. Because I realize how very serious the war situation actually is, I am willing to accept this ultimate assignment to storm into Leyte Gulf.

You must all remember that there are such things as miracles. What man can say that there is no chance for our fleet to turn the tide of war in a decisive battle? We shall have a chance to meet our enemies. We shall engage his task forces. I hope that you will not carry out your duties lightly. I know you will act faithfully and well.[6]

On the same day that Kurita briefed his officers, General MacArthur returned to the Philippines at the head of one of the most powerful armadas the world had ever seen. American forces were able to take advantage of the confusion among the Japanese defenders to quickly establish a beachhead on Leyte. While troops and supplies of the Sixth Army stormed ashore, Kinkaid's Seventh Fleet pounded enemy positions with the guns of its battleships and cruisers.

When the meeting aboard *Atago* adjourned, the Japanese officers returned to their ships and began the preparations necessary to get Kurita's force underway. Japanese sailors, inspired by the sight of the combined fleet anchored at Brunei and believing they had an opportunity to reverse the course of the war, worked diligently throughout the 21st to prepare their ships. By evening everything was ready. On the morning of the 22nd Kurita's First Strike Force sailed from Brunei toward Palawan, with Kurita's flagship in the van just behind a screen of destroyers. As they sailed toward their destination, Kurita was cheered to learn that three cruisers and four destroyers, commanded by Vice Admiral Kihohide Shima, were coming from Formosa and would reinforce his southern wing. The latest additions to Kurita's striking force were instructed to travel south and join Nishimura, who had left Brunei on the 23rd, before entering the Surigao Strait. So far, everything had gone as well as could be expected; the forces had joined and were now traveling rapidly toward the Philippines.[7]

### Strike for Leyte

Lying in the path of Kurita's advancing ships were two submarines that were on patrol near the Palawan Passage, U.S.S. *Darter*, commanded by Commander David McClintock and U.S.S. *Dace*, commanded by Commander Bladen D. Claggett. Just after midnight on the 23rd *Darter*'s radar picked up signals that indicated that an enemy convoy was approaching. Immediately, the two submarines submerged and positioned themselves to attack what they assumed was a relief convoy traveling toward the Philippines' Japanese defenders. As their screens lit up with a number of blips, radar operators on the two submarines soon realized that this was no convoy.

Trained to attack regardless of the odds, the two American submarine commanders positioned themselves immediately in front of the Japanese force and prepared to launch all of their torpedoes at the advancing Japanese ships. Both commanders hurriedly plotted targets at several of the larger blips on their radar operators' screens. Soon, a volley of torpedoes shot out from the two submarines, quickly followed by another. Shortly after the second volley of torpedoes had left their tubes, the crews of the two submarines could hear a series of explosions. Quickly raising their periscopes, the submarine skippers could see two destroyers and a cruiser breaking up under the damage caused by multiple torpedo hits. McClintock later remembered that the cruiser was:

> a mass of billowing smoke from the number one turret to the stern. No superstructure could be seen. Bright orange flames shot from the side along the main deck from the bow to the after turret. Cruiser was already down by the bow, which was dipping under. Number one turret was at water level. She was definitely finished. Five hits had her sinking and in flames. It is estimated that there were few, if any survivors.[8]

With his thoughts focused on the difficulties of bringing his force through the Sibuyan Sea without fighter cover, Kurita was startled by the explosions that erupted to his front and right as two of his destroyers and the heavy cruiser *Myoko* burst into flames and staggered under the blows of enemy torpedoes. The stunned admiral quickly regained his senses, however, and over the objections of some of his officers who wanted to look for survivors, ordered that the fleet continue on toward the Philippines without delay. Aware of the long odds against success, Kurita accepted that his force would suffer casualties; what was most important was that he bring as much of his strength as possible to the north side of Leyte Gulf by the 25th.

Soon after ordering his fleet to continue, Kurita contacted the commander of the First Air Fleet on Luzon, Vice Admiral Takajiro Onishi, and alerted him to the fact that his force had been attacked and that early the next day he could expect to be visited by aircraft of the now alerted American fleet. Onishi agreed and responded with a request to attack Halsey's forces immediately. Even though they had been able to husband a fair number of aircraft throughout the Philippine Islands, Kurita knew that the numbers were insufficient, and the pilots too ill-trained, to launch an air attack on the massive American fleet with any hope of causing serious damage. Kurita denied Onishi's request and instead ordered him to gather as many aircraft as possible to provide what air cover he could to Kurita's force. As if to ensure that his orders would be carried out, Kurita concluded his last message to Onishi with a reminder that, 'the future of the nation rests with the fleet'.[9]

As the Japanese ships sailed on, hurriedly dropping a number of depth charges as they passed, the crews of the two American submarines congratulated themselves on what, by almost any reckoning, had been a tremendously successful evening. What was more important than the sinking of the heavy cruiser *Myoko*, however, was the information that the Combined Fleet had come out to do battle. While the crew of *Darter* began to celebrate, McClintock alerted Admiral Halsey that there was a large Japanese fleet headed toward Leyte Gulf.

## Halsey hits back

Halsey, eager to come to grips with the Japanese, alerted Kinkaid of the approaching enemy force and spent the remainder of the 23rd preparing for their arrival. As soon as it was light enough to launch aircraft, Halsey sent up pairs of Hellcats and Helldivers to search for Kurita's fleet along the most likely approaches to Leyte. One of these search parties consisted of three planes launched from U.S.S. *Intrepid* at 0600 on the morning of the 24th. At 0812, while flying over the Sibuyan Sea, one of these aircraft spotted Kurita's fleet steaming along the western side of the Tablas Strait, headed for the San Bernadino Strait. Within ten minutes this information had been radioed back to Halsey on board U.S.S. *New Jersey*. Following quickly on the heels of the sighting of Kurita's force was news that aircraft from U.S.S. *Enterprise* had located and attacked Nishimura's force of two battleships, a cruiser, and several destroyers. Although he had yet to find the Japanese carriers, Halsey now knew where the bulk of the Japanese forces were located and he quickly devised his plan of attack.[10] His available force was divided into three task groups, Task Group 38.4 commanded by Rear Admiral Ralph E. Davidson (off Leyte Gulf), 38.2 commanded by Rear Admiral Gerald F. Bogan (east of the San Bernadino Strait), and 38.3 commanded by Frederick C. Sherman (east of Luzon). A fourth, Task Force 38.1 commanded by Admiral John McCain, had been detached and sent to Ulithi for rest and re-supply.

Seeking to come to blows with the enemy while at the same time mindful of his order to support Kinkaid's now alerted Seventh Fleet and nervous that the report of Kurita's sighting made no mention of aircraft carriers, Halsey ordered his three remaining task forces to concentrate. While Admiral Sherman was charged with patrolling the northern approaches to Leyte, Admirals Davidson and Bogan were immediately ordered to launch their aircraft against Kurita's advancing forces. Aware of Nishimura's approach, Kinkaid detached all of his larger ships to defend the Surigao Strait and to prepare for the Japanese southern strike force's arrival. Although he cursed himself for the over-confidence that had permitted him to send McCain to Ulithi, Halsey believed, quite rightly, that he still possessed a force potent enough to cause serious damage to Kurita's ships.

After quickly formulating a plan of attack, Halsey contacted his task force commanders, relayed the necessary information on the approaching Japanese formation, and ordered, 'Strike! Repeat. Strike!'[11] Hellcat and Helldiver pilots aboard the carriers of the Third Fleet quickly scrambled and were soon ready to launch attacks on Kurita's fast approaching ships.

Since his radio messages with Kurita the night before, Onishi had been busy preparing to rush his aircraft to the support of the approaching Japanese ships. As soon as it was light, the first of Onishi's planes were in the sky and headed to Kurita's aid. Very early on the morning of the 24th, the skies above the Sibuyan Sea was full of hundreds of Japanese and American aircraft all racing toward Kurita.

Fortunately for Kurita, Onishi's planes won the race. A force of fifty planes had taken position above the Japanese fleet by 0958 and was waiting when the first of the American air attacks reached their target. At 1026 a force of twenty-one fighters, twelve dive-bombers and twelve torpedo-bombers from the aircraft carriers *Intrepid* and *Cabot* reached the Japanese fleet and were staggered by what they saw.[12] Although the size of the enemy force had been reported earlier, actually seeing an armada of such power was truly awe-inspiring. The Americans did not have long to gawk before Japanese aircraft waiting overhead pounced.

Although the Japanese pilots were not as experienced as their American counterparts, they had the advantage of numbers, surprise, and the over-whelming number of anti-aircraft guns of the ships below. A quick pass by Japanese aircraft downed two of the American fighters and three of the dive-bombers before they even had time to react. Soon, American fighter aircraft had engaged the Japanese while the remaining dive bombers regrouped and dove on the fleet, focusing on the huge battleships that lay in the center of Kurita's force.

Despite their bravery, the American dive-bombers never had an opportunity to launch an effective attack. Six of the bombers were blown apart before they even had a chance to launch their weapons. A seventh, badly damaged by enemy fire, crashed into one of the Japanese destroyers in a final act of defiance. Of the remaining eleven aircraft that managed to escape the intense enemy flak, three were destroyed after releasing their torpedoes and the remainder managed to escape intact.

Everything had not gone in favor of the Japanese, however. Of the three torpedoes that the Americans had been able to launch, two found their mark. One struck the battleship *Nagato*. In addition, seven Japanese aircraft had been destroyed. Damage reports from *Nagato* indicated that it could continue, but its speed would be reduced. Kurita knew that although he had driven off the first American force, others would quickly follow. Slowing the speed of his fleet to that of his slowest ship, Kurita awaited the next American attack.

Meanwhile, the stunned survivors of the first American air strike warned their oncoming comrades of what they were about to face. Undaunted, Halsey ordered additional air strikes. At 1245 a second strike force from *Lexington* and *Essex* reached Kurita. Unlike the first failed attack, additional Japanese aircraft sent by Onishi to relieve the initial flight did not surprise the Americans in this second wave. Nevertheless, after twenty minutes of intense aerial combat Kurita drove off the attack, but at far greater cost. Faced by far more experienced pilots who were ready for them, twenty-three of Onishi's airplanes were shot from the sky, at a cost of only three enemy fighters. American bombers had braved the intense anti-aircraft fire and managed to successfully hit the giant *Musashi* with several torpedoes. Although their attack did not sink her, she was sufficiently damaged that she would be unable to keep up with the fleet. While some of the American pilots focused their attention on *Musashi*, others renewed their attacks on the already damaged *Nagato*. Unable to maneuver quickly because of damage suffered during the first strike, *Nagato* could not avoid a string of torpedoes that struck her port side. At 1259, just moments after she had been hit, *Nagato* listed to port and sank.

As the second wave of American aircraft slipped back to their carriers in the east, Kurita surveyed the damage. He had already suffered the loss of two battleships, a cruiser, and two destroyers, losses that under normal circumstances would have sent most naval officers reeling. Several of his staff urged him to retire and save what remained of his fleet before additional American strikes came. Remembering the desperate nature of his mission, however, Kurita decided to continue.

## No matter the cost

Regardless of the losses he had suffered thus far, Kurita reasoned that he still possessed a powerful force that could, if able to reach the transports at Leyte, inflict a crippling blow on the Americans. Unwilling to delay any longer, he silenced critics on his staff and his own fears and continued. For the next several hours the air attacks continued and Kurita's force suffered additional damage. After a 1330 attack, the mighty *Musashi* was so severely damaged that her commander informed Kurita that the battleship was sinking and would have to be abandoned. The news of *Musashi*'s fate staggered Kurita, who wondered if perhaps, they were hoping for too much.

Jubilant American aircrews reported back to Halsey that they had inflicted punishing blows on the Japanese. The commander of the Third Fleet was convinced that his airplanes had eliminated Kurita's force as an effective threat. Now all he had to do was to find the enemy's carrier forces and he could complete the destruction of the Japanese fleet. Unaware of exactly where Ozawa was, Halsey urged Sherman to step up his reconnaissance missions while he prepared to take the three task groups of the Third Fleet wherever was necessary. Aware at the same time that Kurita's battered force remained afloat, he also decided to make arrangements to form another force from his larger ships that would be tasked with protecting the San Bernadino Strait. The new force, dubbed Task Force 34, would consist of four battleships, five cruisers, and nineteen destroyers, and, when organized, would be commanded by Vice Admiral Willis A. Lee. In order to ensure that all of his ships were aware of his plans, at 1512 Halsey radioed all of the ships of the Third Fleet as well as Admirals Nimitz and King describing the contingency force, which would be activated upon his command. Radio monitors from the Seventh Fleet also picked up this message and relayed the information to Admiral Kinkaid.[13]

As Halsey formulated his plans, Kurita contemplated his future. Overcome by the loss of so many men, the admiral ordered three of his destroyers to turn about and pick up any survivors while the crews of his remaining ships repaired some of the damage they had suffered. On board *Atago*, Kurita considered his next move. Having been badly battered by American aircraft throughout the day and having heard little or nothing about the progress of the other *Sho* forces, at 1600 he wired Tokyo that despite the support of a limited number of Japanese aircraft:

> the enemy made more than 250 sorties against us between 0830 and 1530, the number of planes involved and their fierceness mounting with every wave. Our air forces, on the other hand, were not able to obtain even expected results, causing our losses to mount steadily. Under these circumstances it was deemed that were we to force our way through, we would merely make ourselves meat for the enemy, with very little chance of success. It was therefore concluded that the best course open to us was temporarily to retire beyond the reach of enemy planes.[14]

Surveying the remnants of his once powerful force, it was easy for Kurita to assume that the *Sho* plan had been a disaster. The intensity of the air strikes that had been launched against him throughout the day would indicate that Ozawa had failed to draw off the might of the Third Fleet. Having heard nothing further from Nishimura he could only assume the worst there as well. Kurita's fortunes, however, were soon to change.

After repeated efforts to locate Ozawa's force, at 1640 bombers from Sherman's task force spotted the carriers as they steamed south toward Luzon. Locating the Japanese carrier force was just what Halsey – and Ozawa – had been waiting for. Halsey immediately alerted his task group commanders to concentrate and soon had all three of them moving. He radioed McCain to cut short his leave from the Third Fleet and rejoin it as it headed north to destroy the Japanese carriers. With Halsey's force now headed north, the danger of further aerial attack on Kurita's ships had ended. Given a respite from the constant air attacks, Kurita began to recover some of his nerve. Remembering the 'all or nothing' nature of the *Sho* plan, the admiral decided to continue his advance. Perhaps as confirmation of the correctness of this decision, at 1815 Admiral Toyoda responded to Kurita's earlier message informing him 'All forces will dash to the attack, trusting in divine guidance.'[15] His orders now clear and his forces protected by darkness, Kurita proceeded toward San Bernadino Strait. If he experienced no further delays, he planned to pass through the Strait at 0100 on October 25.

While Kurita had been battling for his life in the Sulu Sea, Nishimura's force had proceeded with little interruption from the Americans. Although he had endured one attack early on the morning of the 24th, after he drove off the American planes he proceeded without difficulty. He also received word that the Second Force, commanded by Vice Admiral Kiyohide Shima, was approaching his fleet from the north and would soon be available to reinforce him as he passed through the Strait. Although he had an intense dislike for Shima, Nishimura recognized that the seriousness of the situation demanded that every member of the fleet work together. There would be time enough for personal vendettas after the Americans had been destroyed.

### Remember Pearl Harbor

But Nishimura had been spotted, and although no further attacks were launched against him for the remainder of the day, the Americans were not idle. Given ample warning of the Japanese approach and confident that Halsey had seen to the defense of the San Bernadino Strait, Admiral Kinkaid took his time to prepare for his opponent's arrival at the eastern side of the Surigao Strait. To counter such a move, Kinkaid ordered Rear Admiral Jesse B. Oldendorf to plug the twelve-mile wide northern exit of the strait with a force of six battleships – five of which had been at Pearl Harbor in 1941 – eight cruisers, and twenty-eight destroyers. Oldendorf decided to place his largest ships directly across the mouth of the strait with the destroyers divided and placed along each side. To add depth to the defense, Oldendorf also placed thirty-nine of the diminutive patrol torpedo (PT) boats further down the strait. Unlikely to be able to halt Nishimura's advancing battleships, the PTs would serve as a tripwire that would provide Oldendorf with important up to the minute information about the opponent he was about to face. They would also be able to harass Nishimura as he advanced, perhaps causing some confusion among the enemy.

The evening of the 24th was spent by the men of both navies preparing for the next stage of the battle. While Kurita and Nishimura's crews made final arrangements before their entrance into the Philippine Sea, Halsey's sailors readied their planes for air strikes against Ozawa's carriers and Oldendorf's crews made sure that their guns were well sighted on the northern exit of Surigao Strait.

While aircrews scrambled around the decks of his carriers, Halsey thought it prudent to inform Kinkaid of his plans. At 2024 Halsey radioed Kinkaid that 'Strike reports indicate enemy heavily damaged. Am proceeding north with 3 groups to attack enemy carrier force at dawn.'[16] Kinkaid was pleased with the news. He was ready for Nishimura's force as it headed through Surigao Strait and it appeared that Halsey was ready to knock out Ozawa's force coming from the north with his three task forces. And, although it was not a huge force, Kinkaid believed that Task Force 34 should be more than sufficient to halt Kurita's badly damaged ships from emerging through the San Bernadino Strait. Everything seemed in place to deliver the Japanese a telling blow.

Just ten minutes after Halsey had radioed Kinkaid, word was received that one of Oldendorf's PT boats has spotted Nishimura's advancing fleet. As soon as they had spotted the enemy, the tiny American boats charged ahead in a series of brave, but disappointing, attacks. Despite launching a number of torpedoes, little was accomplished other than disrupting the Japanese advance. Gunners aboard Nishimura's destroyers were able to destroy a number of the PT boats. At 2136 Nishimura radioed Shima, who was following just behind him, that he was 'advancing as scheduled while destroying enemy torpedo boats.'[17]

Opposition to Nishimura's advance, however, was soon to become more intense. Alerted to the advancing Japanese ships just after 0200 on the morning of October 25, Oldendorf's destroyers steamed down Surigao Strait and prepared to deliver a series of torpedo attacks. An hour later the first American torpedoes were sent against the enemy ships. By the time they had finished with these attacks, two destroyers had been sunk and a third badly damaged. Torpedoes had also damaged the battleships *Fuso* and *Yamashiro*. Perhaps most importantly, the PT and destroyer attacks had eliminated all semblance of order among the Japanese ships as they prepared to encounter Oldendorf's waiting cruisers and battleships.

As the badly disorganized enemy force approached within range of his battleships and cruisers, Oldendorf could not believe his luck. the Japanese were approaching in a column dead ahead. For some reason, perhaps the disruptive effects of the earlier PT boat and destroyer attacks, or even Nishimura's obstinacy, the Japanese had neglected to maneuver in such a way as to present a broad front to the enemy. This meant that the American admiral was about to enjoy the advantage, dreamed of by all naval commanders but seldom experienced, of being able to bring all of his guns to bear at the lead Japanese ship. Oldendorf had crossed the 'T'!

At 0351 Oldendorf ordered his ships to open fire. Soon, shells from some of the largest guns in the United States Navy were raining down on the unfortunate Japanese. For the next fifteen minutes salvos quickly shattered what remained of Nishimura's ships. The flagship *Yamashiro* had gone down, *Mogami* and *Fuso* were badly battered and left for dead, and *Shigure*, although she had turned about and begun to retreat, was soon dead in the water as well.

Just as the final salvos of the American battleships began to find their targets, Shima, on board the cruiser *Nachi*, arrived on the scene. He had hoped to join Nishimura earlier, but American PT boat attacks had slowed his advance. Viewing the wreckage of *Fuso* as he sailed northward, Shima soon realized that there was nothing left of Nishimura's force to join. A little after 0400, in a gesture of false bravado, Shima launched a series of ineffectual torpedo attacks at what he believed were American ships, and then turned and headed south. As he sailed away from the scene of Nishimura's demise, Shima came upon the wreckage of *Mogami*, which he believed was lying dead in the water. Unfortunately he was wrong; *Mogami* was moving slowly and, at 0430, Nachi collided with the wounded vessel, causing further damage.

The southern arm of the Japanese advance toward Leyte Gulf had been a disaster. As the sun came up on the 25th, Shima's sailors anxiously awaited the inevitable attacks by pursuing American ships as they began to limp back to Brunei. While Shima was contemplating how he was going to get his battered ships away from the enemy, Kinkaid was meeting with his staff. The Americans were discussing the recently concluded action and, no doubt, congratulating themselves on their stunning victory. Just prior to adjourning the meeting, Kinkaid turned to his chief of staff, Captain Richard H. Cruzen, and asked, 'Now, Dick, is there anything we haven't done?' Cruzen responded that he could think of just 'one thing. We have never directly asked Halsey if TF34 is guarding San Bernadino Strait.' Just to be doubly sure, Kinkaid authorized Cruzen to send Halsey a message to confirm that TF34 was indeed covering the Strait.[18]

Although much of the action on the evening of the 24th–25th had been in the south, Kurita had not been idle. At 0035 his fleet passed unmolested through the San Bernadino Strait and into the Philippine Sea. Kurita, who was still licking his wounds from the air battles of the previous day, could not believe his good fortune. How could the Americans have left such a critical passage uncovered? Had Ozawa's flotilla finally drawn off Halsey's forces? If his luck continued to hold, in just over six hours he would be in a position to attack the American transports in Leyte Gulf. After convincing himself that, indeed, there were no Americans guarding the passage, Kurita radioed Onishi and requested that he have whatever air cover was available rendezvous with him as he rounded the eastern side of Samar. Onishi, who had suffered severe losses defending Kurita's force on the 24th, responded that he would provide what few aircraft remained.

### 'Where is Task Force 34?'

Kurita's passage had been unopposed because of a tragic miscommunication on the part of the Americans. Contrary to what Kinkaid, Nimitz, and King believed, there was no Task Force 34. Halsey's earlier message had simply indicated that the task force would be formed if necessary. Believing that he had so damaged Kurita that he no longer posed a threat, Halsey had elected to take all of his available strength with him, including the ships that would have composed TF34. The misunderstanding was made worse by Halsey's message of the previous evening that declared that he was heading north with '3 groups'. This second message seemed to confirm that Halsey had left San Bernardino protected.

The miscommunication between Halsey and Kinkaid may have been avoided had they been serving under a unified command, but that was not the case. Now, this string of errors meant that as Admiral Kurita sailed around the coast of Samar, all that was guarding the vital American landing beaches at Leyte were sixteen tiny escort carriers and a screen of destroyers divided into three groups – Taffy-1, commanded by Rear Admiral T.L. Sprague; Taffy-2, commanded by Rear Admiral F.B. Stump; and Taffy-3, commanded by Rear Admiral C.A.F. Sprague. The escort carriers, nick-named 'jeep' carriers, were intended to provide air support to forces oper-ating ashore and to conduct anti-submarine patrols. They were armed with only one 5-inch gun and a few anti-aircraft weapons. To make matters worse, most of the aircraft on board had been armed with ordnance more suitable to support operations against Japanese troop formations on Leyte than against enemy warships.

On the bridge of *Atago*, Kurita was still trying to figure out how, despite the battering he had taken the previous day and the silence from the other wings of the *Sho* force, he had been so fortunate. His thoughts were interrupted just before 0600 as he looked up to see thirty-five of Onishi's aircraft overhead. Although he would have enjoyed greater air support, at this point in the operation he was happy with anything he could get. Soon thereafter, a radio report was received from Yamato that announced that radar had spotted American aircraft. Cautious from the previous day's beating, Kurita ordered his fleet to prepare for an aerial attack. Soon, however, reports were received that Onishi's aircraft had splashed an American reconnaissance plane. Sailors aboard Kurita's ships were alert and at their positions when, just visible over the horizon, could be seen the radar masts of Rear Admiral Clifton Sprague's six escort carriers. The news electrified the Japanese crews, Kurita's chief of staff, Admiral Timiji Koyanagi, recalled that soon after sighting the masts 'we could see planes being launched. This was indeed a miracle. Think of a surface fleet coming up on an enemy carrier group? Nothing is more vulnerable than an aircraft carrier in a surface engagement.'[19]

Kurita was astonished. Although his force had suffered a good deal of damage it was still incredibly potent, especially against enemy carriers caught unprepared. He alerted all of the ships of the force to prepare for action and form a battleline. He then steamed toward the American carriers.

At 0658 the massive 18-inch guns of the battleship *Yamato* were fired toward the American carriers. As they approached, additional ships added their salvos to those of *Yamato*.

On board *Fanshaw Bay*, Sprague was horrified to see a huge red geyser of water rise up just off his port bow. The admiral knew that the Japanese often used dye to mark the fall of their incoming rounds. What were the Japanese doing there, he wondered? TF34 was supposed to be guarding the San Bernadino Strait. Sprague had little time to consider what had happened, however, as soon the waters around Taffy-3 were alive with color as Japanese shells came closer and closer. Aware that time was of the essence, he immediately ordered his ships to generate smoke launching their aircraft and to retreat toward Taffy-2. He then radioed to Task Force commander T.L. Sprague and Kinkaid the desperate message, 'Where is Task Force 34?' Kinkaid was alarmed by Sprague's message. He was sure that the strait had been covered. Then he remembered that he had never received a confirmation from Halsey that TF34 was, in fact, off the San Bernadino Strait.

Meanwhile, in a desperate bid to buy time, the aircraft from Taffy-3 were throwing themselves at Kurita's force. Untrained and unequipped for an aerial attack on Japanese ships bristling with anti-aircraft guns and supported by circling land based fighters, Taffy-3's brave pilots were either shot from the sky or driven away before they could do much damage. Later, waves of fighters launched from Taffy-2 and Taffy-1 proved only slightly more successful, launching a torpedo attack that destroyed one of Kurita's destroyers. The beleaguered American carriers of Taffy-3 received a brief respite when they were able to enter the protection offered by a nearby rainstorm. However, even that relief proved to be short-lived. Unable to keep pace with the fast moving storm, the carriers were soon being bracketed by renewed enemy shellfire. Aware that he was sending them to their deaths, but having little other choice, Sprague ordered his destroyers to attack the Japanese. Given the circumstances, the Americans were incredibly successful, severely damaging the cruiser *Kumano* as well as two additional Japanese destroyers.

Even this effort, however, was futile. The overwhelming might of Kurita's battleships and cruisers had soon dispatched the destroyers *Johnston* and *Hoel* and left *Hermann* dead in the water. With his destroyers now gone, Sprague waited for the inevitable, and at 0720, 18-inch shells from *Yamato* ripped into Sprague's flagship, U.S.S. *Fanshaw*, and she quickly went down. *White Plains* and *Gambier Bay* soon followed Taffy-3's flagship to the bottom. Kurita then dispatched a cruiser to deal with the remaining ships of Taffy-3 while the rest of his force continued on toward Leyte Gulf.

Before his ship went down, Sprague was able to alert Kinkaid that unless Taffy-1 and Taffy-2 could do something quickly, it seemed certain that

Kurita would reach Leyte Gulf. In perhaps one of the bitterest ironies of the day, because of the inefficient radio link between the two fleets, at 0720 Kinkaid finally received a response to his message to Halsey of the previous evening. Halsey informed him that TF34 was part of his attack on Ozawa.

Kinkaid now had some difficult decisions to make. He was painfully aware that Taffy-1 and Taffy-2 could do little against Kurita's fleet but he had to sacrifice them in order to buy time. The American battleships and cruisers that had been so successful at Surigao Strait were at least three hours away from Leyte; and although Halsey was reluctantly headed south after a good deal of haranguing and pleading from Kinkaid and a now alerted Nimitz, it would still be several hours before the now formed TF34 could reach the area. As was to be expected, the desperate attacks of Taffy-1 and Taffy-2 did little more than cause Kurita to slow temporarily. Attacks by the aircraft and destroyers of the two groups managed to sink the cruiser *Chikuma* and damage *Tone*, but at the cost of five more of the tiny 'jeep' carriers and most of the destroyer escorts.

## The price of imprudence

Kurita now ordered another cruiser and a destroyer to join his trailing cruiser in finishing off any remnants of Sprague's three carrier groups. Just as *Yamato*'s guns were finishing off the last of Taffy-1, Kurita was informed by an excited Koyanagi that his guns were now within range of the enemy anchorage at Leyte Gulf. Kurita could scarcely contain himself. He immediately ordered that word of this stunning accomplishment be flashed to Tokyo, the troops fighting for their lives around Leyte, and to every ship remaining in the fleet. Elated by what they had accomplished, the Japanese sailors worked relentlessly as the guns of the mighty *Yamato* and the surviving cruisers raked Kinkaid's transports trapped within the confines of Leyte Gulf. What few aircraft remained to Kincaid could do little against the massive barrage of heavy caliber naval shells that came hurtling into the Gulf. The slaughter was on a scale that exceeded that which had occurred at the 1905 Battle of Tsushima Strait, Japan's greatest naval victory. So tightly packed were the transports inside the Gulf that Kurita's gunners barely had to aim their weapons.

Nimitz was startled when he received Kinkaid's desperate message for help. He too believed that Halsey had left TF34 guarding San Bernadino Strait. Aware of the magnitude of what this could mean, Nimitz had immediately radioed Halsey with the question, 'Where is Task Force 34. The World Wonders.'[20] Although the second sentence of the message was meant merely to confuse the enemy, Halsey, perhaps now aware of the tragic mistake that he had made, was enraged. In response, he ignored the pleadings of Kinkaid and the questions of Nimitz for another hour before, reluctantly, making the decision to form TF34 and head it south ahead of the rest of his force. He was far too late to rescue the situation in the south and his momentary confusion meant that Ozawa was able to quickly turn about and escape as well.

Aware that the remaining American ships would soon be rushing to the relief of Leyte Gulf, after a little more than an hour of blasting away at the American anchorage, Kurita turned about and headed back toward San Bernadino Strait. He knew that his battle-scarred ships and exhausted men would have an all but impossible time avoiding Halsey's force, but as had just been demonstrated to him, there were such things as miracles.

As a final bitter end to the rapidly unfolding American disaster, Halsey's final delay in forming Task Force 34 meant that Kurita was able to escape from the Gulf and limp back to Brunei. On the beaches of Leyte, Krueger's Sixth Army was driven back to the water's edge before the guns of the now combined Third and Seventh fleet provided sufficient firepower to halt the Japanese attacks. Although the Sixth Army was able to hold on, the men endured privation exceeding that which the Marines had experienced on Guadalcanal in 1942. Soon, the fighting on Leyte reached a stalemate, with the Americans unable to advance further inland and the Japanese unable to push the Americans into the Gulf. Kurita's stunning victory had set back the timetable for Allied victory in the Pacific by years.

When word of the disaster at Leyte Gulf reached Washington on October 27, President Franklin Roosevelt and his principal military advisors could scarcely believe it. The impetuous Halsey was immediately, and publicly, sacked and replaced by the victor of Midway, the somewhat more prudent Raymond A. Spruance. And although he escaped the fate of his subordinate, Nimitz's strategic plans, much to MacArthur's immense satisfaction, were no longer given much consideration by either King or Roosevelt. After Halsey's removal, there was simply no way to conceal such a disaster from the American public. Mindful of the fact that the election for his unprecedented fourth term as president was just weeks away, aware that many pundits were calling for his removal, and unwilling to see if the American public was prepared to continue to pay the price in blood and treasure necessary to subdue Imperial Japan, Roosevelt made plans for peace.

The American president offered the Japanese a means of escaping from the rain of American B-29 bombers that would soon be unleashed. Roosevelt would agree to a conditional surrender that called for a withdrawal from all of those possessions that the Japanese had taken after December 7, 1941.

Since Tojo's removal after the Saipan disaster, Japanese peace advocates within Emperor Hirohito's government had sought a means of saving the country and the emperor's dynasty while preserving their country's honor. Kurita's victory had provided them with that opportunity. Not only was the emperor allowed to retain his throne, but Japan was able to retain control of its possessions in Indochina, Manchuria, and most of China.

On November 2, 1944, Roosevelt announced to a jubilant American public that the Japanese had agreed to surrender all of the territory conquered after the attack on Pearl Harbor. After giving his unprecedented fourth inaugural speech on Saturday, January 20, 1945, Roosevelt returned to the Oval office to celebrate. Piled upon his desk was a stack of the customary congratulatory telegrams from governments across the globe. He thought it particularly ironic that at the bottom of the stack was a letter of congratulations from Emperor Hirohito.

## The reality

Soon after departing Brunei, the Japanese plans began to come apart. On October 23, Admiral Kurita's flagship was sunk as it was steaming past the Palawan passage and throughout the 24th his ships, lacking any air cover, were battered by Halsey's airplanes. Meanwhile, as described above, Kinkaid destroyed Nishimura's force on the evening of October 24–25.

Believing that he had sufficiently damaged Kurita's force on the 24th, Halsey had steamed northward against Ozawa leaving the San Bernadino Strait unprotected. Despite the battering that the Japanese had received on their way to the San Bernadino Strait, the absence of Task Force 34 meant that all that remained between Kurita and Leyte Gulf were Sprague's escort carriers. In one of the finest displays of courage in the history of the U.S. Navy, the sailors and airmen of Taffy-3 put up a desperate defense against Kurita. Despite the odds against them, Taffy-3's planes – joined later by the pilots of Taffy-1 and Taffy-2 – were able to launch a series of desperate attacks against Kurita. Lacking torpedoes, some planes made dummy bombing runs while others dropped bombs meant for Japanese Army units on Leyte. Meanwhile, the destroyer escorts of Taffy-3 launched determined torpedo attacks against Kurita that sank *Chokai* and *Chikuma* and drove off *Yamato*. So determined were the American attacks that at 0915 Kurita called off his own and, at 1236, on the verge of scoring a great victory, he turned his ships around and headed back through the San Bernadino Strait. Despite all the damage that he had suffered, if Kurita had kept his nerve for just a little while longer, there is every reason to believe that he could have sailed into Leyte Gulf and inflicted the damage described above.

As Taffy-3 was fighting for its life, Halsey began a series of attacks against Ozawa. By the end of the day, the Third Fleet had sunk all of the Japanese carriers. By every estimate, the Battle of Leyte Gulf had been a total disaster for the Japanese. While the Americans escaped with the loss of only three light carriers and three destroyer escorts, the Japanese had lost three battleships, four carriers, ten cruisers, and nine destroyers. They had also lost any chance of stopping the relentless Allied advance on the home islands.

## Bibliography

Cannon, M. Hamlin, *Leyte: The Return to the Philippines* (Department of the Army, Washington, D.C., 1993).

Cutler, Thomas J., *The Battle of Leyte Gulf: 23–26 October 1944* (Harper, New York, 1994).

Humble, Richard, *Japanese High Seas Fleet* (Ballantine, New York, 1973).

Morgan, Ted, *FDR: A Biography* (Simon and Schuster, New York, 1985).

Morison, Samuel Eliot, *Leyte June 1944–January 1945* (Little, Brown, Boston, 1971).

Nalty, Bernard (ed.), *War in the Pacific: Pearl Harbor to Tokyo Bay* (University of Oklahoma Press, Oklahoma, 1991).

Spector, Ronald H., *Eagle Against the Sun: The American War Against Japan* (Free Press, New York, 1985).

Steinberg, Rafael, *Return to the Philippines* (Time Life, Alexandria, 1980).

## Notes

1. Ronald H. Spector, *Eagle Against the Sun: The American War Against Japan* (New York, 1985), p.424.
2. Thomas J. Cutler, *The Battle of Leyte Gulf: 23–26 October 1944* (New York, 1994), p.60.
3. Spector, *op.cit.* p.427.
4. Rafael Steinberg, *Return to the Philippines* (Alexandria, 1980), p.66.
5. Bernard Nalty (ed.), *War in the Pacific: Pearl Harbor to Tokyo Bay* (Oklahoma, 1991), p.199.
6. Richard Humble, *Japanese High Seas Fleet* (New York, 1973), p.38.
7. Cutler, *op.cit.* p.94.
*8. *Ibid* p.100. In reality, the cruiser that *Darter* and *Dace* dispatched was Kurita's flagship *Atago*. Although Kurita survived the sinking of his cruiser he had to be fished from the water. In addition to being understandably shaken by the sinking, he lost much of his staff.
*9. In reality, Onishi did not, as was hoped for, provide air cover to Kurita's hard-pressed forces. Instead, believing that greater honor would be attached to an attack on the American fleet, Onishi sent what remained of his planes against Halsey's Third Fleet. Although able to cause sufficient damage to the carrier U.S.S. *Princeton* that she later had to be sunk by friendly torpedoes, Onishi's inexperienced pilots were shot from the sky in such numbers that they had almost no impact on the battle.
10. Samuel Eliot Morrison, *Leyte June 1944–January 1945* (Boston, 1988), p.174.
11. Cutler, *op.cit.* p.121.
12. Morrison, *op.cit.* p.184.
13. Cutler, *op.cit.* p.161.
14. *Ibid* p.151.
15. Morrison, *op.cit.* p.189.
16. Cutler, *op.cit.* p.170.
17. *Ibid* p.186.
18. Spector, *op.cit.* p.434.
19. Steinberg, *op.cit.* p.60.
20. Spector, *op.cit.* p.438.

# 10
# VICTORY RIDES THE DIVINE WIND
## The Kamikaze and the Invasion of Kyushu

D.M. Giangreco

The lecture on logistic considerations for the recent invasion of Kyushu was going well. Nearly 160 students, faculty, and guests filled Pringle Auditorium at the Naval War College on this blustery Tuesday evening in November, 1946, to hear Admiral Richmond Kelly Turner. A 1908 graduate of the U.S. Naval Academy, Turner had commanded the Pacific Fleet Amphibious Force of more than 2,700 ships and large landing craft during the invasion.[1] The 101 students in the class of 1947 were veterans of the largest war in history, and the transfer of nearly all of the Atlantic Fleet's assets to the Far East after Normandy had insured the participation of every Navy and Marine officer at the college in either the final, mammoth operation at Kyushu or the even more massive operation planned for later in the Tokyo area. Likewise, all but two of the dozen Army, Air Force, and Coast Guard officers – plus the single student from the State Department[2] – had seen service in the Pacific. The college's new president, Admiral Raymond A. Spruance, had himself commanded the Fifth Fleet during the invasion and whispered to an aide that his long-time friend and colleague was 'in top form tonight.'[3]

It was good to see Turner doing well, and Spruance reflected that speaking before the assembled officers – particularly these officers – would do him nothing but good. Turner had only two weeks earlier concluded his testimony in the last of three Congressional inquiries held after the armistice with Imperial Japan, and even before those, he had been summoned back to Washington on three separate occasions in the midst of the war to testify on matters relating to December 7, 1941. During those earlier proceedings, he had been subjected to considerable cross examination because of his pre-war duty in the Navy's War Plans Division[4] and the first hearings after the armistice again dealt with Pearl Harbor. There was very little of substance

231

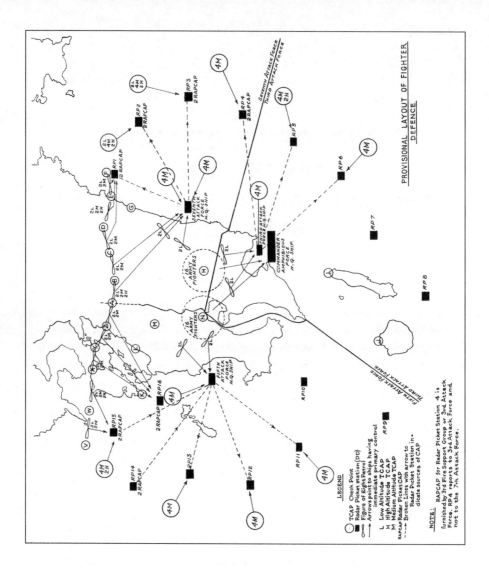

PROVISIONAL LAYOUT OF FIGHTER DEFENCE

LEGEND

TCAP  Check Point
◯  Radar Picket station (DD)
⬭  Figure of Eight Patrol
↗  Arrow point to ships having immediate primary control

L  Low Altitude TCAP
H  High Altitude TCAP
M  Medium Altitude TCAP
RAPCAP  Radar Picket CAP
--→  Broken Lines with arrow to Radar Picket Station indicate sources of CAP

NOTE:  RAPCAP for Radar Picket Station 4 is furnished by 3rd Fire Support Group or 3rd Attack Force. RP4 reports to 3rd Attack Force and not to the 7th Attack Force.

that he had been able to add to the second postwar hearings since the joint House-Senate committee was investigating events surrounding the tactical use of nuclear weapons and the resultant deaths and sickness recorded so far among some 40,000 U.S. military personnel. However, the most recent hearings of the Taft-Jenner Committee had been another matter entirely, and Turner rapidly became the focus of its investigation into why the Navy, after more than a year of experience battling Japanese suicide aircraft, had been 'caught napping' by the kamikazes off Kyushu.

'Pearl Harbor II', as it was dubbed by the press, saw thirty-eight troop-laden Liberty ships and LSTs, along with a score of destroyers and twenty-one other vessels, struck within sight of the invasion beaches during X-Day and X+1.[5] Six other vessels were crashed by *shinyo* speedboats filled with explosives that darted into the assault groups during the confusion, and a further ten Liberty ships were hit by kamikazes from X+2 to X+6. The bulk of the 29,000 dead and missing were ground troops, with an equal number of soldiers and Marines turned into stunned refugees after discarding all their gear during frantic efforts to abandon burning and sinking transports. Finely choreographed assault landings had been terribly disrupted by the incessant attacks and rescue operations. The subsequent lack of proper resupply and reinforcement resulted in nearly triple the anticipated ground-force casualties through X+30 and an unprecedented – and bloody – stalemate until X+20 on the northeasternmost six of the thirty-five invasion beaches.

More men had been lost in the first two weeks at Kyushu than at the Battle of the Bulge and Okinawa combined, and critics were looking hard for someone's head to stick on a pike (an 'Army' pike). Admiral Chester Nimitz, Commander in Chief of the Pacific Fleet, refused to offer up Turner for sacrifice and took full responsibility for the debacle (although it was certainly obvious that there was plenty of blame to go around). Still, the hearings had been brutal and General Douglas MacArthur, from his headquarters in Manila, made it clear that he believed that Turner's 'failure to safeguard the lives of our gallant soldiers and Marines' had forced America into 'an incomplete victory worse than Versailles.' Tonight was the tough old admiral's first public address since the hearings and Spruance did all he could to keep news of the event confined to the tight naval community on Coasters Harbor Island in Narragansett Bay's East Passage. In fact, the only people in attendance not from the Naval War College or Newport Naval Base were retired Marine three-star general Holland Smith, who was visiting the son of a long-time colleague, and George Kennan, an assistant to newly appointed Secretary of State George C. Marshall.

The students were held spellbound by the man that Spruance regarded as the finest example of that rare combination, a strategic thinker and a fighter ready and willing to take responsibility and plunge into battle.[6] Very few of the officers had actually laid eyes on 'Terrible' Turner during the Pacific war and the first round of questions after his presentation were tentative, almost soft-ball. Spruance expected that this wouldn't last long, and it didn't.

'Sir, right from the beginning, at Leyte, when the Japs succeeded in forcing a redisposition of the carriers, we started to lose a lot of ships to the suiciders and even conventional attacks. Was it the loss of those transports and LSTs that slowed down the airstrip construction ashore and just made a bad situation worse from the standpoint of air defense?'

A score of supply ships along with a half dozen destroyer-type vessels had unexpectedly been lost during November 1944. The kamikazes had drawn first blood on October 25–26, when a five-plane raid sank the escort carrier *St. Lo* and damaged three similar carriers. This had prompted many more young Japanese fliers to volunteer for the *Shimpu* (Special Attack Corps) unit, and on October 30 a kamikaze attack damaged three large fleet carriers so severely that they had to be pulled back to the Ulithi anchorage for repairs. Within days, another large flattop fell victim, as did three more toward the end of November.[7] This stunning disruption of carrier airpower spelled the loss of the ships referred to by the questioner, and had a pronounced effect on the conduct of the ground campaign as well. Leyte had not been Turner's show. Vice Admiral Thomas C. Kinkaid had been commanding, and Turner chose his words carefully.

'We expected to take losses, but the nature of the Jap attacks was a complete surprise. We expected that our fighter sweeps would take out most of his airpower in the Philippines before the landings. The feeble response to Bill [Admiral William F.] Halsey's earlier raid in September 1944 led us to conclude that Jap strength in the islands was far weaker than it should have been and we, in fact, canceled intermediate operations and pushed KING II up a full sixty days.[8] There was no way to anticipate the tactics that were used against us. As to airbase development on Leyte, it was not the loss of shipping, but the weather and resultant conditions on the ground that stalled the best efforts of Army engineers. We'd owned those islands for over forty years yet did not have a clue as to just how unsuitable the soil conditions were in the area where we sited the Burauen airfield complex.

'Everyone remembers the newsreels of the theater commander wading ashore from a Higgins boat – I'm sure he did it in one take – [laughter] and his pronouncement that he had 'returned', but what few people know is that he was supposed to have retaken Leyte with four divisions and have eight fighter and bomber groups striking from the island within forty-five days of the initial landings. Nine divisions and twice as many days into the battle, only a fraction of the airpower was operational because of that awful terrain.[9] The fighting on the ground had not gone as planned either. The Japs even did an end run, briefly isolated Fifth Air Force headquarters, and captured much of the airfield complex before the Army pushed them back into the jungle.[10] Colonel?'

Having closed with a comment on the Army, he motioned to a one of several soldiers attending the college. He noted that the officer wore the scarlet crossed-arrow patch of the 32nd Infantry Division which fought battles on Leyte's Corkscrew Ridge, Kilay Ridge, and Breakneck Ridge.[11]

'Thank you, Sir. In light of the fact that the lack of air interdiction allowed the enemy to transfer four divisions plus various independent brigades and regiments to the island from Luzon,[12] do you feel that the amount of time to take Leyte was excessive?'

The admiral was unfazed by the implied rebuke of the question. 'No. Buoyed by pilot reports of both real and imagined losses to our fleet, the Japs decided to conduct their main battle for the Philippines on Leyte instead of Luzon. We had originally intended Leyte to act as a springboard to Luzon in exactly the same way that Kyushu was to act as the last stop before Tokyo. But the important thing to remember is that no matter which island we fought them on, the Japs had only a finite number of troops available in the Philippines. Over eighty percent of Jap shipping used during their effort was eventually sunk during later resupply missions, but we obviously would have liked to have sent them to the bottom sooner. The conquest of Leyte eventually involved over 100,000 more ground troops than anticipated and took us so long to accomplish that the island never became the major logistical center and airbase we intended.[13] My point is that the Japs were turning out to be much more resourceful than we anticipated and this affected operations all across the board. Does that answer your question?'

'Yes, Sir,' said the colonel. But he later told the head of the college's logistics department, Rear Admiral Henry Eccles, that he had considered commenting that the dearth of Army and Navy air interdiction was still being felt months later; that a number of Japanese units were actually evacuated from Leyte when ordered off in January 1945,[14] and that he didn't like fighting the same Japs twice. Eccles said that the colonel had been wise to not press the issue.

Many in the audience now raised their hands with questions, and Turner called on a lieutenant commander from the junior class.

'Admiral, could you comment on the fighter sweeps conducted over southern Japan ahead of the invasion?'

Turner asked him if he could be more specific.

'Yes, Sir. Why was there so little attrition of their air forces ahead of Kyushu?'

This had been a subject of much heated discussion both in the press and in the ward rooms. It had even been rehashed in great detail earlier that day in Luce Hall, with the head of the college's Battle Evaluation Group, Commodore Richard Bates, and about two dozen students.

## Kamikazes 'Glued to the ground'

'To a very real degree, gentlemen, we were the victim of our own success,' said Turner. 'Throughout the war, increasingly effective sweeps by our aircraft – and the Army's fighters and medium bombers – played havoc with Japanese air bases. And we were sure that many of their aircraft would certainly be destroyed by pre-invasion fighter sweeps. But to destroy them on the ground, we would have had to know where they were.[15] Anticipating that attacks would only grow worse as we neared the home islands in force, the Japs stepped up the dispersion of their units and spread aircraft throughout more than 125 bases and airfields that we knew of, and the number was apparently far larger.[16] This effort intensified after we caught hundreds of them on the ground at Kyushu bases preparing for suicide runs at Okinawa.[17] As for the planes slated for use as kamikazes, they didn't require extensive facilities, and were hidden away to take off from roads and fields around central billeting areas.[18] In addition, dispersal fields were being constructed by the dozen, while use of camouflage, dummy aircraft, and propped-up derelicts performed as desired during our strikes against known facilities.'[19]

Spruance suspected that the questioners already knew the answers, or pieces of the answers, almost as well as Turner, but were deeply interested in the admiral's unique insight into Pacific operations. The exchange now moved at a very fast clip.

'Sir, intelligence reports made it clear that there were a large number of aircraft available in Japan,[20] but I was surprised that even though we were bombing virtually everything we wanted at will, they would not come up and fight.'

'You weren't the only one,' replied Turner. 'After some initial sparring with our carriers and Far East Air Force elements flying out of Okinawa, the Japs essentially glued their aircraft to the ground in order to preserve them for use during the invasions. We all know the story. The few high performance aircraft like the Raiden were used against the B-29s, but that was it. There was no significant employment of aircraft, even during the approach of our fleets, since the Japs believed that being drawn out early would cause needless losses and correctly anticipated that we would attempt to lure their aircraft into premature battle through elaborate feints and other deception measures. They planned for a massive response only when they confirmed that landing operations had commenced.'[21]

'Sir,' said another student, 'it has been reported that the Japanese had been planning to use suiciders well before Leyte.'

Turner nodded. 'The codicil to the armistice agreement which allows us to formally discuss the conduct of the war with Japanese officers of equal rank brought out some interesting information on that. These discussions, by the way, are continuing. They are certainly not controlled interrogations and the information is sometimes questionable, but the discussions overall have been frank and useful.' The admiral didn't say it, but he was as amazed as anyone that talks of that nature were even taking place. 'As to your question, the growing supremacy of our fleet prompted some Japanese leaders to contemplate the systematic use of suicide aircraft as early as 1943. But it wasn't until late the following year, after they'd lost many of their best pilots at Midway, the Solomons, New Guinea, and the Marianas, that the kamikaze was seriously considered as a last-ditch alternative to conventional bombing attacks.[22] We'd known this for some time. What we have just learned from our discussions is that the first time that orders were actually handed down for employment of suicide tactics was July 4, 1944, at Iwo [Jima]. Since all the kamikazes were shot down before reaching our ships, we never knew a thing about it.'[23]

'Sir, right to the end there were always Jap pilots who made no attempt to crash our ships. Was that intentional; part of a systematic employment?'

Turner nodded again. 'Yes, experienced pilots, deemed too valuable to sacrifice, were to provide fighter cover or fly conventional strikes. In fact, when some of them volunteered for the one-way missions, they were denied the "honor" of killing themselves for the emperor.'[24]

'Sir, with the benefit of hindsight it seems apparent to me that if the tactics employed at Kyushu had been employed at Leyte, their planes would have been able to crash a lot more ships. When they had altitude, you could pick 'em up without much trouble. But if they'd come out of those hills – coming in low rather than flying up here where we could pick 'em up early around 10,000, 20,000 feet and diving down – frankly, the Japs could have massacred our transports in the Philippines. The only up-side is that it would have made the danger off Japan's coast more clear.'[25]

'You never like to take losses,' said Turner, 'but if the Japs had used their aircraft as you described at Leyte, the lessons learned from that battle would indeed have made a difference at Kyushu. Okinawa represented the first coordinated effort by Jap pilots to use cliffs and hills to foil our radar, but the size of the island and the distances they had to fly from their bases on Formosa and Kyushu, together with the fact that the Japs had only just begun to experiment in this area, initially limited the usefulness of such tactics. Nonetheless, they did enjoy numerous successes when kamikazes appeared so suddenly out of the radar clutter that even fully alert crews of ships close ashore had little time to respond. And, of course, response times naturally stretched out once the fatigue of being constantly at the alert began to set in. All kinds of tactical innovations were developed ad hoc as we gained more experience with the new threat. Ideas were shared throughout the fleet and crews incorporated any innovations they thought would be useful – anything to increase point defense capabilities by shortening anti-aircraft weapons' response times. Would you like to comment on that, Commodore Bates?'

'Certainly, Sir. By summer 1945, slewing sights for the 5-inch gun mount officer's station were helping to ensure quick, non-radar-directed action, and many ships had begun to rig cross connections between their 5-inch guns' slow Mark 37 directors and the 40 mm guns' more nimble Mark 51s. These changes – and a projectile in the loading tray – enabled the 5-inchers to come on line more quickly to counter sudden attacks, but switch back to the longer-range Mark 37 directors if radar found possible targets at a more conventional range. The new Mark 22 radar, which allowed early and accurate identification of incoming aircraft, was also widely distributed by the time of MAJESTIC.[26] It had little impact on the fighting close to shore, but proved its worth over and over again with the carriers.

'Prior to the appearance of the kamikazes, 20 mm anti-aircraft guns had been the greatest killers of Jap planes. After that, however, their lack of hitting power rendered them little more than psychological weapons against plunging kamikazes. Commanders relied increasingly on the larger 40 mm guns, because they could blast apart a closing aircraft. As more became available, we jammed additional mounts of the twin- and quad-40s into already overcrowded deck spaces on everything from minesweepers and LSTs to battleships and carriers.'

A voice rang out from the back of the hall, 'But we wouldn't let you take away our "door knockers"!' [Laughter]

Admirals Turner and Spruance grinned widely at the shouted comment, but the chief of the Battle Evaluation Group offered only a half smile.

'As I was saying, although 20 mm guns had proved ineffective against a plunging kamikaze, that did not mean crews were eager to do away with them in order to free-up deck space. These weapons at least had the advantage of not being operated electrically. Even if a ship's power was knocked out, the "door knockers" could still supply defensive fire.[27] The new 3-inch/50 rapid fire gun is a wonderful weapon. One gun is as effective as two – that's two – quad 40s against conventional planes, and against the Baka rocket bomb the advantage was even more pronounced. It took fully five quad 40s [twenty guns] to do the work of a single 3-inch/50.[28] Unfortunately, very few crews had been properly trained for it by MAJESTIC.

'Reviewing the outcome of the extended radar picket operations off Okinawa,' continued Bates, 'COMINCH [Commander in Chief, United States Fleet] came to the conclusion that one destroyer cannot be expected to defend itself successfully against more than one attacking enemy aircraft at a time – many did, in fact, but were eventually overwhelmed – and noted that, in the future, a full destroyer division should be assigned to each picket station if the tactical situation allowed such a commitment of resources.[29] We were able to do this at four of the sixteen picket stations at Kyushu, but all the other stations had to make do with a pair of destroyers and two each of those special gunboats made especially for operations against Japan [LSMs with one dual and four quad 40-mm mounts], which were far more heavily armed than the gunboats used at Okinawa.

'COMINCH also found that while large warships' and aircraft gunnery was not affected greatly by evasive maneuvers, violent turns by a diminutive destroyer to disturb the aim of the kamikaze, or to bring more guns to bear during a surprise attack, caused extreme pitches and rolls that degraded accuracy. Gunnery improved dramatically when destroyers performed less strident maneuvers, even if fewer guns could be brought into play quickly.'

The officer students were more willing to respectfully interject themselves into Commodore Bates' comments than they were to interrupt Turner, and a former destroyer captain immediately spoke up.

'That's theoretically true, Sir, but anyone who experienced the Philippines and Okinawa, or the raids on Japan, knows that in most instances you can't actually do that and live to tell about it. The suiciders had apparently been told that, since they didn't need the broad targets normally required for aiming bombs, the best results in their type of mission would come from bow – or stern – on attacks that allowed them to be targeted by the least amount of defensive fire.[30] I'd seen new skippers follow COMINCH advice on this matter and the only thing that happened was a sort of Divine Wind "crossing the T", made much easier by less radical destroyer maneuvers.'

A former executive officer chimed in. 'I've been told that even a novice pilot can be trained to perform skids, or side-slips, and when we were hit – I was on the *Kimberly* – the target skidded to always remain in the ship's wake – and we were on hard right rudder! Only the after guns could bear and each 5-inch salvo blasted the 20 mm crews off their feet. The Val came in over the stern, aiming for the bridge, and crashed aft the rear stack between two five inch mounts.'[31]

Admiral Turner was not surprised that, given an opportunity, the talk turned to tactics. He quickly moved to elevate the discussion.

'Early in the war, after Pearl Harbor, Malaya, and the Java Sea, things looked bleak for our surface ships – and those of the Japanese as well. Naval aircraft were clearly dominating any vessels they came up against. The fielding of the proximity fuze[32] in 1942 and 1943 increased the odds that our ships would fight off their aerial tormentors, and by 1943 – just two years after Pearl Harbor – the balance of power had firmly shifted into America's favor as our industrial base; our training base; added warships, attack aircraft, and large numbers of skilled aviators to the fleet. The duel between ships' guns and aircraft, however, came full circle with the advent of the kamikaze. Destroying ninety percent of an inbound raid had been considered a success before Leyte,[33] but the damage inflicted by even one suicide aircraft could be devastating. It was obvious that the invasion of Japan would entail terrible losses and we moved to defeat the threat through increased interdiction, effective command and control, more guns, and everything we could think of to knock them down before they reached our ships.'

'Sir,' interjected a member of his audience, 'one of the points noted over and over again in intelligence reports before Kyushu was that the

Nips didn't even have enough gas to train their new pilots; that, cut off from their oil in the Dutch territories and with all their refineries destroyed by the [B-29] Superforts, they would be hard-pressed to maintain flight operations. I don't really know anyone at my level who bought into this, but was it a factor in why we provided so little air cover at the landing sites?[34]

'I'll answer that in two parts,' said Turner after a moment's deliberation. 'First, everything you said about their ability to import and refine oil was true, but not to the degree that some believed. The other part of the picture dealt with evidence from signals intelligence and the Japs' lack of fleet activity, which appeared to be a clear sign that they had run out of gas. Their navy had drastically curtailed combat operations because of a lack of heavy fuel oil and we were aware that shortages were the primary factor behind the ratcheting down of flight hours in their pilot training. Moreover, reports obtained from neutral embassies also indicated that the civilian population had not only been deprived of liquid fuel but that badly needed foodstuffs, such as potatoes, corn, and rice, were also being requisitioned for synthetic fuel production.[35] We also believed that our attacks had destroyed nearly all of their storage capacity. So, while we were aware that some large number of aircraft had been successfully hidden from us, the recurring weakness of their response to our attacks reinforced the idea that those aircraft were no longer able to defend effectively.

'What we did not know was that the Japs had made a conscious decision early on to build up decentralized fuel reserves separate from those used for training, a reserve which would only be tapped for the final battles. They had seen the writing on the wall when we reestablished ourselves in the Philippines, and succeeded in rushing shipments past our new bases in February and March before that avenue was choked off. Although we sank roughly two-thirds of the tankers running north, four or five got through with 40,000 tons of refined fuel. This shipment and some domestic production formed the core of what became Japan's strategic reserve,[36] which included 190,000 barrels of aviation gas in hidden Army stockpiles and a further 126,000 barrels held by the Navy.[37] To give you an idea of just how much gas we're talking about here, the Japs used roughly 1.5 million barrels during flight operations against our fleet at Okinawa[38] but – and this is important – at Okinawa they had to fly roughly triple the distances they did over Japan.

'Their perceived inability to send up large numbers of aircraft encouraged us to believe that the landing area's immediate defense could be left to our escort carriers, while the nearly 1,800 aircraft of Task Force 58's fleet carriers were assigned missions as far north as 600 miles from Kyushu, well beyond Tokyo. Aircraft from only two of Admiral Spruance's task groups were dedicated to suppression efforts north and east of the screen thrown up by Admiral [Clifton A. F.] Sprague's escorts. I and others argued strenuously – and unsuccessfully – that this was taking a lot for granted. We didn't need a show of force all up and down Honshu. We needed a blanket of Hellcats and Corsairs at the decisive point. We needed them at Kyushu. Yes, command and control would be extremely difficult, maybe impossible, with that many planes concentrated over that airspace. But it would be worth it if the Japs succeeded in massing for an all-out lunge at the transports – and that's exactly what they did.'

'Sir, weren't there also fewer escort carriers taking a direct part in the invasion than there might have been?'

'Yes,' replied Turner, 'but a certain amount of that was unavoidable. A total of thirty-six escort carriers took part in some facet of MAJESTIC, but many had to be siphoned off to protect the far-flung elements of the invasion force. For example, four escort carriers were assigned to provide cover for slow-moving convoys plying the waters between the Philippines and Kyushu against more than 600 Jap aircraft that could be brought into play through their bases on Formosa.[39] Sprague had sixteen flattops with approximately 580 aircraft available for both the direct support of the landing force and defense of the assault shipping.[40] Plans called for roughly 130 aircraft to be on-station from dawn to dusk to provide a last-ditch defense of the landing area.[41] Of course, far more aircraft were required to maintain a continuous, seamless presence, and even more were siphoned away from ground support as they were at Okinawa.[42] The ability of the CAPs [combat air patrols] to actually maintain coverage of this area once battle was joined – the CAP check points averaged fifteen miles apart over a clutter of cloud covered peaks – proved to be extraordinarily difficult and broke down quickly. We didn't have enough depth. The CAPS were drawn away from the barrier patrol by the first Japs coming through. We had expected that there would be some leakers – possibly quite a few – but did not anticipate that they could successfully coordinate and launch as many aircraft as they did.'

'It sounds to me, Sir,' observed his questioner, 'that they had figured us out.'

'It's clear that they'd developed plans based on a comprehensive understanding of the set-piece way in which we do business – our amphibious operations,' acknowledged the admiral, 'and that their plans extended well beyond air operations. In fact, they were so confident in their analyses of our intentions that they moved a number of divisions into Kyushu before our airpower – our ability to interdict them – had been built up sufficiently on Okinawa. The Japs were one step ahead of us. Our intelligence noted the appearance of these reinforcements which, when combined with the units already there and the new divisions being raised from the island's massive population, presented us with an awful picture,[43] but one that we could have dealt with if we had been able to get our forces ashore intact.

'There's an interesting footnote for future historians on this matter. Some of you may know that the original name of the Kyushu operation was OLYMPIC, but do you know why the codename was changed? When intelligence discovered the rapid buildup, it was believed that the invasion plans may have somehow been compromised.[44] The change from OLYMPIC to MAJESTIC represented an effort to confuse Japanese intelligence when, in fact, the changes were based on analyses conducted within Imperial Headquarters. The Japanese had correctly deduced both the location and approximate times of both MAJESTIC and CORONET[45] and decided to expend the bulk of their aircraft as kamikazes during the critical first ten days of each invasion. The landing forces themselves were to be the main focus of Japanese efforts, with additional aircraft allotted to keep the carrier task forces occupied.'[46]

More than a few of the officers present would have liked to have been told how Turner knew this but knew better than to ask, and the next question returned to the kamikazes. It came from another former destroyer captain.

'Sir, irrespective of how many of our own aircraft were used for suppression of Nip bases and defense of the landing zones, it seems to me that the very large number and close proximity of their bases – and Kyushu's mountains – created virtually ideal conditions for the suiciders.'

'Yes. I've had a good deal of time to think about this. The Japanese had seven interrelated advantages during the defense of the home islands that they did not have at Okinawa.

'First, their aircraft were able to approach the invasion beaches from anywhere along a wide arc, thus negating any more victories along the line of the [Marianas] Turkey Shoot or the Kikai Jima air battles [north of Okinawa], where long distances required Jap aircraft to travel relatively predictable flight paths.

'Second, Kyushu's high mountains masked low-flying kamikazes from search radars, thus limiting our response time to incoming aircraft. Plans were made to establish radar sites within our lines and on the outlying islands as quickly as the tactical situation allowed, but this had only a minor effect on the central problem – the mountains. In addition, most shore-based radar units during MAJESTIC were not slated to be operational until after $X+10$[47] – by then the kamikaze attacks were drawing to a close.

'Third, we knew that the Japs were suffering from a severe shortage of radios, and some among us discounted their ability to coordinate attacks from dispersed air fields and hiding places through use of telephone lines. At this point in the war, however, Jap reliance on telephones was more a strength than a weakness. No communications intercepts there.[48] Our forces could neither monitor nor jam the land lines and, like the Jap electrical system, it presented few good targets for air attack.

'The fourth advantage was related to the second and had to do with the virtually static nature of our assault vessels while conducting the invasion. Because the ships disembarking the landing force were operating at a known location, kamikazes didn't have to approach from a high altitude, which allowed them the visibility needed to search for far-flung carrier groups yet also made them visible to radar. Instead, they were able to approach the mass of transports and cargo ships from the mountains and then drop to very low altitudes. The final low-level run on the ships offered no radar, little visual warning, and limited the number of anti-aircraft guns that could be brought to bear against them. It wasn't difficult to see that this was going to be a problem during MAJESTIC, since a much larger percentage of kamikazes got through to their targets when flying under radar coverage to fixed locations, like Kerama Retto anchorage [Okinawa], than those approaching ships at sea from higher altitudes.

'I want to stress, however, that despite the advantages offered by radar picking up the high-flyers, ships operating at any fixed location invited concentrated attack, and the radar pickets near certain Japanese approach routes to Okinawa suffered much more than those on the move with fast carrier task forces. The lack of predictable approach routes at Kyushu only exacerbated the situation.

'Fifth, we had begun extensive use of destroyers as radar pickets as early as the Kwajalein operation in January 1944, and by the end of that year comparatively sophisticated CICs [combat information centers] were effectively providing tactical situation plotting and fighter direction from select destroyers. Unfortunately, coordination within and timely communications from the radar pickets' newly installed CICs presented a problem, with the centers frequently becoming overwhelmed by the speed of events and sheer quantity of bogies. Add a nearby landmass to the equation, and things got dicey in a hurry.

'Sixth, as previously noted, radar coverage of the countless mountain passes was virtually nil during the Kyushu operation, and the Fifth Fleet CAPs attempting to form a barrier halfway up the island were essentially on their own because they were frequently out of direct contact with the pickets assigned to control the checkpoints. The barrier patrol over the 120-mile-wide midsection of Kyushu and Amakusa-Shoto, an island close to the west, were able only to find and bounce a comparatively small percentage of attackers coming through the mountains, and this number shrank even further in areas with a modest amount of cloud cover. As it turned out, MAJESTIC was launched at a time that the weather was ideal for Japanese purposes – and, I might add, the same would have been true for CORONET. Not only did the moderate-to-heavy cloud cover, ranging from 3,000 to 7,000 feet, tend to mask the low-level approach of aircraft to the landing beaches, but the inexperienced Jap pilots searching for carriers out to sea from high altitudes also found that these clouds provided good cover from radar-vectored CAPs while being no great hindrance to navigation.

'Last, and perhaps most important of all, a proportionately small number of suicide aircraft got through to the vulnerable transports off Okinawa because of the natural tendency of inexperienced pilots to dive on the first target they saw. As a result, the radar pickets had, in effect, soaked up the bulk of the kamikazes before they reached the landing area. Accomplishing this entailed terrible losses even though the destroyers had their own CAPs and were sometimes supported by LCSs and LSMs acting as gunboats. At Kyushu, however, there were no radar pickets on the landward side of the assault shipping to absorb the blows meant for the slow-moving troop transports and supply vessels, which had to lock themselves into relatively static positions offshore during landing operations. These were the ships that kamikaze pilots were specifically to target, and circumstance and terrain went a long way toward helping them achieve their goal of killing the largest number of Americans possible.

'While all this must seem like a wonderful example of twenty-twenty hindsight, I believe that we would have anticipated much more of this ahead of time if we had not been lulled by the lack of air opposition in the months preceding MAJESTIC. It was simply inconceivable to many of us that they would be willing to take the degree of punishment that they did from the air without fighting back. It crossed few minds that they were, in effect, waiting to see the whites of our eyes. Next question.'

'Sir, wouldn't this also tie in with why we didn't disperse our blood supplies ahead of the invasion?'

The young captain's question touched on one of the most grim facets of the invasion. Five LST(H)s,[49] one for each set of invasion beaches, had been outfitted as distribution centers for plasma and whole blood needed by the wounded ashore.[50] Even before the first waves of landing craft hit the beaches, one had been turned into an inferno and another had been sunk by mid morning of X-Day. For many thousands of wounded ashore, this was a disaster of terrible proportions. The landing beaches now denied blood supplies had been unable to receive assistance from the remaining three vessels because of excessive casualties in those ships' own assigned areas. Although it was difficult to calculate precisely, estimates ran as high as 4,100 for the number of wounded whose deaths might have been prevented if the immediate blood supply had not been nearly halved. Emergency shipments were rushed up by destroyer from Okinawa and flown direct to escort carriers off Kyushu aboard Avenger torpedo bombers from the central blood bank on Guam. These emergency shipments, together with blood donated by bone-tired sailors after the last air raids of the day, enabled the situation to be stabilized by X+4.

'The care and storage of blood products is a complicated matter. It is a valuable – and highly perishable – commodity that requires it to be stored and distributed from refrigeration units. The system for blood distribution at Kyushu made perfect sense in light of these requirements and past experience.[51] The blood supply expert on MacArthur's staff had, in fact, pointed out the vulnerability of the system to be employed, but lack of proper facilities had rendered any worthwhile changes impossible on such short notice.'

Even Turner realized that his answer sounded like it had been written by a press officer and he quickly moved on to the next question by pointing to an officer in the third row who had raised his hand twice before.

## Deception operations

'Sir, with all the ships we produced during the war, why didn't we create a dummy invasion fleet? Why didn't we make more of an effort to draw their planes out early so that we could get at them?'

The admiral did not immediately answer, but instead cast a glance at the poker face of Spruance sitting to his left. Had the young captain thought of this himself or had he picked up on clues in the newspapers where references to an elaborate deception operation – not carried out – were already beginning to leak from an unannounced, closed-door session that Turner had with the Taft-Jenner Committee? The room was deathly quiet as the admiral looked back to the podium and drew a deep breath. The men – the veterans – in the room deserved to get an answer.

'Certain deception operations were conceived ahead of MAJESTIC.[52] Codenamed PASTEL, they were patterned after the very successful BODYGUARD operations conducted against the Nazis before, and even well after, the Normandy invasion. Through those operations, very substantial German forces were held in check far from France in Norway and the Balkans, and a well-equipped army north of the invasion area was kept out of the fight until it was too late to intervene effectively.[53] Deception operations of this type were particularly effective in Europe, with its extensive road and rail nets, but were a waste of time against Japan proper. They all assumed a strategic mobility that the Japanese did not possess for higher formations – corps and armies – and were made even less effective by our own air campaign against the home islands which essentially froze those formations into place. Distant movements could only be made division by division and only at a pace that a soldier's own feet could carry him. Likewise, the success of the blockade rendered the deception operations against Formosa and the Shanghai area unnecessary.

'The Japanese, themselves, had realized this early on and their system of defense call-up and training during the last year was reoriented toward raising, training, and fielding combat divisions locally in order to minimize lengthy overland movements.[54] With major population centers within easy marching distance of threatened areas, they could actually get away with this. The most useful comparison to our own history might be the Minutemen.'

Turner could see that some of the students were questioning the rele- vance of his comments and were wondering if he was going to dodge the question altogether.

'In short,' he continued, 'we spent far too much time and energy trying to keep the Japanese from doing something that both we and the Japs knew they couldn't do anyway. To the specifics of your question, in May of last year I, along with admirals Spruance and [Marc A.] Mitscher, were replaced by Bill Halsey and his crew so that we could begin planning for Kyushu. I regretted not being able to see Okinawa through to the finish, but ICE-BERG was to have been wrapped up in forty-five days, and since the Fifth Fleet of Admiral Spruance had been selected to handle Kyushu, what was then called OLYMPIC, planning could not be delayed any further.[55]

'Our work was conducted back at Guam and took full account of what we had learned at Okinawa. It was my conclusion that kamikaze attacks of sufficient strength might so disrupt the landings that a vigorous resistance ashore against our weakened forces would put our timetable for airfield construction in serious jeopardy. Four months was the minimum time judged necessary for base construction and subsequent softening up before our landings near Tokyo. These, in turn, had to be conducted before the spring monsoon season, when use of our armored divisions from Europe would become impossible on the Kanto, or Tokyo, Plain.[56] The landing force had to get off to a running start and it was up to us to get them there in the best possible shape. What we proposed was exactly what you sug-gested, form a fleet – a dummy fleet carrying no men; no equipment – escorted by the usual screen but with the air groups rearranged to carry a preponderance of Hellcats and Corsairs.[57]

'It had to look credible, especially from the air. Feints at Okinawa, that we had considered quite impressive, had absolutely no discernible impact on the course of the campaign.[58] Moreover, communications intelligence made it clear that the Japs were expecting us to try something like that again and we estimated that we would have to utilize 400 ships, not counting the escort, in order to provide enough mass to be convincing.[59] Assault ship-ping and bombardment groups would form up at multiple invasion beaches. We would follow all normal procedures; heavy radio traffic; line of departure; massive bombardment. All of this would take time, of course, and the Japs would be able to get a real good look at us. They would judge it to be the real thing because it was – minus a half-million troops! They would send up thousands of aircraft to come after us and we would be able to concentrate virtually all of our airpower, by sectors running from Nagoya [south-central Honshu] through Kyushu, and we would knock them down.

There would be leakers. We would loose ships and many good sailors. But at the end of the day – actually three days – we'd pull out.

'The Japs would undoubtedly believe that they had repelled the invasion. Those same ships and others, however, would be at Okinawa, at Luzon, at Guam, loading for the real knockout. We would be back at Kyushu in just two weeks and this time there would be so few meatballs left that we could handle them easily. Preparations for Operation BUGEYE[60] were begun in early June at Pearl [Harbor] and Guam.'

A slight pause in Turner's commentary precipitated a sea of hands to be raised across the floor. The Class of '47 was a sharp group and it was not hard to guess what was on their minds.

## Typhoon Louise strikes

'Was it Louise,' asked one, 'was it the October typhoon[61] which killed the plan?'

'Ultimately, yes. It had been a hard sell to begin with. The shipping crisis that had come to a head at Leyte[62] had never been completely solved and there was a legitimate concern that if too much was lost during BUGEYE we would be hard-pressed to fulfill our needs during MAJESTIC. We received the go-ahead for BUGEYE only after certain numbers of assault ships of every category had been pulled from the operation. Vessels like the thirty-eight to be used as blockships for CORONET's "Mulberry" harbor[63] would have been completely satisfactory for the feint, and yet even though many were virtual derelicts, we were nevertheless required to preserve them for Tokyo. I need not remind you that construction of the artificial harbor carried a priority second only to development of the atom bomb[64] and that we were producing seven unique, heavy-lift salvage ships in two classes especially for the invasion.[65] As things turned out, four of the six that had arrived in-theater survived Typhoon Louise and were fully employed with salvage operations at Okinawa till nearly Thanksgiving.

'Everyone in this room is painfully aware of the disaster at Okinawa. Every plane that could be gassed up was sent south [to Luzon] and most were saved. The flat bottoms [assault shipping and craft designed to be beached] weren't so lucky. Six-hours' warning was not enough. Shifting cargoes in the combat-loaded LSTs sent 61 of 972 LSTs to the bottom; 186 of 1,080 LCTs went down or were irretrievably damaged; 92 of 648 LCIs;[66] the list goes on.[67] Plus, a half-dozen Liberty ships and destroyers. At least they couldn't blame this one on Bill.[68] This storm took on mystical proportions to the Japanese war leaders who had defied the Emperor and taken over the government when he tried to surrender during the first four atomic attacks in August.[69] Hearkening back to the original 'divine wind', or kamikaze, which destroyed an invasion force heading for Japan in 1281, they saw it as proof that they had been right all along. Their industrial base in Manchuria was gone because of the Soviet invasion, their cities were in ashes, but the Japs were even more certain that we would sue for peace if they just held out.

'Any chance of carrying out the feint was gone. With a little more time, the shipping losses – greater in tonnage than Okinawa – could be made up. But there was no time. The Joint Chiefs originally set December 1, 1945, as the Kyushu invasion date with CORONET, Tokyo's Kanto Plain, three months later on March 1 this year. That's three months.

'What I'm about to say is an important point and I'll be returning to it in a moment. To lessen casualties, the launch of CORONET included two armored divisions shipped from Europe which were to sweep up the plain and cut off Tokyo before the monsoons turned it into vast pools of rice, muck, and water crisscrossed by elevated roads and dominated by rugged, well-defended foothills.

'Now, planners envisioned the construction of eleven airfields on Kyushu for the massed airpower which would soften up the Tokyo area. Bomb and fuel storage, roads, wharves, and base facilities would be needed to support those air groups plus our Sixth Army holding a 110-mile stop-line one third of the way up the island. All plans centered on construction of the minimum essential operating facilities, but most of the airfields for heavy bombers were not projected to be ready until 90 to 105 days after the initial landings on Kyushu,[70] in spite of a massive effort. The constraints on the air campaign were so clear that when the Joint Chiefs set the target dates of the Kyushu and Tokyo invasions for December 1, 1945, and March 1, 1946, respectively, it was apparent that the three-month period would not be sufficient. Weather ultimately determined which operation to reschedule, because CORONET could not be moved back without moving it closer to the monsoons and thus risking serious restrictions on all ground movement – and particularly the armor's drive up the plain – from flooded fields, and the air campaign from cloud cover that almost doubles from early March to early April.[71] MacArthur's air staff proposed bumping MAJESTIC ahead by a month and both my boss, Admiral Nimitz, and the Joint Chiefs immediately agreed. MAJESTIC was moved forward one month to November 1.[72]

'The October typhoon changed all that. A delay till December 10 for Kyushu, well past the initial – and unacceptable – target date was forced upon us, with the Tokyo operation pushed to April 1 – dangerously close to the monsoons. We were going to get one run, and one run only, at the target. No BUGEYE. One of the greatest opportunities of the war had been lost.'

At first there were no hands appearing above the audience since they were still absorbing everything that Admiral Turner had said. A Navy captain in the second row was the first to break the silence.

'Sir, was there reconsideration at this time of switching to the blockade strategy that we, the Navy, had been advocating since 1943?'

Turner's host that evening, Admiral Spruance, had been outspoken in his belief that such a move was the best course[73] but, like Turner, had followed orders to the fullest of his ability and beyond. Turner knew that he had already said far more than he should on BUGEYE and moved to wrap things up.

'I can't tell you what others were advocating. All I can say is that I was fully, very fully, engaged in carrying out my orders. On a personal note, I would have to say that I believe that the change in plans regarding the use of atom bombs during MAJESTIC was fortuitous. After the first four bombs on cities failed in their strategic purpose of stampeding the Japanese government into an early surrender, the growing stockpile of atom bombs was held for use during the invasion. Initially, though, we did not intend to use them as they were eventually employed, against Japanese formations moving down from northern Kyushu. Initially we were going to allot one to each corps zone shortly before the landings.'[74]

Audible gasps and a low whistle could be heard from the some in the audience, who immediately recognized the implications of what the admiral was saying.

'Yes,' Turner acknowledged, 'the radiation casualties we suffered in central Kyushu were bad enough, but they were only a fraction of what would have been experienced if we had run a half-million men directly into radiated beachheads – and all that atomic dust being kicked up during the base development and airfields construction! The result hardly bears thinking about. It was clear, after the initial bombs in August, that the Japs were trying to wring the maximum political advantage from claims that the atom bombs were somehow more inhuman than the conventional attacks that had burnt out every city with a population over 30,000. At first their claims about massive radiation sickness were thought to be purely propaganda.[75] However, over the next few months it was determined that there was enough truth to what they were saying to switch the bombs to targets of opportunity after the Jap forces from northern Kyushu moved down to attack our lodgment in the south. They had to concentrate before they could launch their counteroffensive and that's when we hit 'em. As for the original landing zones, repeated carpet bombing by our heavies from Guam and Okinawa produced the same results that the atom bombs would have and, besides, the big bombers had essentially run out of strategic targets long before the invasion. The carpet bombing gave them something to do. [Laughter]

'The Jap warlords were unmoved when atom bombs were employed over cities, but the extensive use of the bombs against their soldiers is what finally pushed them to the conference table. Yes, they changed their tune when they faced the possibility of losing their army without an "honorable" fight, but so did we when it became undeniably clear that our replacement stream would not keep up with casualties.'

Turner looked over at General 'Howlin Mad' Smith, and continued, 'One man in this room tonight served in the trenches of World War I. An incomplete peace after that war meant that he and the sons of his buddies had to fight another war a generation later. We can only pray that the recent peace will not end in a bigger, bloodier, perhaps atomic, war with Imperial Japan in 1965. Thank you.'

## The reality

The coup attempt by Japanese forces unwilling to surrender was thwarted by Imperial forces loyal to the Emperor Hirohito, and the Japanese government succeeded in effecting a formal surrender before the home islands were invaded. Occupation forces on Kyushu were stunned by the scale of the defenses found at the precise locations where the invasion was scheduled to take place. The U.S. Military Government eventually disposed of 12,735 Japanese aircraft.

On October 9–10, 1945, Typhoon *Louise* struck Okinawa. Luckily, Operation MAJESTIC had been canceled months earlier. There was considerably less assault shipping on hand than if the invasion of Kyushu had been imminent, and 'only' 145 vessels were sunk or damaged so severely that they were beyond salvage.

## Bibliography

Asada, Sadao, 'The Shock of the Atomic Bomb and Japan's Decision to Surrender – A Reconsideration' *Pacific Historical Review* 67, November 1998.

Bartholomew, Charles A., Captain, USN, *Mud, Muscle and Miracles: Marine Salvage in the United States Navy* (Department of the Navy, Washington, D.C., 1990).

Bix, Herbert P., *Hirohito and the Making of Modern Japan* (Harper Collins, New York, 2000), p.519.

Bland, Larry I. (ed.), *George C. Marshall Interviews and Reminiscences for Forrest C. Pogue* (George C. Marshall Foundation, Lexington, 1996).

Brown, Anthony Cave, *Bodyguard of Lies, vol.2* (Harper & Row, New York, 1975).

Buell, Thomas B., *The Quiet Warrior: A Biography of Admiral Raymond A. Spruance* (U.S. Naval Institute Press, Annapolis, 1987).

*The Campaigns of MacArthur in the Pacific, vol.1: Reports of General MacArthur* (General Headquarters, Supreme Allied Command, Pacific, Tokyo, 1950).

Cannon, M. Hamlin, *Leyte: The Return to the Philippines* (Department of the Army, Washington, D.C., 1954).

Cline, Ray S., *Washington Command Post: The Operations Division* (Department of the Army, Washington, D.C., 1954).

Coakley, Robert W., and Leighton, Richard M., *The War Department: Global Logistics and Strategy, 1943–1944* (Department of the Army, Washington, D.C., 1968).

Coox, Alvin D., 'Japanese Military Intelligence in the Pacific: Its Non-Revolutionary Nature' in *The Intelligence Revolution: A Historical Perspective* (Office of Air Force History, Washington, D.C., 1991).

Coox, Alvin D., 'Needless Fear: The Compromise of U.S. Plans to Invade Japan in 1945' *Journal of Military History*, April 2000.

Drea, Edward J., *MacArthur's Ultra: Codebreaking and the War Against Japan, 1942–45* (University Press of Kansas, Lawrence, 1992).

Dyer, George Carroll, Vice Admiral, USN, *The Amphibians Came to Conquer: The Story of Admiral Richmond Kelly Turner* (U.S. Navy Department, Washington, D.C., 1972).

Frank, Bemis M., and Shaw, Henry I., Jr., *History of U.S. Marine Corps Operations in World War II, vol.5: Victory and Occupation* (Historical Branch, U.S. Marine Corps, Washington, D.C., 1968).

Gallicchio, Marc, 'After Nagasaki: General Marshall's Plan for Tactical Nuclear Weapons in Japan' *Prologue* 23, Winter 1991.

Giangreco, D.M., 'Operation Downfall: The Devil Was in the Details' *Joint Force Quarterly*, Autumn 1995.

Giangreco, D.M., 'The Truth About Kamikazes' *Naval History*, May–June 1997.

Giangreco, D.M., 'Casualty Projections for the Invasion of Japan, 1945–1946: Planning and Policy Implications' *Journal of Military History*, July 1997.

Hattendorf, John B.; Simpson, B. Michael, III; and Wadleigh, John R., *Sailors and Scholars: The Centennial History of the Naval War College* (Naval War College Press, Newport, Rhode Island,1984).

Hattori, Colonel, *The Complete History of the Greater East Asia War* (500th Military Intelligence Group, Tokyo, 1954).

Huber, Thomas M., *Pastel: Deception in the Invasion of Japan* (Combat Studies Institute, Fort Leavenworth, 1988).

Inoguchi, Rikihei, Captain, IJN, and Nakajima, Tadashi, Commander, IJN, *The Divine Wind: Japan's Kamikaze Force in World War II* (U.S. Naval Institute Press, Annapolis, 1958).

*Interrogations of Japanese Officials, vol.2* (United States Strategic Bombing Survey, Tokyo, 1946).

'The Japanese System of Defense Call-up' *Military Research Bulletin*, no.19, 18 July 1945.

Kendrick, Douglas B., Brigadier General, USA, *Medical Department, United States Army: Blood Program in World War II* (Office of the Surgeon General, Washington, D.C., 1964).

Morison, Samuel Eliot, Rear Admiral, USN, *History of United States Naval Operations in World War II, vol.12: Leyte, June 1944–January 1945* (Little, Brown, Boston, 1958).

Morison, Samuel Eliot, Rear Admiral, USN, *History of United States Naval Operations in World War II, vol.13, The Liberation of the Philippines: Luzon, Mindanao, the Visayas, 1944-1945* (Little, Brown, Boston, 1959).

Morison, Samuel Eliot, Rear Admiral, USN, *History of United States Naval Operations in World War II, vol.14: Victory in the Pacific, 1945* (Little, Brown, Boston, 1960).

Morison, Samuel Eliot, Rear Admiral, USN, *The Two Ocean War: A Short History of the United States Navy in the Second World War* (Little, Brown, Boston, 1958).

*Oil in Japan's War: Report of the Oil and Chemical Division, United States Strategic Bombing Survey, Pacific* (United States Strategic Bombing Survey, Tokyo, 1946).

O'Neill, Richard, *Suicide Squads: Axis and Allied Special Attack Weapons of World War II, their Development and their Missions* (Ballantine Books, New York, 1984).

Potter, E.B., *Nimitz* (U.S. Naval Institute Press, Annapolis, 1976).

Roland, Buford, Lieutenant Commander, USNR, and Boyd, William B., Lieutenant, USNR, *U.S. Navy Bureau of Ordnance in World War II* (U.S. Navy Department, Washington, D.C., 1955).

Sakai, Saburo; Caidin, Martin; and Saito, Fred, *Samurai* (Bantam Books, New York, 1978).

Sherrod, Robert, *History of Marine Corps Aviation in World War II* (Presidio Press, Bonita, 1980).

Stanton, Shelby L., *Order of Battle, U.S. Army, World War II* (Presidio Press, Novato, 1984).

Walker, Lewis M., Commander, USNR, 'Deception Plan for Operation OLYMPIC' *Parameters*, Spring 1995.

## Notes

1. Vice Admiral George Carroll Dyer, USN, *The Amphibians Came to Conquer: The Story of Admiral Richmond Kelly Turner* (U.S. Navy Department, Washington, D.C., 1972), p.1109.

2. John B. Hattendorf, B. Michael Simpson III, and John R. Wadleigh, *Sailors and Scholars: The Centennial History of the Naval War College* (Naval War College Press, Newport, Rhode Island, 1984), p.329.

3. Dyer, *op.cit.* pp.1118–19.

4. *Ibid* p.1117.

5. The Joint Chiefs of Staff designated the invasion of Kyushu (Operation OLYMPIC, later MAJESTIC) as X-Day, December 1, 1945, and the invasion of Honshu (Operation CORONET) as Y-Day, March 1, 1946.

6. Thomas B. Buell, *The Quiet Warrior: A Biography of Admiral Raymond A. Spruance* (U.S. Naval Institute Press, Annapolis, 1987), pp.417–18.

7. Rear Admiral Samuel Eliot Morison, USN, *History of United States Naval Operations in World War II, vol.12: Leyte, June 1944–January 1945* (Little, Brown, Boston, 1958), pp.300–6, 339–49, 354–60, 366–8, 380–5.

8. M. Hamlin Cannon, *Leyte: The Return to the Philippines*, in the series *The United States Army in World War II* (hereafter USAWWII) (Department of the Army, Washington, D.C., 1954), pp.8–9. See also Rear Admiral Samuel Eliot Morison, USN, *The Two Ocean War: A Short History of the United States Navy in the Second World War* (Little, Brown, Boston, 1958), pp.422–3.

9. Cannon, *op.cit.* p.306.

10. *Ibid* pp.294–305.

11. Shelby L. Stanton, *Order of Battle, U.S. Army, World War II* (Presidio Press, Novato, 1984), pp.112–13.

12. Cannon, *op.cit.* pp.92–4, 99–102.

13. *Ibid* pp.306–8.

14. *Ibid* pp.365–7.

15. Operations of U.S. aircraft as recent as the Gulf War's 'Scud hunt' illustrate that this is generally not as easy as some presume it to be.

16. Hattori Takushiro gives the number of Japanese airfields on the home islands, including those under construction and ninety-five concealed airfields, at 325. Figures from the July 13, 1945, 'Central Agreement Concerning Air Attacks' between the Japanese Army and Navy in vol.4 of Colonel Hattori's *The Complete History of the Greater East Asia War* (500th Military Intelligence Group, Tokyo, 1954), p.165. Translated from Hattori's *Daitoa Senso zenshi*, 4 vols (Masu Shobo, Tokyo, 1953).

17. *Ibid* vol.4, p.234. Hattori states that the blow destroyed fifty-eight Navy and two Army aircraft on the ground. Smoke and decoys prevented an accurate U.S. assessment and Morison calls it 'indeterminate' in *History of United States Naval Operations in World War II, vol.14: Victory in the Pacific, 1945* (Little, Brown, Boston, 1960), p.100.

18. *Oil in Japan's War: Report of the Oil and Chemical Division, United States Strategic Bombing Survey, Pacific* [hereafter USSBS] (Tokyo, 1946), pp.87–9; and Hattori, *op.cit.* vol.4, p.165.

19. See Captain Rikihei Inoguchi, IJN, and Commander Tadashi Nakajima, IJN, *The Divine Wind: Japan's Kamikaze Force in World War II* (U.S. Naval Institute Press, Annapolis, 1958), pp.81–2, for an examination of high-grade decoy production and employment at an austere facility. The quality of dummy aircraft construction varied considerably from location to location, but even simple constructions of straw and fabric were effective since pilots under fire in speeding fighters had little time to closely examine aircraft on the ground.

20. U.S. estimates in May 1945, that 6,700 aircraft could be made available in stages, grew to only 7,200 by the time of the surrender. This number, however, turned out to be short by some 3,300 in light of the armada of 10,500 planes which the enemy planned to expend in stages during the opening phases of the invasion operations – most as kamikazes. After the war, occupation authorities discovered that the number of military aircraft actually available in the home islands was over 12,700. See *MacArthur in Japan: The Occupation: Military Phase, vol.1: Supplement, Reports of General MacArthur* (General Headquarters, Supreme Allied Command, Pacific, Tokyo, 1950), p.136; and Hattori, *op.cit.* vol.4, p.174.

21. *Ibid* vol.4, p.191. Transports had always been a high priority for suicide aircraft but did not become the main focus of Japanese planning until the spring and summer of 1945. See *Interrogations of Japanese Officials, vol.2* (USSBS Naval Analysis Division, Tokyo, 1946), Admiral Soemu Toyoda, p.318; Vice Admiral Shigeru Fukudome, p.504.

22. Inoguchi and Nakajima, *op.cit.* pp.25–6.

23. Saburo Sakai with Martin Caidin and Fred Saito, *Samurai* (Bantam Books, New York, 1978), pp.254–6, 263.

24. Inoguchi and Nakajima, *op.cit.* pp.58–9, Sakai, *op.cit.* pp.294–5.

25. From Jack Moore, in D. M. Giangreco, 'The Truth About Kamikazes' *Naval History*, May–June 1997, p.28.

26. COMINCH P-0011, *Anti-Suicide Action Summary*, August 31, 1945, p.20.

27. Lieutenant Commander Buford Roland, USNR, and Lieutenant William B. Boyd, USNR, *U.S. Navy Bureau of Ordnance in World War II* (U.S. Navy Department, Washington, D.C., 1955), pp.245–7.

28. *Ibid* pp.267–8.

29. *Anti-Suicide Action Summary*, p.21. See also Confidential Information Bulletin no.29, *Anti-Aircraft Action Summary, World War II* (COMINCH, October 1945) for an overview of gun, ammunition, and fire control development.

30. Inoguchi, *op.cit.* pp.85–91.

31. From a March 25, 1945, combat report of the *Fletcher* Class destroyer U.S.S. *Kimberly*, DD-521, excerpted in Richard O'Neill's *Suicide Squads: Axis and Allied Special Attack Weapons of World War II, their Development and their Missions* (Ballantine Books, New York, 1984), pp.164–5.

32. A miniature radio device that automatically exploded projectiles when they passed close to their targets.

33. Rear Admiral Samuel Eliot Morison, USN, *History of United States Naval Operations in World War II, vol.13: The Liberation of the Philippines: Luzon, Mindanao, the Visayas, 1944–1945* (Little, Brown, Boston, 1959), p.58.

34. A useful window to the thinking of some senior members of Nimitz's staff can be found in *Joint Staff Study, OLYMPIC, Naval and Amphibious Operations*, CINCPAC, 5, produced under the direction of Admiral Forrest Sherman, Deputy Chief of Staff, COMINCH. Updated through at least July 8, 1945, it echoes the intelligence reports referred to in this comment and states that attacks by U.S. forces 'will have served to reduce the enemy air force to a relatively low state' by the projected November 1 invasion. However, the assessment in *Staff Study, Operations, CORONET*, General Headquarters USAFP, August 15, 1945, demonstrates a detailed understanding of Japanese plans for employment of kamikaze aircraft.

35. *Oil in Japan's War*, USSBS, pp.40–1.

36. *Interrogations of Japanese Officials, vol.2*, USSBS, Vice Admiral Shigeru Fukudome, p.508.

37. *Oil in Japan's War*, USSBS, pp.68, 88.

38. Hattori, *op.cit.* vol.4, p.166.

39. *Joint Staff Study, OLYMPIC, Naval and Amphibious Operations*, CINCPAC, May 1945, Annex 1 to Appendix C, June 18, 1945; and *Staff Study, Operations, OLYMPIC*, General Headquarters USAFP, April 23, 1945, p.13 and map 8.

40. *Ibid* Joint Staff Study, OLYMPIC.

41. See CINCPAC map 'Appendix 35, Provisional Layout of Fighter Defense' in *Report on Operation 'OLYMPIC' and Japanese Counter-Measures, part 4, Appendices by the British Combined Observers (Pacific)*, Combined Operations Headquarters, August 1, 1946.

42. Bemis M. Frank and Henry I. Shaw, Jr., *History of U.S. Marine Corps Operations in World War II, vol.5: Victory and Occupation* (Historical Branch, U.S. Marine Corps, Washington, D.C., 1968), pp.187, 671; and Robert Sherrod, *History of Marine Corps Aviation in World War II* (Presidio Press, Bonita, 1980), pp.385–6. Marine ground support sorties at Okinawa amounted only to 704 of the 4,841 launched between April 7 and May 3, as protection of the escort carriers and the landing/support areas from kamikazes remained the top priority.

43. See 'Amendment No.1 to G-2 Estimate of Enemy Situation with Respect to Kyushu' G-2, AFPAC, July 19, 1945, in *The Campaigns of MacArthur in the Pacific vol.1: Reports of General MacArthur* (General Headquarters, Supreme Allied Command, Pacific, Tokyo, 1950), pp.414–18; and Edward J. Drea, *MacArthur's Ultra: Codebreaking and the War Against Japan, 1942–45* (University Press of Kansas, Lawrence, 1992), pp.202–25.

44. A comprehensive and insightful treatment of this subject was produced by Alvin D. Coox shortly before his death. See 'Needless Fear: The Compromise of U.S. Plans to Invade Japan in 1945' *Journal of Military History*, April 2000, pp.411–38.

45. *Ibid*; see also Hattori, *op.cit.* vol.4, pp.185–7; and Coox, 'Japanese Military Intelligence in the Pacific: Its Non-Revolutionary Nature' in *The Intelligence Revolution: A Historical Perspective* (Office of Air Force History, Washington, D.C., 1991), p.200.

46. Hattori, *op.cit.* vol.4, pp.171–4, 183, 191.

47. See CINCPAC map 'Appendix 36, Radar Build Up' in *Report on Operation 'OLYMPIC' and Japanese Counter-Measures*, part 4.

48. There are no circumstances in which Admiral Turner would even mention, let alone address in detail, U.S. code breaking of Japanese radio transmissions other than to use the very general term 'communications intelligence', which includes a variety of methods for divining an enemy's intentions. See Drea, *op.cit.*

49. The 'H' designation stands for hospital. These were tank landing ships converted to serve as forward medical and evacuation facilities.

50. Brigadier General Douglas B. Kendrick, USA, *Medical Department, United States Army: Blood Program in World War II* (Office of the Surgeon General, Washington, D.C., 1964), pp.639–41.

51. *Ibid* pp.633–9.

52. Thomas M. Huber, *Pastel: Deception in the Invasion of Japan* (Combat Studies Institute, Fort Leavenworth, 1988).

53. Anthony Cave Brown, *Bodyguard of Lies, vol.2* (Harper & Row, New York, 1975), especially pp.900 and 904.

54. 'The Japanese System of Defense Call-up' *Military Research Bulletin*, no.19, July 18, 1945, pp.1–3; and 'Amendment No.1 to G-2 Estimate of Enemy Situation with Respect to Kyushu' G-2, AFPAC, July 29, 1945.

55. Admiral Nimitz was also worried that the strain of extended combat operations might be taking a toll on senior Fifth Fleet commanders. For Nimitz's worries about fatigue, see Buell, *op.cit.* pp.391–3. Whether or not such fears were justified, biographer E.B. Potter states categorically in *Nimitz* (U.S. Naval Institute Press, Annapolis, 1976), p.456, that they were the cause of the reliefs.

56. D.M. Giangreco, 'Operation Downfall: The Devil Was In the Details' *Joint Force Quarterly*, Autumn 1995, pp.86–94.

57. Commander Lewis M. Walker, USNR, 'Deception Plan for Operation OLYMPIC' *Parameters*, Spring 1995, pp.116–57, for all references from '400 ships' through the following paragraph.

58. Hattori, *op.cit.* vol.4, p.124; Frank and Shaw, *op.cit.* pp.51, 107.

59. Walker, *op.cit.* pp.116–17.

*60. 'BUGEYE' is a fictitious name.

61. On October 9, 1945, a typhoon packing 140 mph winds struck Okinawa. This key staging area would have been expanded to capacity by that date if the war had not ended in September. Even at this late date, the area was still crammed with aircraft and assault shipping – much of which was destroyed. U.S. analysts at the scene matter-of-factly reported that the storm would have caused up to a forty-five day delay in the invasion of Kyushu. For a review of the damage see Rear Admiral Samuel Eliot Morison, USN, *History of United States Naval Operations in World War II, vol15: Supplement and General Index* (Little, Brown, Boston, 1962), pp.14-17.

62. Robert W. Coakley and Richard M. Leighton, *The War Department: Global Logistics and Strategy, 1943–1944* in USAWWII (Department of the Army, Washington, D.C., 1968), pp.551–62; and Cannon, *op.cit.* pp.6–7, 34, 38, 276.

63. *Staff Study, Operations, CORONET*, General Headquarters USAFP, August 15, 1945, Annex 4, Basic Logistic Plan, Appendix H.

64. Ray S. Cline, *Washington Command Post: The Operations Division*, in USAWWII (Department of the Army, Washington, D.C., 1954), p.348.

65. Captain Charles A. Bartholomew, USN, *Mud, Muscle and Miracles: Marine Salvage in the United States Navy* (Department of the Navy, Washington, D.C., 1990), pp.449–51.

66. LST, tank landing ship, 1,625 tons; LCT, tank landing craft, 143 tons; LCI, infantry landing craft, 209 tons; LCS (referred to elsewhere), 246 tons.

67. Assault shipping totals from Dyer, *op.cit.* p.1105. See also Morison, *Supplement*, pp.14–17.

68. Reference to a pair of earlier typhoons that had severely damaged fleet elements under Admiral Halsey's command. The December 18, 1944, typhoon had capsized three destroyers and heavily mauled seven other ships. Nearly 800 lives had been lost and 186 planes were jettisoned, blown overboard, or irreparably damaged. The June 5, 1945, typhoon wrenched 130 feet of bow off of a heavy cruiser; heavily damaged thirty-two other ships, including one escort and two fleet carriers that lost great lengths of their flight decks; and resulted in the loss of 142 aircraft. Totals from E.B. Potter, *op.cit.* pp.423, 456.

69. The coup attempt by officers intent on pursuing the war has been recounted in numerous works, but the original document upon which these accounts are based is *Japanese Operations in the Southwest Pacific War, vol.2, part 2: Reports of General MacArthur*, pp.731–40. See also Sadao Asada, 'The Shock of the Atomic Bomb and Japan's Decision to Surrender – A Reconsideration' *Pacific Historical Review* 67, November 1998, pp.477–512, especially pp.592–5 on the insistence by mid-level and senior Japanese officers that the war be continued at all costs. For a different opinion see Herbert P. Bix, *Hirohito and the Making of Modern Japan* (Harper Collins, New York, 2000), p.519.

70. See CINCPAC chart 'Appendix 43, Air Base Development' in *Report on Operation 'OLYMPIC' and Japanese Counter-Measures, part 4*; see also *Staff Study, Operations, CORONET, annex 4, appendix C*.

71. *G-2 Estimate of the Enemy Situation with Respect to an Operation Against the Tokyo (Kwanto) Plain of Honshu*, General Headquarters USAFP, G-2 General Staff, May 31, 1945, section I–2, 1.

72. *Reports of General MacArthur*, vol.1, p.399.

73. Buell, *op.cit.* pp.394–6, and Dyer, *op.cit.* p.1108.

74. Larry I. Bland (ed.), *George C. Marshall Interviews and Reminiscences for Forrest C. Pogue* (George C. Marshall Foundation, Lexington, 1996), p.424; and Marc Gallicchio, 'After Nagasaki: General Marshall's Plan for Tactical Nuclear Weapons in Japan' *Prologue* 23, Winter 1991, pp.396–404. See also D.M. Giangreco, 'Casualty Projections for the Invasion of Japan, 1945–1946: Planning and Policy Implications' *Journal of Military History*, July 1997, pp.521–82, especially pp.574–81.

75. *2605, section 3, Japanese Propaganda Efforts*, Headquarters United States Army Forces Middle Pacific, November 1, 1945, pp.70–1.